# The 21st Century
# Superhero

# The 21st Century Superhero

## Essays on Gender, Genre and Globalization in Film

*Edited by*
RICHARD J. GRAY II *and*
BETTY KAKLAMANIDOU

McFarland & Company, Inc., Publishers
*Jefferson, North Carolina, and London*

LIBRARY OF CONGRESS CATALOGUING-IN-PUBLICATION DATA

The 21st century superhero : essays on gender, genre and
    globalization in film / edited by Richard J. Gray II and Betty
    Kaklamanidou.
        p.        cm.
    Includes bibliographical references and index.

    ISBN 978-0-7864-6345-9
    softcover : 50# alkaline paper ∞

    1. Superhero films—History and criticism.   2. Motion
pictures—History—21st century.   3. Motion pictures and
globalization.   4. Masculinity in motion pictures.   5. Sex
role in motion pictures.   I. Gray, Richard J., 1971–
II. Kaklamanidou, Betty, 1972–   III. Title.
PN1995.9.S76A88   2011
791.43'652 — dc22                                    2011017365

BRITISH LIBRARY CATALOGUING DATA ARE AVAILABLE

Cover art © 2011 Digitalvision. Front cover design by David Landis
(Shake It Loose Graphics)

Manufactured in the United States of America

McFarland & Company, Inc., Publishers
    Box 611, Jefferson, North Carolina 28640
    www.mcfarlandpub.com

Richard dedicates this book to his family.

Betty dedicates this book to Petros,
her everyday superhero.

# Acknowledgments

The editors would like to thank the contributors for their stimulating chapters, and our families for their patience for the long hours that we spent preparing this collection. We would also like to thank Andrea L. Menz for her careful proofreading. As we approach the 10-year anniversary of 9/11, this book serves to examine superheroes in television and film in the wake of a tragedy that forever changed the world in which we live. At no other time in world history, perhaps, has the need for superheroes been so great.

# Table of Contents

# Introduction

The first decade of the new millennium will certainly be remembered for many things: The 9/11 attacks, the War on Terror, the first African-American in the White House, natural disasters, the fear of a long-term global financial crisis, the birth of YouTube, and the widespread use of internet social networks which have changed the way that people communicate with each other. However, for the Hollywood film industry, it will also be remembered as the "superhero" decade. Never before in the history of cinema have so many "spectacular narratives"— to borrow Geoff King's term — been released and met with unprecedented box-office success. From *The X-Men* (2000) to *Kick-Ass* (2010), more than thirty superhero films from Marvel, DC, and Dark Horse Comics were adapted for the silver screen. The television landscape also succumbed to this tendency. *Smallville* (The WB, 2001–2006/The CW, 2006–2011) and *Heroes* (NBC, 2006–2010), among countless animated superhero series, are only two of the most well-known and syndicated television shows whose global appeal has become the subject of numerous articles, internet debates, fan sites and forums.

The revival of the genre has surpassed all expectations, which according to boxofficemojo.com has resulted in three of the top five highest opening-weekend box office grosses in film history being held by superhero films. There are many potential theories as to why these films have become and remained so popular over the last decade, from desperate attempts for escape to an honest yearning for real-life heroes. One such theory is that the notion of the word "hero" has evolved since the attacks of 9/11 and their subsequent fallout. Joseph Campbell, the literary scholar who outlined a hero archetype from the mythology of numerous cultures, defined a hero as "someone who has given his or her life to something bigger than oneself" (151). Since 9/11, however, overuse of the word has both diminished its power and undermined the accomplishments of real modern heroes. In the Pixar animated film *The Incredibles* (2004), a film in which each of the members of the Parr family has a super power, the dialogue exchanged between Dash (Spencer Fox), the son gifted with super speed, and Helen (Holly Hunter), also known as Elastigirl, underscores this particular perspective:

DASH: Dad always said our powers were nothing to be ashamed of. Our powers made us special.

HELEN: Everyone's special, Dash.

DASH: *[sullenly]* Which is another way of saying *no one* is.

This same view is furthered by a comment made by the nemesis of the Parr family, Syndrome (Jason Lee): "I'll give them heroics. I'll give them the most spectacular heroics they've ever seen! And when I'm old and I've had my fun, I'll sell my inventions so everyone can be superheroes! Everyone can be super! And when everyone's super, *[laughs maniacally]* no-one will be." Thus, these two passages highlight a very important reality: In the real world, most of us are nothing more than regular people who live regular lives.

Thus, as regular people living regular lives, we seek a way to cope with the truths brought to light following the attacks of 9/11. A recent Associated Press article maintained that in a decade "that brought harsh reality home with the war on terror and an economy gone bust, Hollywood became more of a dream factory than ever, embracing fantastic escapism at a time when audiences needed it most" and started producing or reviving superhero fantasies that provide the frustrated, disappointed and even somber audience with a few hours of respite through audiovisual fantasy (*www.msnbc.com*). As of February 2010, *Avatar* (2009) had claimed the coveted position of highest-grossing movie of all time with more than $2 billion in admissions receipts worldwide. In 2008, *The Dark Knight* grossed more than $1 billion worldwide, and in 2007, *Spider-Man 3* reached nearly $900 million.[1] This unprecedented commercial success not only confirms the global popularity of superhero films, but also raises interesting questions regarding the reasons behind this success.

This astonishing abundance of superhero narratives in the first decade of the 21st century combined with their staggering box-office numbers initiated this collection and led to the decision to exclusively focus on the film and television superhero genre. Although the cinematic narratives discussed in the ensuing chapters are adaptations and do not constitute original stories *per se*, we believe that a comparative analysis with their origins, the comics — however constructive — would not serve the main purpose of this book, which is to examine the films against their particular sociocultural circumstances in order to discern the main issues which are raised in them and which constitute the three different sections of the book. Furthermore, adopting Gardies' position, we consider the filmic adaptations of literary or comic sources as autonomous narratives who claims that it is much more fruitful to consider the source as a kind of database from which the film team draws a sum of directions which they should handle cinematically (5). In addition, it should also be noted that in cases where the filmic adaptation is produced and released with a delay of several decades and/or even centuries, the film is used as a comment on the contemporary sociocultural circumstances and does not respond to the time period in which the source was written and/or published (McFarlane 9–10).[2] For instance, Superman and Batman, both "born" at the end of the Great Depression, not only served as escapist past-times, but were "read" as symbols of selfless heroism, the fight against evil and most importantly, hope. However, the same figures are used in the new millennium to provide today's global audience with possible outlets and/or solutions to contemporary concerns. Although today's globalized dilemmas echo those dark years, they differ in ways that have to do with the progress the world has known since the 1930s and have also altered and/or differentiated the fictional superheroes/superheroines to better "fit" the current trends, which have created exciting and thought-provoking new narratives.

If we consider mainstream films to be a form of escapism, which offer a mixture of education and entertainment, superhero films of the new millennium lean greatly toward the latter characteristic. Further, historically, during times of war (or in the periods immediately following), films have become a source for the renewal of patriotism. Since the beginning of the War in Afghanistan, which began on October 7, 2001, and the Iraq War, which began on March 20, 2003, the United States and many other nations of the world have been embroiled in both local and international armed conflict. Against this backdrop, superheroes have become civilians who are charged with restoring peace during troubled times. Moreover, many superheroes serve as a hope-inspiring figure, an image of someone (like Batman) who can pull the endangered individual from the dark abyss. Superhero films promote the ideas of peace, safety and freedom and seek to restore the planet to a nostalgic harmony.

In their comic form, Superman and Batman have been in existence since the 1930s, while many other superheroes appeared in the ensuing decades (Wonder Woman, The Hulk, The X-Men, etc.). Comic aficionados have never lost interest in the stories of their favorite superheroes/superheroines, whose number was significant. Nevertheless, one cannot argue that film has the power to attract a global audience and acquaint even the unfamiliar spectator with characters with super powers they never knew existed. When talking about film, and especially Hollywood, one of the first things one must consider is the economic factor. The film industry does not spend hundreds of millions of dollars unless it will make a profit. Therefore, after the enormous financial success of the first superhero films in the early 2000s, the industry continued to invest in similar narratives following a business tradition that goes back to the 1920s.[3]

> Moreover, in an age in which the big Hollywood studios have become absorbed into giant conglomerates, the prevalence of spectacle and special effects has been boosted by a growing demand for products that can be further exploited in multimedia forms such as computer games and theme-park rides—secondary outlets that sometimes generate more profits than the films on which they are based [while these narratives] might also be driven by the increased importance of the overseas market in Hollywood's economic calculations [King 1–2].

In the process, a new genre was born or, to be more accurate, re-born. Film and television alike both invested in superhero stories in earlier decades the four Superman films (1978, 1980, 1983, and 1987), the four Batman films (1989, 1992, 1995, and 1997), and the television *Batman* (ABC, 1966–1968) among many others with impressive box-office results and ratings respectively, which means that there must be an additional reason for the production of an impressive number of superhero films in the last decade. The reason put forth in this collection relates to the discussion of how films reflect or respond to contemporary sociopolitical and cultural events. Traditionally, films have been attacked for inaccuracy and/or tampering with historical facts to the detriment of the "truth." William Palmer holds the following opinion:

> Since the New Historicists have presented their arguments that historical "fact" is much more complex than conventional historians have portrayed it, and historical "reality" is extremely difficult to re-create and may not even exist, those charges against Hollywood's exploitation of history have been rendered even more moot... Hollywood creates a discourse in clearly defined texts that not only comment perceptively upon contemporary social history but actually participate in it [William Palmer xi].

It becomes clear that the events of the 2000s could not help but enter into the film medium even in the form of mainstream action narratives which use superheroes, the iconic figures of the American pop culture mythology. These new superhero texts, however, not only comment on contemporary sociopolitical events, but also disseminate American ideology throughout the world. Franklin claims that each American motion picture contains part of the nation's political ideology, which is based primarily on classical liberalism put forth by John Locke during the 17th century (20). On the same note, Franklin also observes that some of the tales, which are most often repeated on the silver screen, deal with the conquest of the west, the cult of the individual, and the "rags to riches" motif (24–27). The main theme that can be applied to superhero narratives is the cult of the individual; that is the focus on a single person with a great kind of power, usually a combination of mental and physical strength, who succeeds against all odds. Daniel Franklin describes this narrative as follows:

> a resilient resourceful individual with personal courage and ingenuity overcomes the odds and succeed without help against the grain of an oppressive environment often depicted as the government. This focus on the individual ... promotes a dynamic, vibrant, and creative society [25].

However, close to the core of the superhero narrative, this theme is presented with some alterations in the films. First of all, superhero films focus on special individuals and not ordinary human beings—whether human, alien, or mutant (Batman, Superman, X-Men)—or teams of special individuals which act as one (Watchmen, Fantastic Four). Secondly, these "super" individuals and/or teams of superheroes/superheroines fight against Evil and not necessarily an oppressive government, although the X-Men's, Batman's and Iron Man's fictional worlds often place their superheroes opposite cruel, unjust and/or illegal governmental policies and/or corrupt officials. Finally, superhero films do not exactly encourage "a vibrant, and creative society" in the way that films such as *The Pursuit of Happyness* (2006), *Erin Brockovich* (2003), and *Schindler's List* (1993) do. The aim of these cinematic texts is to "lead" spectators to admire the psychological strength and perseverance of an ordinary individual against every kind of personal difficulty and/or societal pressures and to uphold the notion of how a single person can overcome what seem to be insurmountable obstacles and triumph in the end, thus confirming and perpetuating the basic American belief in the power of the individual and the necessity of a government with limited authority.

Thus, as part and parcel of an overall attempt to convey a better understanding of both the function and the importance of the superhero film and television genre in the new millennium, this collection explores the ways that superhero narratives in both film and television negotiate, respond to and/or defuse some of the most significant socio-political issues in the new millennium. We believe that the increasing number of these narratives requires an in-depth academic study of the concept of the hero/heroine in a globalized society that is dealing with terrorist attacks and increasing fanatic activity of every kind. In such a society, the concept of hero constitutes something strange, admirable and even enviable. Using some of the most recognizable American pop culture symbols, the Hollywood film and television industries turned them not just into highly profitable products, but more importantly into modern day myths (according to the Barthesian definition which views myth as discourse). What is more, we argue that such a discussion is also important insofar as popular culture is one of the most fecund terrains for this kind of dialogue. Harriett Hawkins rightly observes the following:

> Whenever we "identify ourselves with a collective past" or as members of a given generation, those books and films and television shows and popular music that we especially enjoyed as children and adolescents (from *King Kong*, *Casablanca* and *Gone with the Wind* to *Star Wars* and *E.T.*) "are what constitute our collectively shared experience" [xv].

Indeed, popular culture is a domain that has, for several decades, received significant academic attention because it produces multilayered narratives that contain and spread ideological and political messages to a wide audience. Hollywood films—still the most powerful pop culture product in the new millennium—are nowadays released the same day all over the globe and are watched and/or "consumed" by hundreds of millions if not billions of people. Saturation mass booking may be the distribution method that the industry prefers for these films which are already considered as blockbusters even in their pre-production phase and are more often than not regarded as fatuous "pop-corn movies," but their extensive marketing and advertising campaigns cannot and should not condemn them as unworthy of systematic scholarly analysis *a priori*. Of course, one could not easily deny that many of these films rely more on their special effects and technological excellence, aspects which King explained:

> ... have led some to announce the imminent demise of narrative as a central or defining component of Hollywood cinema, or at least its dominant spectacular form... These films still tell reasonably coherent stories, even if they may sometimes be looser and less well integrated than some classical models." [While] "contemporary spectaculars also continue to manifest the kinds of underlying thematic oppositions and reconciliations associated with a broadly 'structuralist' analysis of narrative" [2–4].

In addition, drawing from Claude Lévi-Strauss' views on myth, King believes that, more often than not, not only do these "spectacular narratives" find a balance between the spectacle — which may seem to sometimes exist solely for the sake of grandiosity — and the narrative, but more importantly they "entail a move towards the imaginary resolution of contradictions that cannot be resolved in reality" (King 2–10). Superhero films and television shows can be a wonderful way to relax and escape from reality, but they can also be "profoundly thought-provoking" (Moriss and Moriss ix).

Consequently, this edited collection brings together diverse international scholars who investigate what we consider to be a true cultural phenomenon whose momentum has not subsided here at the beginning of the 21st century. Our main goal is to study the superhero film narratives from three main perspectives (globalization, gender, and genre) and to end with a chapter which examines one of the longest superhero television series, as this is an area which has yet to be adequately addressed in contemporary scholarship. We argue that superheroes in film and television have not only evolved as super individuals to encompass a wide range of human emotions — blurring and sometimes even rejecting the strict binary opposition between good and evil of the past — but the narratives which constitute their field of action, however fantastic, abstract, futuristic or simplistic they may be, resonate with specific events in the globalized world and could be used as starting points for a discussion about contemporary sociopolitical conflicts.

Finally, it should be underlined that this superhero trend is far from over, as it appears that superhero films are here to stay; The animated *Megamind* (2010) became an instant box-office hit in its first month of release, while several new titles, such as *Green Lantern, Green Hornet, Thor, X-Men: First Class, Captain America: The First Avenger, Ghost Rider: Spirit of Vengeance, The Dark Knight Rises, The Wolverine, Spider-Man Reboot, The Avengers, Kick-Ass 2* and *Iron Man 3* are scheduled for release between 2011 and 2013. At the same time, NBC has already announced a new superhero show, entitled *The Cape*, which debuted on January 9, 2011. It seems that the world still craves stories about super-powerful individuals who believe in basic human values such as honor, truth, and justice, despite their inner conflicts which may result from their corrupt, dangerous and immoral surroundings. The global audience not only needs an escape from harsh realities, but also needs to feel safe and protected even if this takes place in a dark theater or in their living room.

## The Collection

This collection of essays is divided into four parts. Each part addresses a different aspect of the superhero cinematic narrative. The first part of the collection deals with the notion of globalization. Here, globalization refers to the superhero film and geopolitical discourse after the events of 9/11.

Anthony Peter Spanakos' "Exceptional Recognition: The U.S. Global Dilemma in *The Incredible Hulk, Iron Man,* and *Avatar*" explores how superhero narratives in popular culture, specifically films, produce a pedagogical anthropology which creates and subverts signposts of self/otherness. Most people consume the global through popular culture, often packaged in superhero narratives, in which films and television shows perform a pedagogical anthropology explaining and shaping the tastes, desires, and fears of the self and other. These narratives indirectly, but powerfully, help answer fundamental anthropological questions. Analyzing *Hulk* (2003), *The Incredible Hulk* (2008), *Iron Man* (2008), *Iron Man 2* (2010) and *Avatar*, Spanakos notes that the self/other distinction becomes blurred as Western-created superheroes find themselves entering in the cultural and political struggles of the other. Additionally, the Western produced films are viewed by audiences in Rio de Janeiro, the Muslim world, and China, who produce their own interpretations of the superhero narrative as they see themselves both as the self and the other. Thus, in *The Incredible Hulk*, the Hulk character — known as much for his rage and power as for his constant, lonely wandering of the U.S. — has gone global. He is living in Latin America's largest shantytown and his gamma-infected blood gets into bottles which make their way into the U.S. markets. In *Iron Man*, Tony Stark is an overachieving engineer, entrepreneur, womanizer, and alcoholic. Tony's encounter with the global changes him physically and ethically. Finally, in James Cameron's *Avatar*, which creates two new worlds, one human and one Na'vi, the main character suffers the anthropological dilemma of going native and romanticizing the traditional, while the forces of modernization scorch the forest to steal its resources. *Avatar* is very obviously a cautionary and critical commentary on imperialism, on U.S. military adventures in Iraq and Afghanistan, and on the U.S.'s historic treatment of Native Americans.

In "You Took My Advice About Theatricality a Bit ... Literally": Theatricality and Cybernetics of Good and Evil in *Batman Begins, The Dark Knight, Spider-Man,* and *X-Men*," Johannes Schlegel and Frank Habermann examine the eternal struggle of Good versus Evil as constitutive for superhero films. They argue that postmodern representatives such as *Unbreakable* (2000) not only reflect this, but also question this assumption massively. While older films were still able to depict an ontological distinction between Good and Evil, recent films increasingly subvert this premise. Their chapter, therefore, focuses on this observation from two different perspectives. Their main thesis argues that Good as well as Evil is performatively generated in the first place; that is, they do not exist per se. Ultimately, their indifference stems from both being equally staged theatrically. Thus, Habermann and Schlegel aim to describe this theatricality and scenography as "self-fashioning" (Greenblatt) in a "public realm" (Arendt). By means of the active performativity of this staging, however, ethical issues emerge, since the decision for Good or Evil is only one among other equal options of action. The theatricality of Good and Evil, therefore, becomes the dominant pattern of postmodern superhero films and is applied to various films such as the *X-Men* trilogy, Sam Raimi's *Spider-Man*, *Hellboy* (2004) and Christopher Nolan's *Batman* franchise. Furthermore, the chapter argues that the general questioning of this formerly stable difference is a means of reflecting new or altering political discourses after 9/11. Due to the fact that superheroes negotiatively observe what is Good and Evil, they transform this seemingly inflexible difference into a rather dynamic relation. Thus, recent superhero films sketch a poetics of indifference as a crucial moment of indistinguishability which coincides with the superhero and where the constitutive distinction between Good and Evil can no longer be drawn.

Christine Muller's "Power, Choice, and September 11 in *The Dark Knight*" explores how this film serves as a fraught confrontation with September 11 as a cultural trauma. A promotional poster for *The Dark Knight*'s (2008) theatrical release, which now serves as DVD cover art, features a bat-shaped fiery crash zone penetrating the upper floors of a skyscraper's façade, an image reminiscent of passenger planes penetrating the World Trade Center towers' upper floors. Yet, this image never appears in the film itself, evincing a provocative self-consciousness about how *The Dark Knight* engages September 11. Since contemporary audience members can be considered at least witnesses, if not survivors, of September 11, dramatic allusions invite viewers to connect their own personal experiences with the film's staged exigencies. As the film depicts "good guys" Wayne, Gordon, and Dent stymied by — and in Dent's case, finally succumbing to — the Joker's relentless no-win scenarios, which ultimately also target the average Gothamite, audiences might revisit similar no-win scenarios of September 11 and its wake: victims with a choice only of how, and not whether, to die; those communicating by phone or email with loved ones mortally trapped in the Twin Towers or on the airliners; and the subsequently equivocal efforts to formulate a coherent, effective, just response. Therefore, Muller illustrates how by anchoring troubles with current ramifications in a pre-existing genre, *The Dark Knight* permits consideration of, without prescribing or proscribing definitive conclusions about, the responsibilities of those who act on behalf of others, as well as those who allow others to act on their behalf, in matters of justice and public safety. In effect, *The Dark Knight* instantiates and leaves unresolved the kinds of moral quandaries September 11 has posed.

The second part of the collection centers on the concept of gender. Inherently a social construction, both masculine and feminine gender (and sexuality) are perceived here, in part, as negotiated and performed through a patriarchal construct.

In "The Mythos of Patriarchy in the X-Men films," Betty Kaklamanidou explores the mythos of patriarchy in the four X-Men films (*X-Men*, 2000; *X2*, 2003; *X-Men: The Last Stand*, 2006; and *X-Men Origins: Wolverine*, 2009) by arguing that the patriarchal structure of modern society is a myth constructed to uphold its hegemonic interests and perpetuated via the widely popular film medium. In 1957, Roland Barthes defined myth as discourse; a message that is not confined to oral speech, but is hidden in many representations such as photography, sports, and cinema. Barthes argued that although there may be ancient myths, no one can last forever, because it is only human history that can regulate and decide on the life and death of mythic language, since the messages it contains are used to resolve social conflicts. In this chapter, Kaklamanidou analyzes the trajectory of the main female heroines in the four films and shows how those who defy the patriarchal authority are subtly and progressively stripped of not only their powers, but also their cinematic presence. This characteristic culminates in *Wolverine*, which could be categorized as a "buddy" movie. The patriarchal structure of the X-Men world, defined by the male, paternal figures Xavier (Patrick Stewart) and Magneto (Ian McKellen), which personify the poles of good and evil, may allow women to assume important positions in their world and the film narratives but only insofar as those heroines (Jean, Storm, Mystique) abide by their rules and answer to them. With rare exceptions, superheroes are male individuals who operate in a strictly patriarchal context, one of the most durable mythic environments in the western world.

Richard J. Gray II's essay, "Vivacious Vixens and Scintillating Super Hotties: Deconstructing the Superheroine," "fleshes out" what makes millennial superheroines the vivacious vixens and scintillating super hotties who continue to attract both adolescent and adult males. Through an application of Laura Mulvey's notion of the "male gaze," Gray examines the filmic superheroine as "bad girl art," a term which originated in the 1990s that referred to comic book women who were both violent and sexually-provocative in nature. These (anti-) superheroines have "super-sized" breasts, strong thighs, and thin waists, and are often depicted in uncomfortable, erotic positions. Though a host of authors have written about the depiction of superheroines in comic books, there has yet to be a significant study that evaluates the portrayal of superheroines as "bad girls" in the new millennium within the medium of film. Therefore, in this chapter, the author deconstructs superheroine identity by examining the physical representation of the superheroine in the new millennium against a theoretical backdrop informed by theorists such as Betty Friedan, Judith Butler, Julia Kristeva, Laura Mulvey, Jacques Lacan, and Sigmund Freud. On a path toward developing an even greater understanding of how superheroines are portrayed in the 21st century, this essay examines a range of characters taken from several popular films, including Lara Croft (*Lara Croft Tomb Raider*, 2001), Rogue, Jean Grey, Storm (*X-Men*, 2000), Kitty Pryde (*X-Men: The Last Stand*, 2006), Catwoman (*Catwoman*, 2004), Elektra (*Elektra*, 2005), Invisible Woman (*Fantastic Four*, 2005), and Æon Flux (*Æon Flux*, 2005).

In "Evolving Portrayals of Masculinity in Superhero Films: *Hancock*," Christina Adamou discusses a different kind of superhero. On the surface, John Hancock, a drunk, outcast, African-American with no alias has little in common with Superman/Clark Kent, Spider-Man/Peter Parker and Batman/Bruce Wayne, who are all white, male model citizens. Adamou's aim is to show how Hancock's obstacles and difficulties are inextricably linked to issues around masculinity and its cinematic representation, which in the film seems to oppose the conventions of the genre, as well as those of classical Hollywood narration. Using genre and gender theories as well as close analysis, Adamou argues that both the plot and the audiovisual codes of the film focus on issues of masculinity in a post-feminist era. As heterosexual genders in the film are still constituted through binary oppositions, Hancock's masculinity can only "unproblematically" exist when the hero is in control of his body, space and action, while the superheroine is contained within the private sphere. Nevertheless, the masculine hero cannot be fully accepted by society, unless he becomes more sensitive and socially conscious, thus approaching the ideal of a model citizen as well as that of the "new man."

The third part of the collection focuses on issues of genre as film genres are not "ahistorical in nature," strictly stable narratives which follow their respective conventions to the letter (Altman 218). Genres can only continue to exist if they evolve and adapt to the specific cultural ambiance of their inception and production time.

Vincent M. Gaine's "Genre and Super-Heroism: Batman in the New Millennium," considers the definition of the body of films commonly referred to as the "superhero genre." While the term may seem self-explanatory, close consideration of the tropes, themes and iconography of this body of films reveals problems and contradictions with the concept of "superhero film." The chapter identifies various features and elements from diverse film genres that feed into the superhero film, including the martial arts adventure and the spy thriller. As particular case studies, the essay focuses on *Batman Begins* and *The Dark Knight*, superhero narratives which, according to the author, create problems regarding the borders of film genre and which are largely caused by the films' engagement with debates within contemporary society and culture, particularly debates around the War on Terror and the clash between public safety and civil liberties. Through close attention to the concept of borders and the crossing of social thresholds, Gaine aims to show how these two films demonstrate the flexibility of the superhero genre.

Justin S. Schumaker's "Super-Intertextuality and 21st Century Individualized Social Advocacy in *Spider-Man* and *Kick-Ass*" uses Barthes' conception of text alongside Bolter and Grusin's idea of remediation to explore the parallel layers of intertextuality at discursive and narrative levels as well as across metafictional associations and generic categorization in the new millennium Spider-Man trilogy and *Kick-Ass*. The author argues that attention to this formal aspect of contemporary superhero cinema can offer important insight into the characterization of superheroes, aside from traditional figurations of heroism and with greater emphasis on issues of advocacy, social justice, and individual rights. In spite of the obvious function of superhero characters which is to protect those who cannot or choose not to care for themselves, existing scholarship rarely discusses the responsibilities that the superhero adopts, the rights of the citizenry they protect and serve, and the assumptions built into this advocacy. Furthermore, the degree of characters and themes reappearing and being repurposed within the genre of superhero cinema has remained largely ignored. And yet the similarities in imagery, cinematic connections through *mise-en-scène* and montage among these four films stand in stark contrast to the differences in characterization of the superhero (and villain, much more ambiguously addressed) between the earlier and the later film references and across the genre. This chapter aims to clarify definitive features of contemporary superhero cinema and shows a shift toward individual responsibility and social advocacy through the super-intertextuality of key examples in and across the *Spider-Man* franchise and the controversial *Kick-Ass*.

Phillip Davis' "The *Watchmen*, Neo-Noir and Pastiche" explores noir and neo-noir influences in the cinematic adaptation of *Watchmen*. Starting from the emergence of neo-noir and its relationship with the classic film noir of the 1940s and 1950s, the author traces the neo-noir dimensions of the 2009 *Watchmen* film, arguing that this superhero narrative also depends upon the tropes of noir and neo-noir to indicate contemporary social crises. Davis argues that in a world increasingly defined by media saturation and globalization, the clear boundaries between genre and nation become increasingly difficult to maintain. *Watchmen* identifies this facet of contemporary culture through its use of pastiche to critique settled notions of genre and nationalism. The chapter shows how the film troubles the conventional representation of the noir and neo-noir protagonist through its characterizations of Rorschach, who is both a representation of a classic (neo) noir protagonist and an exaggeration: a character who takes the implicit violence associated with the noir detective to psychotic extremes. Davis also explores questions of nationalism which emerge from the question of genre, and proves how the very concept of "American" culture itself becomes a form of pastiche, as the film creates an alternate representation of American history.

This collection would not be complete without a chapter dedicated to the oldest and one of the most revered superheroes of all time: Superman. *Smallville*, the longest-running comic book-based series in television history, belongs to an exclusive and prestigious grouping of television shows that lasted ten years and more (such as *Murder, She Wrote* [CBS, 1984–1996], and *Beverly Hills 90210* [Fox, 1990–2000]). But, it is also part of the new golden age that American television has being enjoying for at least the past ten years.[4] *Smallville* will end its ten-year run in 2011 after 217 episodes, 26 awards and 112 nominations.[5] We, therefore, felt it appropriate to end our collection with a chapter focusing on this series. We think that this discussion will hopefully initiate a new scholarly debate revolving around television superheroes, which will cast further light on the reasons behind their surprising audience attraction through narratives that last much longer than a film text and, as a result, provide the opportunity to investigate the nature, actions, instincts, and emotions of the superhero/ superheroine from every possible angle, as well as the sociopolitical issues that are examined in the weekly stories.

Shahriar Fouladi explores the adolescent Superman in "*Smallville*: Super Puberty and the Monstrous Superhero." Fouladi argues that *Smallville* creates a version of the first superhero that showcases the underlying monstrosity of most superheroes—a dark potential which lies at the root of the genre itself. Like most superheroes of this era in film and TV, Clark Kent on *Smallville* is coming of age. However, he experiences a kind of super puberty while he gradually discovers a number of new, powerful abilities and struggles to control them, questioning his moral mission at the same time. The author explains that the show combines aspects of the teen, horror, and superhero genres, and presents the pre–Superman Clark Kent as potentially either a savior or a destroyer, confirming the monstrous inverse that the superhero contains. Through close textual analysis, Fouladi demonstrates how Clark's monstrosity is exemplified in episodes in which he loses control of his super body, goes "bad" due to some alien or magical affliction, and faces doubles and fellow aliens who reflect the dark path that he could take. Finally, the chapter looks at the frequency in which the monstrous Superman appears on *Smallville*, how he is contrasted with the more heroic side of the protagonist, the social/cultural fears and fantasies engaged, and how viewers writing on the internet and in popular media respond to these depictions.

## Notes

1. http://boxofficemojo.com/alltime/world/
2. For example, *Dangerous Liaisons* (1988) is not only a film that discusses the French society of the late 18th century but also "very much a late-twentieth-century film, and one aspect of its metaphorical contemporaneousness is its feminist critique." (Palmer 257).
3. For a more detailed analysis on how Hollywood uses "generic formulas in order to assure production simplicity, standardization and economy," see the history of the biopic (Altman 38–44).

4. According to Janet McCabe and Kim Akass, the main reasons behind this change in the U.S. television landscape are "changes in broadcast delivery, new systems of production and distribution, economic restructuring based on brand equity and market differentiation, and the rise to prominence of Home Box Office (HBO) (3).This era witnessed a variety of different television narratives, such as *Sex and the City* (HBO 1998–2004), *The West Wing* (NBC, 1999–2006), *The Sopranos* (HBO, 1999–2007), *Six Feet Under* (HBO, 2001–2005), *24* (FX, 2001–2010), *Nip/Tuck* (FX, 2003–2010), *Lost* (2004–2010), among many others, which were not only different in that they preferred location shooting and film techniques to ameliorate the final product, but also because they touched upon provocative and socially controversial issues that proved to respond to the concerns and needs of the audience, who rewarded them with not only high ratings, but unprecedented fascination and even adulation.

5. These data are drawn from imdb.com.

# Exceptional Recognition

## The U.S. Global Dilemma
## in The Incredible Hulk,
## Iron Man, and Avatar*

ANTHONY PETER SPANAKOS

In *The Incredible Hulk* (2008), *Iron Man* (2008) and *Iron Man 2* (2010), and *Avatar* (2009), U.S. heroes go global and even intergalactic. They are all post–September 11 fantasies of self-preservation, but what is noteworthy is that the consistent enemy is not the distant other, but the military industrial complex (henceforth MIC) which gave initial life and meaning to the protagonists. The heroic struggle is to offer an alternative patriotism by defending what is just against official versions and representatives.

Interestingly, these post–September 11 Hollywood blockbusters deliberately contest an officialist and simplistic vision of patriotism and disqualification of the other, presenting awareness of the other as central to finding one's authentic self and struggle. They do this by showing the global superpower's tendency to both exploit and colonize the other, while identifying an authentic patriotism with recognition of the other. This chapter will examine this counter-patriotism by analyzing *Hulk* (2003), *The Incredible Hulk* (TIH), *Iron Man* (IM), *Iron Man 2* (IM2), and *Avatar* based on the notions of the exceptional state as articulated by Giorgio Agamben's *State of Exception* (2005) and *Homo Sacer* (1998) and the concept of recognition as developed by Paul Ricoeur in *The Course for Recognition* (2005). Once the films have been analyzed, this chapter will make some preliminary conclusions about how these films articulate the global dilemma of the U.S. state, which has become especially visible since September 11, 2001.

*The author thanks Despoina Kaklamanidou, Richard Gray, and Photini Spanakos for their comments on different iterations of this paper.*

## The Incredible Hulking Exception to Recognition

Carl Schmitt argues that the dominant ontology is one in which miracles are interventions into a neutral natural world (Schmitt, *The Concept of the Political*). Superheroes, accordingly, are "miraclemen." The Hulk, whose strength and physical invulnerability appear to be only limited by his potential for rage is, obviously, an exception to the rules that govern the natural and political world. He himself is an ontological exception, as he does not have an origin as much as he has a genesis, "created" not by a loving God but by scientists, some ambitious, some well-meaning, who work for the utterly unloving USMIC (*Hulk*). The USMIC creates a miracle by contravening the natural world and thoroughly transforming the nature of Banner's being. Since creating the Hulk, the USMIC wants to control him. But superheroes, like the Hulk, are exceptions to forms of rule. Like Batman, the Watchmen and other superheroes, they can hardly be reined in and, for this reason, cannot be controlled by the state, which is nominally sovereign over a given territory (Spanakos 2009). Non-superheroes, however, are different, and the state is more capable of demanding obedience of them. The visibility of the state as sovereign is greatest during periods when the state annuls the law.

In *Hulk*, there are two "sovereigns," in the sense of beings that are capable of suspending the laws that bind citizens under ordinary conditions: the first is Banner (Eric Bana and Ed Norton) *qua* Hulk, or even potential Hulk, as normal constraints do not apply to him. As Hulk, he grows into superhuman size and form, traverses huge swathes of territory by jumping, resists the most powerful shelling of ammunition, and has, apparently, limitless strength. As potential Hulk, otherwise normal operations become potentially life threatening. This is particularly evident in *The Incredible Hulk*. When confronted by local toughs in a factory in Rio, Banner coyly tells them that he is a different person when he is angry. More banal, but more attention-grabbing is when Banner's elevated heart rate during an almost sex scene with Betty Ross (Liv Tyler) brings him close to, literally, releasing the inner beast, losing control of not only his body but his self. Thus, even when he is not in the form of the Hulk, the potential to become the Hulk threatens to suspend the normal laws of nature.

The second, and more dangerous, sovereign is the USMIC, who, unlike the Hulk, has institutional and symbolic power as well as the material and symbolic interests of a sovereign. This is the sovereign which is the implicit enemy, the "bad guy," of the film. Obviously, the antagonist for Banner is Emil Blonsky (Tim Roth), hyped up on super-soldier serum. However, Emil was a soldier before he was transformed into a beast, so both of his incarnations are dependent upon the U.S. Military Industrial Complex. This takes a critical view of the USMIC, especially when compared with the origin of Captain America, the pinnacle of superhero patriotism. Both Steve Rogers and Blonsky volunteered to be part of the super serum experiment. But unlike Steve who was too sickly and weak to join the U.S. armed forces and was given the serum because he insisted on serving his country in World War II, Blonsky was a soldier whose decision to take the superhero serum was based on ego; that is his taking vengeance on the Hulk. These perversions in patriotism are fomented, rather than constrained, by the USMIC in both Hulk movies. The perversion of U.S. patriotism by the USMIC can be seen in the life of Bruce Banner. Pre-gamma rays, Banner was either a peace loving scientist or a geeky scientist pushed around by more aggressive and macho personalities, such as potential father-in-law General Ross. He was within the USMIC, but at its social and ethical margins. Yet he still saw himself within that structure. Indeed, his love interest was the daughter of the General, the personification of the greed, arrogance, and bellicosity of that system.

Ricoeur's *The Course of Recognition* aims to present a philosophy of recognition, and does so with a progressive typology which moves from the verbal "recognize" to the substantive "recognition" (19). As one moves towards the latter, one becomes more aware of the other, while also reaching a higher form of knowing (instead of recognizing an object, one can recognize and be recognized by self and others) (ibid. 21). But this process is neither smooth nor easy. In an earlier essay, Ricoeur writes that "the discovery of the plurality of cultures is never a harmless experience.... When we discover that there are several cultures instead of just one ... it becomes possible that ... we ourselves are an 'other' among others" (Ricoeur, *History and Truth*, 277–278). Recognition by others may begin with misrecognition, or "the refusal of recognition," but it "anticipates," without "accomplishing," mutuality (Ricoeur, *The Course of Recognition*, 161, 255). Over time there is a shift "[...] from disregard toward consideration, from injustice toward respect," which finds its rational end in the then institutionalization of recognition in hierarchies (like the state) (ibid. 171).

Prior to becoming the Hulk, Banner had a residual misrecognition, a "refusal of recognition" (ibid. 161) of the USMIC, even though he was literally and figuratively at its very epicenter. Nevertheless, it is only once he is bombarded by gamma rays that he fully recognizes this. This makes him more aware of how he is mis-recognized by the USMIC father-figure. To it, he becomes a guinea pig, a science project of the system that once employed him, rather than a creative scientist with a voice that is heard. *The Incredible Hulk* shows the clear conflict over Banner's identity: he sees himself as a human afflicted with an illness that he wants to cure, and the USMIC refuses him his humanity and considers him military property, a military experiment which will lead to better scientific knowledge and still more powerful weapons. The USMIC's misrecognition of Banner and Banner's refusal to continue to see himself within the USMIC create a search for a new identity on the part of Banner and open the possibility of awareness of others. This is the beginning of the hero's quest. Fleeing dehumanization and persecution, he travels, helping others who face issues that are similar in nature, if not in degree. *The Incredible Hulk* television series (CBS, 1978–1982) was most characterized by Banner's lonely peregrinations, constantly pursued by the USMIC which had created but, curiously, could not understand him. Or rather, they mis-recognized him as a weapon, a technological missing link, but certainly not a man. Globalization and September 11 shrank the world for the constant traveler who was previously largely confined to the United States, particularly the U.S. Southwest (in *IM2* there are references made to Banner in the form of "problems in the Southwest"), making it more difficult to disappear. In his post–September 11 film version, however, Banner, like the U.S., goes global, not to the Rio de Janeiro of upscale *Barra de Tijuca* or *Ipanema*, or even the commercial Copacabana, but to Rio's *favelas* (shantytowns).

When Steve Weintraub interviewed *The Incredible Hulk* director Louis Leterrier and asked why he filmed in Brazil and its *favelas*, Leterrier responded: "We needed a place in the world where Bruce Banner could truly disappear...."[1] The *favela*, he explained, "is madness... It is a place that is a little at the margins of the law, with so many people packed in together."[2] Marvel comics had been concerned about security, Leterrier says, "[b]ecause for them... Brazil is no-man's land. You are going to get shot if you go there..." but "[n]othing happened. The place worked very well for our goal of a sea of humanity. The panoramic view in the beginning is not computer graphics. It is our helicopter flying over the *favela* of Rocinha for two minutes."

The *favela* could only be other to a U.S. born scientist who grew up in military bases and was a product of the highest levels of techno-modernity. But the current Bruce Banner no longer recognizes himself in the USMIC and, remarkably, finds tranquility in the *favela*. Given that the *favela* represents danger in the mind of Brazilians (Caldeira 2000), it is interesting that only here is Banner able to settle down. After being on the run in his native land, the *favela* becomes the space in which he is able to maintain an address, build a remarkably well-equipped lab, and get a regular job. So settled is he that he is able to regularly meet with a Brazilian jiu jitsu master who tries to teach him to control his breathing and anger (the mystical sage of the developing world solving the problems of technology and development), develop feelings for a local woman and irritate local men who sexually harass her (the outsider protects the woman from her macho society). All of this, clichés and romanticization of the other aside, requires a certain stasis, a stability, which is normally absent from the life of a man whose anger triggers a transformation into the Hulk.

Although he is certainly not "home," and he does not become the other (he is still a "gringo" to coworkers, and a foreigner to the woman in the factory), he becomes a friend to the woman and a valued employee to his boss. Bruce recognizes them as they begin to recognize him, incompletely, but at least they see him as a human being. There is, of course, dissymmetry in these relations. The heckling chauvinists stand no chance against an enraged Banner, he is overqualified to work at a bottling factory, and he is unable to communicate linguistically adequately with his possible female love interest. This is akin to

Ricoeur's analysis of the ultimate form of recognition, mutual recognition, which he likens to a gift exchange. In that exchange, the goal is not to pay that which is owed for a service or to match exchange equal goods, but to establish mutual relations. "The one is not the other. We exchange gifts, but not places ... [and a] just distance is maintained at the heart of mutuality, a just distance that integrates respect into intimacy" (*The Course of Recognition*, 263).

The irony is that the anarchic space at the margins of global society, a space of high rates of crime, murder, and gang activity, is a space of peace and healing to the itinerant superhero until the global sovereign enters, transforming it into a space of danger and anarchy. Although Leterrier described the *favela* as "madness," prior to the arrival of the USMIC, it is an overcrowded island of peace for the perpetually pursued gamma-particle–enhanced physicist. Once the USMIC discovers that Banner is in Rio, it invades Brazil, literally occupying the *favela* and setting off an exhilarating chase scene in which the cramped, uneven, and spontaneous topography of the *favela* transforms from backpacker *chic* to labyrinthine danger. While in Brazil, Banner displays an orientation towards mutual recognition, reflective of a U.S. search for understanding and respect of the other in coming to terms with itself, a self that has become unrecognizable as ethics have not developed as quickly as technology. But Banner's time in Brazil, and later, Central America, is brief. The majority of the film chronicles his time facing the USMIC in the U.S. This is because the time in which he "lives a normal life" and "finds himself" is cut short when the USMIC essentially declares an exception regarding the new, peaceful state of affairs.

Regardless of whether it operates on U.S. soil or not, the USMIC is a sovereign in Agambenian terms. It has neither the right to enter into Brazil nor to comb its *favelas*, and it is utterly unaccountable for its doing both. Yet, in *TIH*, the Brazilian government and the population of the *favela* are unable to resist the constitutive power of the USMIC, the power to constitute the system of relations from which power may become authority, fear and obedience (de la Durantaye 339). This is, of course, an exaggeration of U.S. power, but the U.S. invasions of Afghanistan and Iraq, as well as a host of other countries, including many in the Americas, display a preoccupying precedent. What is interesting in *The Incredible Hulk* is that the USMIC does not simply, *de facto*, declare an exception in a Brazilian *favela*, a territory over which it has no jurisdiction, but it operates within the United States itself with little regard for the legal sovereign, the U.S. government. This lack of concern for the powers of government and the constraints that they place on government agents, one of which is this unit of the USMIC, is analogous to Agamben's critique of the November 13, 2001 declaration of U.S. president Bush "which authorized the 'indefinite detention' and trial by 'military commissions' (not to be confused with military tribunals provided for by the law of war) of noncitizens suspected of involvement in terrorist activities" (Agamben, *Homo Sacer*, 3). The state, possessing the ability to declare emergency powers to suspend constraints, had created the conditions for the recurrent and regular recourse to exceptional powers which placed citizens in a space of indistinction between living a good life and barely living.[3]

## I(ron Man) Am the Exception and You Can't Have Me

*Iron Man 2* begins with the outrageous Tony Stark (Robert Downey, Jr.) declaring "I have privatized peace" (IM2). It is little wonder that the rest of the movie consists of the U.S. government trying to "nationalize" peace by getting control over his armor and technology. In fact, in both *Iron Man* and *Iron Man 2*, Tony Stark's primary enemies are the USMIC and the U.S. government itself. This may surprise fans of the comic book who watched him fight a host of Cold War enemies, "such Communist super villains as the Mandarin, Crimson Dynamo, the Red Ghost and Titanium Man" (McCoy B10). Of course, the official villain in *IM2* is former Soviet scientist, Ivan Vanko (Mickey Rourke), but the psychological drama that drives the "origin" of Vanko *qua* supervillain centers on U.S.–Soviet Cold War military complexes which encouraged scientific investigations, as well as the personal betrayal of Anton Vanko (Ivan's father, played by Yevgeni Lazarev) by Howard Stark (Tony's father, played by John Slattery), who commercialized the elder Vanko's research. If the USMIC produced a Hulk, it also produced Vanko the villain.

What makes Stark politically interesting as a superhero is that he is aware of the exceptionalism that power entails—that it suspends rules (Schmitt *The Concept of the Political*; Agamben *State of Exception*). *Iron Man* begins with Tony Stark's trip to Afghanistan, where he oversees some of the battle sites in which the weaponry made by his company is being used by U.S. soldiers.[4] He goes as the leading military contractor, a man at the very heart of the USMIC. Afghanistan, like the *favela*, may be seen as a "no-man's land," an anarchic space in which competing armed groups jockey for position and dominion. As an arms dealer, it is a great market. Stark, however, is not just an arms dealer but a patriot who wants to supply U.S. soldiers with weapons so that they can more effectively and safely serve their missions. He makes no apologies, telling one reporter "[t]he day weapons are no longer needed to keep the peace I'll start making bricks and beams for baby hospitals" (Dennis C5). The *naïveté* of his position is betrayed when he discovers that his weapons were used against U.S. soldiers and, worse, that his company was funding both sides of the conflict.

This should hardly surprise, since the USMIC inserts itself into states of exception where it operates with little oversight. According to Agamben, the U.S. has used the global War on Terror to declare a permanent state of exception wherein the U.S. as "sovereign" can not only intervene into the activities of another *de jure* sovereign state, but can replace it altogether, or eliminate it without quite replacing it (the famous "Pottery Barn rule" applies to the invasions of Afghanistan and Iraq). The U.S. authorized its intervention in Afghanistan, with considerable support among most nations in the world, and the U.S. invasion of Iraq was equally self-authorized, although it received much less support within the international community. Additionally, not only are U.S. military police and military performing duties for which they have not been trained, but the U.S. relies heavily on private security forces like Blackwater, indicating that normal rules of accountability do not apply.

At the heart of the "global state of exception" and the U.S. military engagement in exceptional spaces is the USMIC, and the fictional Stark Industries is the beast. Tony Stark has a "moment of clarity" in Afghanistan. While Banner is shocked by what he has become, Stark is horrified by who he is and of what he is a part. Stark is only able to escape, and then to continue living, because he pioneers a new technology in Afghanistan. The obvious technology is that of the Iron Man suit, but the real technology (seen in greater depth in *IM2*) is the device that keeps his heart running. Stark not only develops a new conscience in Afghanistan, but he has a literal change of heart. When he returns from Afghanistan, he tells the press "I saw young Americans killed by the very weapons I created to defend and protect them... And I saw that I had become part of a system that was comfortable with zero accountability" (Dennis C5).

The new Tony is subject to derision by an old family friend, Obadiah Stane (Jeff Bridges) at the company his father founded and built. Given how well Stane knows Tony, it is only fitting that he completely misrecognizes the new version of him. He tries to convince Tony that he is experiencing Post-Traumatic Stress Disorder, is being unrealistic in thinking that a weapons company will promote peace, and, finally, that he is not himself. Few people should understand Tony better, since few people are so much "like" Tony. But Tony's identity has shifted as his experience in Afghanistan has forced him to take accountability for his recognition before others as a producer of arms, which, ultimately, kill people, including American soldiers. Tony no longer countenances the ability of the USMIC to declare a state of exception (Agamben, *State of Exception,* 86) and eliminate discussions of how military technologies are used, what sort of missions are possible, how to evaluate success, and so on.

The shift in identity encourages the quirkily solipsistic Stark to not just consider his image (recognition before others), but to think of the gifts he can give in a dissymmetrical exchange of mutual recognition. In *IM*, his interaction with Yinsen (Shaun Toub), the captured scientist whose research he admired, creates the possibility for him to continue living (with his new heart) and to be someone new (through the Iron Man suit). Although he continues to appear to be a self-centered *bon vivant*, he becomes far more aware of others. Tony tries, but is unable, to save Yinsen from a gang of terrorists armed with Stark

International weapons. On a personal level, in both *Iron Man* films he moves from playboy towards something resembling monogamy as he becomes willing to acknowledge (and reciprocate) how his faithful assistant and subsequent manager of his company, Pepper Potts (Gwyneth Paltrow), recognizes him.

For all the changes in his life and the good he tries to do, Tony works under adverse circumstances. He may be able to use the Iron Man suit to fight his enemies, but he is less able to suspend the rules to punish injustice more generally. The same cannot be said for Stane. Stane, a personification of the USMIC, exerts the sovereign power to declare exceptions throughout *IM*, just as the U.S. government does throughout *IM2*. If Agamben's sovereign is visible most clearly in his suspension of a constitutional order, a sovereign is excessively visible when it suspends the most fundamental rights within a given constitutional order. In both *Iron Man* films, the USMIC and the U.S. government do exactly this by using their power (control over stockholders, secretly charging James Rhodes [Don Cheadle] to steal the Iron Man suit) to abrogate Stark's control over his company, his intellectual property rights, as well as his personal liberty. Fittingly, during his appearance before Congress in *IM2* when he is asked to turn over the Iron Man technology to the government, he says "I am Iron Man. You can't have me." But that is just the sort of power that the sovereign has in a state of exception when anomie and *nomos* overlap, where the sovereign strips away rights and dignity, leaving only "bare life" (Agamben, *State of Exception*, 87–88). If this is the state of affairs led by the USMIC in the post–September 11 approach to global encounters with the other, Tony Stark's demand of autonomy and rejection of the ability of the USMIC/U.S. state's declaration of a state of exception to strip him of fundamental U.S. values (liberty, property rights) are counter-patriotism. The enemy is the perverse and bellicose patriotism promoted by those who will and do profit from facilitating warfare, not the former Soviet scientist.

After all, Vanko is hired by Justin Hammer (Sam Rockwell), a competitor in the provision of military goods for the express purpose of besting Tony Stark. Rather than be horrified, or at least concerned, by the violence and egoism that motivates Vanko's use of his technology in his first confrontation with Iron Man, Hammer gives him virtual *carte blanche* to develop a new army of robotic warriors (*IM2*). That Hammer cannot control Vanko is not because of who Vanko is, but the nature of the MIC, whose aim is to transform violence into power and then into authority. In a state of exception, this is possible. Stark is the fly in the ointment that shakes the viewer out of the idea that the events of September 11 created an ongoing condition of lawlessness in which the U.S. state could act as sovereign without regard to the fundamental liberties and rights that constitute the authentic legitimacy of the state.

## Exceptional Anthropology

The prototypical patriot in U.S. film narratives is a soldier, usually not an officer, but a "grunt," a John Wayne–like character, who genuinely represents the values of the USA. This patriotism is not limited to the well behaved, disciplined soldier, but even to those on the criminal and emotional margins of the armed forces as seen in *The Dirty Dozen* (1967). The soldier is, of course, a type for the superhero. Protagonists in science fiction fantasy films may not be "superheroes," but their access to technology-enabling abilities to contravene the normal and natural limitations on viewers blur the line between science fiction and superheroes. Jake Scully (Sam Worthington) may not be a superhero *per se*, but his ability to link into an avatar essentially gives him super-heroic abilities, and the epic tale of super-powered groups fighting over who has the legitimate claim to a specific territory and/or its people are central to the super-hero mind. Central to *Avatar*, and indeed most of James Cameron's science fiction films, is the way in which technology intervenes into the normal — changing expectations, inverting who may be a hero and under what conditions. Although technology, like the powers of the Hulk, Iron Man, or even the Watch-men and Miraclemen, has liberating and utopian potential, Cameron's films are consistently interrupted by the way that power captures technology.[5] The same could be said of Agamben's state of exception where the break in the normal state of affairs could bring an authentic shift (*State of Exception*, 57), but most of Agamben's writings focus on what state of exceptions actually do.

If Bush's USA, according to Agamben, creates a global state of exception through which the nation can reconstitute global political space, Cameron's humans in *Avatar* create an intergalactic exception in the form of an allegory — pregnant with appropriations from various folk tales and historical events — of the exploitation of the noble savage by the cruelly civilized. At the root of this colonialism is a politic of necessity, the usual justification for the state of exception, as the humans who have bankrupted their own world of resources now seek to destroy the world of another to fuel their own empire and needs. In so doing, the humans employ a private military force to conduct observations and military research on the possibility of extracting untold wealth of "unobtainium" from the Na'vi people. Key to that mission is Jake Scully, a wheelchair-bound marine who gives regular observations of the other, its customs and world, to the intergalactic military industrial complex. Along the way, he goes native as he discovers the "humanity" of the Na'vi and questions the humanity of his own people. This quest from misrecognition to recognition is made possible through the richness of the depiction of the Na'vi world in *Avatar*.

Cameron wanted the world to be credible "because the audience is invited to relate to [the Na'vi], not as aliens but as creatures which express some aspect of ourselves which we admire and aspire to" (Keegan 254). In one discussion, his creative group asked the following questions: "What is the lifespan of the average Na'vi? What is the composition of the atmosphere on Pandora? Why does unobtainium float?" (ibid. 253). The goal was to produce a real world, a real people, with whom the viewer would sympathize, whom Jake Scully could come to know once he was capable of overcoming his military background and orders. Cameron also enlisted Paul Frommer, a University of Southern California trained linguist, to create the language of the Na'vi people, building on elements of Malay, Persian, Hebrew, and Chinese among other languages (ibid. 242; Zimmer 20).[6]

Cameron's meticulous concern for building a world that was credible and yet alien facilitates the viewer's belief that a genuine and morally equal world exists on Pandora, so that the Na'vi can be seen as victims of human violence. The film consistently displays securing unobtainium as the sole motivation for the military industrial complex's interest in understanding the Na'vi, and when the MIC becomes convinced that the unobtainium can only be obtained by destroying the other, it literally destroys the "tree of life" (Hometree) that spiritually and socially sustains the Na'vi people. While explaining what unobtainium is, Cameron says "It's diamonds in South Africa. It's tea to the nineteenth-century British. It's oil to twentieth-century America. It's just another in a long list of substances that cause one group of people to get into ships and go kick the [*&#@] ... out of another group of people to take what is growing on or buried under their ancestral lands" (Keegan 253). Here, it is worth returning to Agamben.

Although the politics of "necessity" are used to justify exceptional powers (the emergency powers of the governments in World War II, changes in rights of detainees in the U.S. following September 11), Agamben pushes the claim of necessity into the ontological realm, where a biopolitical machine creates a fictive state of exception to perpetuate its control over human life and its reduction of humans to *homines sacri*, people who have no legal standing within the state and can be disposed of at the state's pleasure (*State of Exception*, 87). Cameron's blasé description of unobtainium shows how very inessential it is to his plot. If not unobtainium, there would be some other reason for his humans to use their techno-military superiority to extend their dominium over territories, and that reason would be used to contravene and suspend diplomatic, ethical, and inter-species norms. And yet, amidst the *machtpolitik* and sovereign exceptionalism of the military industrial complex, there is the love story, and the heroic journey of Jake Scully.

Importantly, Scully's heroism cannot be a military one, as he has lost his ability to use his legs, and he can only "serve" his country/race/private security corporation by entering into the unit link chamber and merging with his avatar. He was chosen as the replacement for his brother, a scientist, who was part of scientist Grace Augustine's (Sigourney Weaver) study of the Na'vi, and he is given a secret mission by Colonel Quaritch (Stephen Lang) to bring information back to him so that the humans can defeat the Na'vi. Scully, initially, is thrilled at the chance to be back in the field as a soldier and to have a fully functional body. The discovery of his new body and the world that it allows him to enter gives the audience the opportunity to observe the various stages of recognition for Ricoeur (from active to passive, from knowledge of objects to recognition by others) by understanding the "humanity" of the other, as Cameron alluded to earlier.

Scully begins the path of recognition, as Ricoeur suggests, by focusing on objects: getting used to his new body (that he can walk, run) and the world of the Na'vi (its particular flora and fauna). He is looking for knowledge about the world and about his new body, but this knowledge is unreflective, as he does not think about who he is or how the new body has changed him. Rather his concern is the object (the body) that he now occupies. As he becomes more accustomed to linking into his avatar, he literally loses himself in the forest that is the home of the Na'vi. He meets Neytiri (Zoe Saldana) as she both saves his life and shows utter disdain for him, recognizing him, probably fairly accurately, for what he is. In an early report, he says: "'It's hard to put into words the connection the people have to the forest... They see a network of energy that flows through all living things. They know that all energy is only borrowed—and one day you have to give it back'" (Fitzpatrick 61). The report shows a certain respect Scully has developed for the Na'vi—a romanticization perhaps—but he has yet to identify with them. Nevertheless, he is not seeing them as objects as much as he recognizes them as similar beings.

As the film narrative and love story progress, Scully's avatar becomes increasingly "the real" Jake. Neytiri is revealed as a real, but flawed, "person" who can be loved, and the "primitive," "bestial" Na'vi become a group that Scully not only respects, but wants to join. The ritual of his joining the Na'vi, as well as the later love/marriage scene, are indicative of his rejection of his old self, the one that winked at Colonel Quaritch while giving reports to Dr. Augustine. In the end, it is Scully who leads the Na'vi in battle against his former colleagues.

Jake Scully is not an obvious superhero, since that term connotes beings with powers that are outside of what is possible for normal humans. But that is a bit of a misconception. Superhero is a trademark owned by Marvel and DC comics, publishers who have produced storylines with protagonists and antagonists with and without powers in many different genres (war, fantasy, science fiction, detective, among others). Some of the most beloved superheroes have no powers at all (Batman, Robin, Iron Man, Hawkeye, Punisher, Phantom, most of the Watchmen) as do some of their supervillains (Penguin, Joker, Mr. Freeze, and so on). However, by dressing up in costume, changing their identity, and relying on wits and gadgets, they are able to do what others (their readers) cannot, but wish they could. Jake Scully has no powers; in fact, he is bound to a wheelchair. But through the linking chamber he adopts a new physical identity and is able to contravene the restrictions of his natural body. In the process, he conquers a force of heavily armed robotic soldiers. This gives him affinity with Batman and Iron Man, but his superheroism is not the definitive characteristic that makes him compelling. It is not becoming the massive and powerful Na'vi, but the transformation (thanks to his "deprogramming" and "training" by scientist Grace Augustine and lover Neytiri) into a thinking being who understands, loves, and almost dies defending the other (Talalay 2010) that makes him heroic. Scully becomes a being capable of "recognizing" another and being recognized by others (from snoop to traitor to leader). Midway through the film, Neytiri, her parents, and the Na'vi, at one point, believe Scully was responsible for the destruction of their world (Hometree). They "misrecognize" Scully, believing him to be the man he was an hour earlier in the film and only when he returns riding on the back of a Toruk and proposes a new battle against the humans is he "recognized" by the Na'vi as the person he has become: the one who feels community with them. Neytiri recognizes him there and later, in the fullness of his identity, when the unit link chamber in which Scully's body sleeps is attacked. This gives her the opportunity to see Scully for "who he is," and she sees in this disabled veteran the man she loves.

Dr. Augustine, who had been unreceptive to his joining the mission initially, also recognizes this change. Her name, Grace Augustine, immediately references the Christian Saint who justified Christian participation in military action. Saint Augustine explained that a Christian could unite "thou shalt not murder" and "love thy neighbor" if he goes to battle out of love for a neighbor that he seeks to defend. The Parable of the Good Samaritan is the answer that Christ gives to the question of "who is my neighbor?," and in Dr. Augustine's vision, the neighbor is the Na'vi. Certainly Jake, similar to Banner, remains Jake, although, through the link chamber, he is able to occupy the body of the other. Nevertheless, he is not so much transformed into the Na'vi as he becomes a being capable of understanding them, one who is careful to not exploit the asymmetries between them (Ricoeur, *The Course of Recognition*, 263).

## The Patriotism Project

Scully is interesting not simply because he is a superhero, but more importantly because he is "the embodiment of the hero's journey" (Dargis 2009). *Avatar* shows not only the quest of a superhero but a superpower as well, since it highlights the integrity of the U.S. patriot who seeks to do what is right, even if it means "betraying" one's government or official mission. This is necessary because of how corrupt the patriotism of the USA, or, in this case, the humans, have become as a result of the greed and violence promoted by the military industrial complex. Scully's success in his battle against the military industrial complex (and a snarling Neytiri protecting her "man/atar" by killing Quaritch) represents a liberal fantasy of the overcoming of power by reason, a project that is central to Ricoeur's *The Course of Recognition.*[8] But there are no Scullys without a "sovereign" capable of suspending the norms, laws, and rights that exist in non-exceptional situations, and this sovereign in post–September 11 films is intimately tied to the U.S. government, the USMIC, and visions of official patriotism.

What has dominated U.S. news, and its perception, since 2001, is not its victimization at the hands of a sophisticated global terrorist network, but its willingness to enter into moral grey areas and its excessively bellicose pursuit of its interests in the land of the "other." The U.S. government has invaded and occupied two countries, adding to the already considerable number of countries where the U.S. has a physical military presence. Military action into the affairs of other countries was justified by necessity, echoing the words of Agamben's sovereign, and U.S. citizens were expected to fall into rank behind U.S. foreign policies because "you are either with us or against us."

The selling of war and the efforts to transform the meaning of patriotism were not without its limits. Scandals emerged immediately following the fall of the Saddam Hussein government in Iraq when military contracts were limited to U.S. companies with ties to Dick Cheney, who had been the CEO of Haliburton for the five years prior to becoming Vice President. More challenges emerged when Blackwater, a private military force, which was employed by the occupying government to reduce the financial, legal, and human cost to the U.S. Armed Forces, was involved in a number of scandals, raising questions about what law a private armed force operates under. The case for supporting official U.S. policies became more difficult when images of torture and humiliation emerged from a prison in Iraq. Torture, previously denied, was justified, like the use of military action, on the basis of necessity, getting information so that victory could be secured in the war against insurgents in Iraq — insurgents who in-surged only after the invasion. The tail seemed to be wagging the dog. This became more apparent when, long after the invasion, it was clear that the evidence that the Hussein regime possessed weapons of mass destruction was not especially credible.

Had the USA misrecognized the "other"? Had it allowed the military industrial complex to drag it and its citizens into conflicts with the other (Iraq) that it essentially did not know? The films analyzed here suggest that their filmmakers believe that both are the case. Superheroism in their films involves finding an authentic and just patriotism while rejecting official accounts and/or the narrative of the U.S. military industrial complex. Importantly, superheroes find themselves in the moral and physical territory of the other and, as a result of the encounter, they emerge as legitimate heroes. The films, then, point to the danger of a politics of "exception" and the need for re-education in the "course of recognition." They also strike at the heart of a fundamental dilemma that the USA faces: as the most powerful country it engages in periodic diplomatic and military missions to ensure global security, but doing so necessitates understanding the many global others with which it must deal. Far more attention has been given to force, and less to recognition.

*Hulk, The Incredible Hulk, Iron Man* and *Iron Man 2,* and *Avatar* warn that as long as the U.S. military industrial complex shapes patriotism and U.S. encounters with the other, the USA will continue to "misrecognize" too many people as *homines sacri,* stripping them of their rights and the completeness of being human, reducing them to "bare life." And they, like Odysseus's countrymen, "a savage race that hoard, and sleep, and feed," are likely to continue "to know not" "us." The dangers of this in a post–September 11 world are potentially catastrophic. An antidote, Ricoeur would suggest, adds to the Delphic oracle, saying that to "know thyself" one must recognize and be recognized properly by the other.

## Notes

1. There are two versions of this interview. It was originally posted in Portuguese and then an English version was posted. The interview appears to be carried out in English, but the English version that was posted does not seem to be the original. The quotes included here are the author's translations of the Portuguese text.

2. Leterrier had originally thought of shooting parts of the film somewhere in Asia, particularly Hong Kong, but when he learned that *Batman* was being filmed there, he looked elsewhere. It is not incidental that the efforts of two blockbusters to reimagine solitary superheroes fleeing from injustice in their own society so that they could "recover" would take place towards the margins of the Western mind. For readers interested in the use of Rio in the film, the panoramic initial shot in the movie was Rocinha, Latin America's largest shantytown, but most of the time in "Rocinha" was filmed in the *favela* "Tavares Bastos," one of the safer *favelas.* In truth, the *favela* is used essentially for Banner's home space and the chase scene, where it serves as a labyrinth where Thomas Malthus meets Karl Marx. The rest of "Rio" was filmed in Canada. However, while Canada is transformed into Brazil, Brazil transforms into other Latin American locations. The parts of the film that claim to take place in Chiapas, Mexico, and in Guatemala, were filmed in Santa Teresa, Lapa and the Floresta de Tijuca, neighborhoods of Rio de Janeiro.

4. See Agamben, *Homo Sacer* 82.

5. This is a reworking of the *Iron Man* origin in the comics where Stark was captured in Vietnam, not Afghanistan. Thus U.S. imperialism has always played a part in his "becoming" Iron Man.

6. His influential account of robots and Skynet are, perhaps, the most well-known contemporary popular culture expression of exceptionalism into the human condition (see his *Terminator* series).

7. Cameron is not the first to have his fictional language become real. Marc Okrand, a University of California Berkeley trained linguist, created the "Klingon" language which is now spoken by many Star Trek fans throughout the world.

8. This is especially true as he follows the way that Hegel tried to de-fang the violence in Hobbes's state of nature.

# "You Took My Advice About Theatricality a Bit ... Literally"

## Theatricality and Cybernetics of Good and Evil in Batman Begins, The Dark Knight, Spider-Man, and X-Men

JOHANNES SCHLEGEL *and*
FRANK HABERMANN

## Introduction

It comes as no surprise that one of the basal narrative patterns of superhero films (and comic books alike) is the eternal Manichean struggle of good versus evil. The eminent comic book writer and former president of Marvel Comics Stan Lee phrased it this way: "After all, the battle between a hero and a villain (which is what virtually all our stories get down to) is basically a conflict between a good guy and a bad guy, or between good and evil" (165). In his movie *Unbreakable* (2000), director M. Night Shyamalan illustrates how the genre of the superhero film as such is constituted by this dichotomy from the outset — and subverts it at the same time: *Unbreakable* tells the story of David Dunn (Bruce Willis), who, after being the sole survivor of an atrocious train crash, is contacted by Elijah Price (Samuel L. Jackson). Price reveals that he suffers from *osteogenesis imperfecta*, or brittle bone disease, and believes that Dunn has a complementary "gift," that is to say he is almost invulnerable. In the final sequence, however, which is another example for Shyamalan's notorious trademark twist endings, Dunn comes to understand that Price is the mastermind behind a series of horrifying terrorist attacks and therefore responsible for hundreds of deaths. Price's revelation, significantly set in a comic bookstore, appears to be a rather cynical version of the concept of *felix culpa*: evil exists in order to bring forth a greater good. Accordingly, the villain of

Shyamalan's film construes a connection between his suffering and Dunn's ability, and therefore bestows meaning upon it: "You know what the scariest thing is? To not know your place in this world. To not know why you are here. [...] Now that I know who you are, I know who I am. I am not a mistake. It all makes sense. In a comic, you know how you can tell who the arch villain's going to be? He is the exact opposite of the hero."

This account is self-referential indeed, as it obviously exceeds the villain's somewhat perverse justification by unfolding the underlying, constitutive principle of the genre as such: while the film seemingly starts as a thriller, it turns into a superhero film in the end, cumulating in the final confrontation of "good" and "evil."[1] By means of this twist, therefore, and by putting emphasis on the fact that the dichotomy is not given, but first and foremost construed and, thus exhibiting it explicitly, Shyamalan subverts the said premise. This feature renders *Unbreakable* postmodern and separates it from its predecessors, which still were able to depict an ontological, that is, given distinction between good and evil. Richard Donner's *Superman* (1978), for instance, even pictures its eponymous hero as a "Christ or Messiah-like figure" delivering man from evil (Schenk 33). In 21st-century superhero film, however, the situation seems to be more complicated. Significantly, in Guillermo del Toro's pertinent films even the devil Hellboy (Ron Perlman) chooses to fight metaphysical evil—notwithstanding that he is not only a descendant from hell ("son of the fallen one"), a beast of the apocalypse whose destiny is "to bring about the destruction of the earth" (*Hellboy II*, 2008) but that he is also conjured by the Nazis with the help of the sinister, diabolical occultist Rasputin (Karel Roden). A greater disposition to evil could scarcely be dreamt up—yet there is hardly any doubt what side Hellboy is actually on. The boundary between good and evil, therefore, seems to be at least permeable—and, consequently, the very distinction no longer absolute. In the following, this paper shall argue that, at least as far as the postmodern superhero film is concerned, a fundamental ambiguity stems precisely from this.[2]

If the notion of such an ambiguity should prove correct, however, it is of vital importance to avoid two diametric fallacies: first, to normatively postulate or assert an ontological distinction *a priori*, and second, to abrogate the distinction entirely. By no means are both of these polar positions merely theoretical differentiations. John Kenneth Muir, for instance, states in his *Encyclopedia of Superheroes on Film and Television* that after 9/11

> We all wanted desperately to believe that good can defeat evil, and, perhaps more to the point, that there is a clear line differentiating these opposing philosophies [...]. Superheroes became comforting and safe, like creamy vanilla ice cream, reflecting pure American values and innocence [7].

While Muir's account relies completely on a distinct, stable differentiation between good and evil, the German scholar Bernd Scheffer, on the other hand, most recently stated apodictically that the well-proven differentiation could not be wielded any longer at all (257–270).[3] Quite contrary to these points of view, the present paper seeks to argue that recent superhero film does not allow for presupposing such a "clear line" — and neither does it for abolishing that distinction totally. Circumventing these fallacies, therefore, the dichotomy of good and evil in contemporary superhero films is first and foremost negotiated, performatively generated and constantly debated, rendering it an unstable phenomenon of produced *and* ascribed meaning that has to be reaffirmed perpetually. Instead of focusing on representations of evil, which would require a secure, *linear* relation between a signifier and the signified, this paper aims at investigating two modes that provide a *processual* approach towards both the performative origin of the ambiguity *and* its negotiation and (re-)evaluation: first, theatricality and second, cybernetics. In order not to give a comprehensive survey, but instead a sequence of exemplary case studies highlighting different, complementary aspects of such processes, we will predominantly focus on Christopher Nolan's *Batman Begins* (2005) and *The Dark Knight* (2008), Sam Raimi's *Spider-Man* trilogy (2002, 2004, 2007), and, last but not least, on Bryan Singer's *X-Men* (2000) and *X2* (2003), and Brett Ratner's *X-Men: The Last Stand* (2006).[4]

## The Will to Act

Given the presence of constitutive and frequently campy costumes in this genre, theatricality seems to be intrinsic to it from the outset — just as the Manichean plot structure. Neither of them, however, should be taken for granted. Christopher Nolan's *Batman Begins* takes this premise seriously and self-reflexively features and thus exhibits the motif of theatricality as a rather overt subtext, being explicitly addressed at least four times by various characters.

It is referred to for the first time in an approximately five-minute-long sequence, in which Bruce Wayne (Christian Bale) is trained by Ducard (Liam Neeson) after being released from the prison camp. In a cross-cut sequence, shots of both men in combat training alternate with shots of Ducard explaining the "methods" of the League of Shadows, while parts of this explanation serve as voice-over in the training shots and thus guarantee continuity: "You have learned to bury your guilt with anger. I will teach you to confront it and to face the truth. You know how to fight six men. We can teach you how to engage 600. You know how to disappear. We can teach you to become truly invisible."

Ultimately, the means to achieve this end is the staging of a daunting spectacle, including the utilization of explosive powders to create distractions. Accordingly, Ducard states that "theatricality and deception are powerful agents. You must become more than a man in the minds of your opponents." Thereby, *Batman Begins* draws upon the Aristotelian connection of theatre (in a more general sense) and fear (phobos)—both of which are addressed throughout the whole film and more often than not are intertwined, as, for instance, in the sequence that inevitably results in the murder of Thomas (Linus Roache) and Martha Wayne (Sara Stewart): The family attends a production of Arrigo Boito's opera *Mefistofele*, but leaves early as Bruce is too terrified by the events on stage.[5]

It is not merely by chance that *Batman Begins* substitutes the cinema for the theatre and thus theatricality, which does not only signify consciousness of class—the alleged elitist medium opera as opposed to the egalitarian cinema[6]—but furthermore serves to illustrate the birth of the vigilante Batman from the spirit of theatre. During the aforesaid practice session, Ducard confronts Wayne's feelings of guilt and his denial of his father's failure resulting from the murder: "Your parents' death was not your fault. It was your father's. Anger does not change the fact that your father failed to act. [...] The training is nothing. The will is everything. The will to act"—an obvious pun on the double meaning of the verb *to act*, which means to take action, but also to perform a (fictional) role.

Consequently, performances are constitutive for superheroes and all the world is literally a stage. This is what clearly separates Batman from Ra's Al Ghul (Ken Watanabe), as the latter ironically, yet correctly asserts when he sees Bruce Wayne in his Batman disguise for the first time: "Well, well," Ra's Al Ghul says, "you took my advice about theatricality a bit ... literally." Indeed, Ra's Al Ghul appears almost "truly invisible"—precisely as he instructed Bruce Wayne earlier—whereas Batman constantly stages public appearances. The fact that at the same time divergent sets of ethics seem to stem from this difference is even more decisive. On the one hand, Batman's relation to the law is at least arguable[7]: as a floating signifier he serves as a means to negotiate the binary opposition of good and evil. Ra's Al Ghul, on the other hand, exceeds this opposition, and his standpoint, therefore, is actually beyond good and evil. The extent to which Ra's Al Ghul differs from other, rather stereotypical, supervillains is correctly observed by Keith M. Booker, who puts forward that he is a much more complex figure, as "he seeks neither revenge nor personal gain. He is not even evil in the usual sense, but seems genuinely to believe that he is doing a good thing for the world by attempting to destroy Gotham City. He is not a man without morals but simply a man with his own unconventional system of morals" (28). In other words, he is not just the representative of utilitarian morals; he *is* the utilitarian principle as such.

Unconventional as they may be, Ra's Al Ghul's morals are by no means discretionary. Rather, he embodies a morally indifferent concept and thus enforces some sort of equilibrium: "Justice is balance. You burned my house and left me for dead. Consider us even," he informs Bruce Wayne as the League of Shadows burns down the family mansion. This pursuit for balance again stresses the moral distinction between the alleged hero and the equally alleged villain, since, morally speaking, the latter's pursuit for balance outranks the former's quest for vengeance. Thus, comparing Batman and Ra's Al Ghul indicates that the evaluation of what can be observed as good or evil, depends on theatricality, which, since it is explicitly and self-referentially exhibited as the medium of these negotiations becomes their *conditio sine qua non.*

The notion of theatricality and its relation to fear, however, does not only account for Batman/Bruce Wayne himself, but obviously for his antagonists as well: As it turns out, Ducard is merely a persona of the real Ra's Al Ghul, "a man greatly feared by the criminal underworld." Furthermore, the whole idea behind Dr. Jonathan Crane (Cillian Murphy), also known by the telling name Scarecrow, is to cause overwhelming fear in his opponents. Significantly, he achieves this with the help of his mask, or, in other words, with the help of a theatrical prop: "There is nothing to fear but fear itself." As both Batman and Scarecrow employ theatricality in order to cause fear, the assumption of a fundamental difference between them is put into question. Unsurprisingly, then, it is the sequel *The Dark Knight* that radicalizes this notion and thus depicts good and evil as profoundly ambivalent. This already becomes obvious at the very end of *Batman Begins*, which functions as a transition between the two films, as the arch-villain Joker (Heath Ledger) is introduced by Jim Gordon (Gary Oldman) wondering

> What about escalation? [...] We start carrying semi-automatics; they buy automatics. We start wearing Kevlar; they buy armor piercing rounds [...]. And you're wearing a mask, jumping of rooftops. Take this guy: Armed robbery, double homicide. Has a taste for the theatrical, like you.

Therefore, in Gordon's account it becomes obvious that both superhero and villain are comparably staged, which, in turn, renders the dichotomy of good and evil, albeit existing, unstable — a fact that necessitates complex, reaffirming negotiations. The fact that good and evil are generated reciprocally ultimately implies that neither good nor evil has ontological status. Rather, both are conceptualized through storytelling,[8] and are therefore mere constructs. As ciphers, they serve various purposes, since the dualism of good and evil is one of the most fundamental diametric patterns functioning as a means not only to interpret the world as a whole, but also to understand what shapes identity and, moreover, constitutes the human as an inevitable part of the *conditio humana.* Thus, this dualism is an important facet of the "webs of significance" man constantly spins and is suspended in (Geertz 5), and accordingly is a cultural phenomenon of ascribed meaning being negotiated in diverse media. Given the constitutive underlying dichotomy, an eminent genre in which these negotiations take place and thus become observable is that of the superhero film.

Due to the fact that superheroes have been perpetually subject to revisionism,[9] they become symptomatic signifiers of contemporary consciousness and thus can serve as embodiments of specific needs in a given time — last but not least, a fact that becomes manifest in their economic success and thus renders the superhero film a far more popular medium than superhero comics[10]: At present, Christopher Nolan's *The Dark Knight* ranks fifth in the IMDB's *all-time box office: world-wide* list, and the films of Sam Raimi's *Spider-Man* trilogy rank among the top thirty.[11] By exhibiting and displaying negotiations and ascriptions of meaning, post-millennial representatives seem to question the established and well-proven distinction of good and evil massively — and thus obviously offer something that is met with a receptive audience. The necessity, therefore, to re-negotiate and re-evaluate the binary opposition of good and evil is the manifestation of a radical confusion, which ultimately affects the individual. As the sketched final sequence of *Unbreakable* demonstrates, identity is brought about by dialectics of self and other, but once one comes to understand that evil does not exist *per se* but is ascribed in the first place, a specific tradition in which evil functions as a momentous signifier of the other, who is accordingly rendered inferior, becomes questionable, and identity, therefore, unstable — a problem which at the present time seems to be exceptionally pressing.

While in the 1990s a "loss" of evil was lamented — the late French post-structuralist Jean Baudrillard nostalgically stated that due to a "transparency of evil" it was no longer possible to speak of "evil" — things got more complicated after the 9/11 attacks. On the one hand, a proper renaissance of discourses of evil began in various discursive fields, while on the other hand the notion of evil became controversial and uncanny in itself. As a result, evil is increasingly conceptualized not as the external other, but rather as a diffuse intrinsic quality, finally rendering good and evil ambivalent, if not indifferent. In this regard, Baudrillard — who maybe was not so much a stringent or even systematic theoretician as he was a provocative, yet at times sensitive diagnostician of present culture — sketches the post–9/11 introversion as follows:

> The faultless mastery of this clandestine style of operation is almost as terroristic as the spectacular act of September 11, since *it casts suspicion on any and every individual.* Might not any inoffensive person be a potential terrorist? If *they* could pass unnoticed, then each of *us* is a criminal going unnoticed (every plane also becomes suspect) [*Spirit of Terrorism* 20, italics added].

The implied impossibility of distinguishing the innocent from the criminal is decisive. As far as the differentiation of good and evil is concerned, recent superhero films seems to reveal such general uncertainties and discontents in culture, which stem precisely from this ambivalence. How, after all, is one supposed to tell good and evil apart? Contrary to John Kenneth Muir's conviction, contemporary superhero film does not respond soothingly to that challenge — but fuels it. It is at this point that theatricality comes into play.

Christopher Nolan's re-imaginations of the *Batman* narrative are sensitized to the fact that, first, theatricality becomes the predominant mode for negotiating good and evil in the genre, and, second, that this mode consists of two reciprocal facets: while it requires the production or staging of certain events or, more generally, signs, it is essential that these productions are performed in the face of an audience. Therefore, as Erika Fischer-Lichte points out, theatricality is a "process of production whose product is consumed" simultaneously (87). Our notion of theatricality thus differs from the one conceived by Elizabeth Burns, who defines it solely as "a particular viewpoint, a mode of perception" (13). Such an approach, however, does not seem sufficient, as it falls short of the fact that the perceived sign does not precede its performative genesis. It is this creation of signs, though, that renders theatricality an intriguing model of culture, since "the signs engendered by theatre denote the signs produced by the corresponding cultural systems. Theatrical signs are therefore always signs of signs" (Fischer-Lichte 88).

Christopher Nolan's title illustrates precisely this. Given the ceaseless addressing of fear, the spectator is constantly reminded that theatricality is a performance in view of a specific audience — regardless of its quantity and whether it is imagined or actually present. The costumes, the props, in fact every single aspect of the mise-en-scène contributes to the thrill and thus doubles the aesthetic experience of the film's reception on the level of its diegesis. Furthermore, they allow observation of the semiotic drift that is triggered once "particular signs [...] are employed as signs of signs" (Fischer-Lichte 88). The central characters of superhero films serve as symbols, as Bruce Wayne duly notes: "People need dramatic examples to shake them out of apathy and I can't do that as Bruce Wayne. As a man of flesh and blood I can be ignored, I can be destroyed. But as a symbol, as a symbol I can be incorruptible, I can be everlasting."

As conceived by Charles S. Peirce, a symbol is a sign signifying something else without being that thing in itself, and whose meaning is merely conventional — that is, in other words, ascribed in the first place and subject to negotiation and eventually to historical change (par. 292–302). That Batman is indeed a floating signifier, whose fundamental semantic openness is theatrically induced, becomes manifest in the last sequence of *The Dark Knight*. After Batman rescues Gordon and his family, which results in the death of Harvey Dent (Aaron Eckhart), he decides to assume a new role in order to ensure the future stability of Gotham's legal system and society: "You either die a hero, or you live long enough to see yourself become the villain [...] I am whatever Gotham needs me to be." What ultimately enables him to fully embrace the role of the eponymous dark knight, if nothing else, is the public and at times vigorous debate concerning his moral quality, which, more often than not, is amplified by the mass media. In other words: Batman can convincingly play the dark knight only because his role was perceived as (potentially) evil from the outset — at least by a few. While Batman is the one who theatrically produces signs, those few represent the constitutive counterpart.

## Acting Lessons

Although Batman emanates from the universe of DC Comics, and Spider-Man is the driving force behind the economic success of its rival Marvel, Sam Raimi's cinematographic adaptations of the latter's adventures and the superhero films of Christopher Nolan have two surprising characteristics in common: First, the almost complete absence of genuine evil, and second, the significant subplot of the theatre and the theatrical, which are intertwined. However, while in the *Batman* films theatricality is depicted as the source and the cause of the aforementioned ambiguity, in Sam Raimi's *Spider-Man* it seems to be the response to it. Each and every part of the trilogy endeavors to point out the contingency of evil and thus rationalizing it, which, for instance, becomes palpable in the editing of the beginning of the first installment, clearly aiming at establishing analogies between the future opponents. By means of montage, indicating that distinct, yet parallel actions occur simultaneously, and by adopting various motives such as intimidation, and the modification of DNA, it becomes obvious that hero and villain differ not in kind but in degree: "Not only is there no essential opposition between monster and superhero, the illusion of that opposition as inevitable or natural is a function of narrative expectation" (Sönser Breen 183). Neither good nor evil, therefore, exist *per se*. A match cut intensifies the analogy: The instance the Green Goblin (Willem Dafoe) breaks free, Parker/Spiderman (Tobey Maguire) awakens as if from a bad dream, while Osborne's sardonic growl is still audible and thus ensures the analogy. Ultimately, what turns the Green Goblin into a malevolent creature are merely the side effects of the "human performance enhancers," which are, as is explicitly stated, insanity, violence, and aggression. Not only are those enhancers quite similar to the ones transmitted by the spider, but their side effects also hardly qualify as indicators for genuine evil: Aggression is a bio-anthropological constant, an inevitable part of the human condition,[12] and thus cannot be employed categorically in order to define evil. Furthermore, Harry Osborne (James Franco), Norman's son and formerly Parker's best friend, underwent basically the same procedure as his father. Yet, in the end he becomes Spider-Man's brother-in-arms. Finally, by means of a sequence depicting a "dialogue" between Norman Osborn and his reflection in a mirror, he is unambiguously depicted as schizophrenic, which means that he does not embrace his new powers consciously and thus cannot be made responsible for his deeds.

This notion proves to be true for all the villains in the *Spider-Man* films, be it that they are governed by a higher, artificial intelligence as is Otto Octavious, a.k.a. Doctor Octopus (Alfred Molina) in *Spider-Man 2*, or an extraterrestrial "symbiote," which "enhances aggression," as Dr. Curt Connors (Dylan Baker) states in *Spider-Man 3*. In the case of the Sandman (Thomas H. Church), another villain from the third installment, the explanation basically consists of

a combination of bad luck and being at the wrong place at the wrong time— and thus is profoundly contingent.

This holds true for Parker/Spider-Man as well: "*Spider-Man* does not represent a paragon of goodness who simply protects the innocent because it is the right thing to do" (Richardson 696). Rather, he is truly fallible and his actions are driven by his feelings of shame and guilt deriving from his failures (like Batman), most notably in his refusal to arrest the man who will become the murderer of his uncle Ben (Cliff Robertson). Given that these observations are correct, however, the question arises how the increasingly permeable and thus unstable distinction of good and evil is negotiated in the films. We suggest that this happens by means of self-reflexively exhibiting these negotiations as such in the mode of theatricality—which is most prominently featured in the character of Mary Jane (Kirsten Dunst), an aspiring actress, who, at first, finds it hard to break into show business—or, as she puts it: "They said I needed acting lessons. A soap opera told me I needed acting lessons" (*Spider-Man*)—but eventually becomes an acclaimed theatrical performer on Broadway, starring in a production of Oscar Wilde's *The Importance of Being Ernest* (*Spider-Man II*), which in turn ironically points out the relation of identity and performance.[13]

However, keeping in mind that theatricality was defined as the simultaneous process of production and consumption of signs, it becomes obvious that it is of eminent importance to Raimi's films. The single most important sequence, in which the word *evil* is used, is theatrical to an extremely high degree. In the first *Spider-Man*, Aunt May (Rosemary Harris) is assaulted by the Green Goblin while she is reciting the Lord's Prayer. Just as she reaches the crucial words—"Lead us not into temptation, but deliver us"—an explosion marks the appearance of the Goblin, forcing the frightened Aunt May to finish her prayer and thus to designate him as "evil." Rather than being a representation of *genuine* evil, the ascription is the outcome of the production and reception of a spectacle, or, in other words, of a self-fashioning on the part of the Goblin.[14] The irony of this sequence thus reveals that evil, or at least what traditionally could be perceived as such, is entirely dislocated from metaphysical explanations and relocated within the human and solely depends on "the presentation of the self in everyday life."[15] The most striking sequence illustrating this can be found in *Spider-Man 3*. After Parker/Spiderman is infested by the symbiote, the audience can observe how the dark facets of their personalities slowly take over. But what does "evil" Parker do, finally being released from categorical, moral imperatives? Nothing but performing a humiliating dance in front of and for the benefit of Mary Jane: "That was all for her?," Parker's dancing partner disgustedly asks and thus emphasizes the theatrical aspects. Even though this sequence might be disappointing in that it fails to live up to expectations of what a truly evil Spider-Man could have done, it is, in a certain way, telling, as it circumvents depictions of evil *a priori*. Instead, it displays the generation of a specific meaning as a process between three poles: production, reception, and evaluation.

Such presentations and fashioning are a constant in almost every post-millennial superhero film: for instance, Parker's tenacious struggle to create an appropriate costume in *Spider-Man*, the creation of Batman as discussed above, the unexplained requirement for consistent uniforms in *X-Men*, or *Hellboy* trying to grind down his horns, let alone the Joker in *The Dark Knight*, who tells two divergent stories of how he got his scars. The "moral" evaluation and the judgment of these self-fashionings, however, predominantly occur in a public space in view of an audience. In some cases, the audience is even created by the hero or villain himself. The prime example is Tony Stark (Robert Downey, Jr.) at the end of *Iron Man* (2008); when during a press conference the public exclusively focuses on him, Stark acts as a real show-off — and theatrically reveals his true identity as Iron Man. Spider-Man creates an audience as well, taking his own photographs. On the one hand, of course, these pictures guarantee Parker's livelihood. On the other hand, they are utilized by J. Jonah Jameson (J. K. Simmons), the opportunistic and exploiting editor-in-chief of the *Daily Bugle*, in order to trigger and fuel public debate: "Spider-Man: Hero or Menace?" The insistence and frequency with which Jameson's suspicion is shown renders him more than just a comic relief. In his skepticism, the general ambiguity of good and evil is reflected: everyone with superhuman powers has to account for their action in view of the public.

This notion becomes most apparent in a film that questions the dichotomy most radically: "Ladies and gentlemen, the truth is that mutants are very real," Senator Kelly (Bruce Davison) states in a public debate at the beginning of Bryan Singer's *X-Men* (2000), concluding that "they are among us. We must know who they are, and, above all, we must know what they can do." In other words, he demands that the mutants "come forward," to "reveal themselves publicly" so they can be judged. The public, therefore, is the *ultima ratio* to reaffirm lost beliefs, to challenge the postmodern *i*llegibility of the world. According to Hannah Arendt, "being seen and being heard by others derive their significance from the fact that everybody sees and hears from a different position. This is the meaning of the public life" (57). Theatricality therefore allows the observation of a fundamental negotiation that consists of the alignment of heterogeneous perspectives and thus serves as a medium: "Whether as audience or spectator, listener or reader, the addressee is called upon to bear witness to a turn of events that as such can never be seen. This and only this constitutes theatricality as medium" (Weber 157).

In the following, this notion shall be addressed from a theoretically advanced point of view: namely that of second-order cybernetics. This approach allows not only for abstractly reformulating abstractly the processual, dynamic relation between the perception ("bear witness") and the production of signs ("events") as intrinsic to the story, but also for exhibiting it as an inevitable part of its observation and thus avoiding a mere representational mode of discourse. Both the necessity and the legitimacy to do so derive from the films themselves.

## Through the Eyes of the Other — Cybernetics and the Superhero Film

Despite his demonic appearance, the mutant Kurt Wagner, a.k.a. Nightcrawler (Alan Cumming), a blue skinned man with yellow eyes and a prehensile tail, is a faithful Catholic. In Bryan Singer's *X2* (2003) he explains to Storm (Halle Berry) his empathy for mankind: "Do you know, outside of the circus most people were afraid of me. But I didn't hate them. I pitied them. Do you know why? Because most people will never know anything beyond what they see with their own two eyes." As he was praying beforehand, his revelation clearly has a religious undertone. Nevertheless, if taken literally, a further possible reading is evoked, providing an alternative approach to handle the dualism of good and evil as primary function of superhero narratives. Rather than being mere representations of good and evil, superheroes and supervillains display the capacity of differentiating between good and evil as a persevering process. Hence, they do not only see with their own eyes, but, additionally, through the eyes of the Other.

Significantly, despite his stereotypical outer appearance, it is Nightcrawler who points out both his ability and the importance to alternate perspectives. His initial performance and presumed attack against the President of the USA in the White House mark him as a potential assassin, and when Storm and Jean (Famke Janssen) are looking for him in the dark uncanny church, he declares, in German, to be the messenger of the devil ("Ich bin der Bote des Teufels") and a spawn of evil ("Ich bin die Ausgeburt des Bösen") in order to get rid of the strangers. His alleged evil is thus the product of a theatrical staging: Like Hellboy, in other words, he assumes a role. Nightcrawler not only sees through his own eyes— additionally, he is able to see *that* he sees through his own eyes. In terms of second-order cybernetics and the theory of observation as proposed by the German sociologist Niklas Luhmann, Nightcrawler observes his observation. Hence, as he himself as neither solely good nor evil, he handles good and evil as a distinction; not to unify the duality of good and evil into a "particular singularity," as Rebecca Housel sketches the "main premise of the second X-Men film" (76), but to exhibit the distinction *as* distinction.

Heinz von Foerster points out that second-order cybernetics is "the cybernetics of *observing* systems" as opposed to first-order cybernetics, i.e., "the cybernetics of *observed* systems" (*Understanding*, 285, italics added). It is important to note that in second-order cybernetics the observer is always related to his observations, which, in turn, means that he is part of the world that he observes: "Observations are not absolute but relative to an observer's point of view" (ibid. 274). Moreover, observations affect the observed, which is why von Foerster rejects the idea of "true" objectivity — in terms of an independent and always reproducible observation — as "nonsense."[16] By rejecting "true" objectivity and due to the fact that the observer enters his observation, second-order cybernetics advances to an epistemological premise for doing theory (ibid. 229–246). Luhmann's adaptation of second-order cybernetics allows him to draft a general theory of observation "which is not tied to, say, the concept of intelligence, the mind of human beings." He uses "second-order observation" as "a very formal concept of observation" in order to "describe relations of social systems to each other, or minds to social systems, or minds to minds, or maybe bodies to neurophysiological systems, *or whatever*" (Luhmann and Hayles 8, italics added). Corresponding to this formal concept of observation and referring to George Spencer Brown's *Laws of Form*, Luhmann defines observation very basically as "nothing but making a distinction to indicate one side and not the other, regardless of the material basis of the operation which does the job" (Luhmann 773–74). Luhmann thus formulates a "postontological theory of observing systems" (776), a theory of difference and differentiation that allows considering the metaphorical speech of seeing and observing as operations of second-order cybernetics.

Implicitly, such a processual theory has already been applied to superheroes by Shaun Treat, describing them as "morally ambiguous SuperAntiheroes who are flawed or conflicted *dystopian cyborgs*" (105, italics added). According to Donna Haraway, a cyborg is a "cybernetic organism, a hybrid of machine and organism" that renders thoroughly ambiguous the difference between natural and artificial, mind and body [...], and many other distinctions" (149). Post 9/11 superheroes as "ambiguous SuperAntiheroes" and "dystopian cyborgs" have indeed made a specific distinction ambiguous: precisely the one that allows seeing them as superheroes. But instead of reading the superhero as cyborg, which would mean incorporating the difference of good and evil as ontological, i.e., that he is good *and* evil at the same time, we prefer to apply the second-order perspective by proposing to redefine the superhero as a second-order observer.

By definition, every observation has its blind spot, that is to say something that is literally out of sight. In addition, "we do not see that we have a blind spot. In other words, we do not see that we do not see" (Foerster, *Understanding*, 284). A second-order observer, however, observes other observers and their observations. Therefore, he is able to see the blind spot of such an observer and thus can obtain his perspective: "if you observe that observer, then you see how he or she sees the world" by making a specific distinction (Luhmann and Hayles 11). It is crucial to understand that every second-order observer is also a first-order observer precisely because he observes on his part. It follows that even second-order observers cannot see their own blind spots. This triggers a self-reflexive loop, as observations of other observers serve as a means to indirectly see oneself. By seeing that others inevitably fail to see something, one comes to understand that oneself always fails to see something, too. "It is the other, through whose eyes we may see ourselves" (Foerster, 1991, 73). Due to these multiplications of perspectives, it becomes evident that every distinction framing an observation is only one among equal other distinctions and can be rejected or accepted any time. Thus, Luhmann concludes that "At the level of second-order observing, everything becomes contingent" (769).

Applied to superheroes, second-order observation does not only offer an approach towards an alternative interpretation of post 9/11 negotiations of an essential dualism, but also a modality in which good and evil are observed through superhero narratives. If M. Keith Booker argues that *X2* was the most successful part of the trilogy as it most clearly established the dichotomy of good and evil, then he lumps several distinctions of good and evil, which the film provides, together (82). After all, the film does not correspond to the distinction of humans and mutants, or to the one of rivaling groups of mutants who are led by Professor Xavier (Patrick Stewart), and Magneto (Ian McKellen), respectively. The X-Men are not mere flawless, infallible superheroes confronting their vicious counterparts. Ultimately, their ambiguity is staged in the last sequences of *X2*. During a live TV broadcast, in which President McKenna (Cotter Smith) addresses the recent paranormal phenomena that nearly extinguished mankind, his office darkens and time seems to stand still. Accompanied by a tempestuous noise of thunder and lightning, the X-Men seem to appear from nowhere and expose their threatening powers. They submit secret files from the private office of William Stryker (Brian Cox), sworn enemy to all mutants, who almost succeeded in starting a war between mutants and humans, and try to convince the president "to work together for a better future" instead of repeating "the mistakes of the past." After Wolverine's (Hugh Jackman) final and slightly threatening words—"We'll be watching"—they disappear. Indeed, the X-Men are "watchmen" who observe the distinction of good and evil drawn by humans and their opponent mutant group. Therefore, precisely because they are observers and thus employ that very distinction themselves, *X2* proliferates a range of observers who observe the same, and consequentially points out the contingency of the utilization of that distinction.

The ambiguity that is generated by the multiplication of observers who operate with the help of the distinction of good and evil in order to render the world intelligible is impressively negotiated in *The Dark Knight*. The reinterpretation of Batman's exceptional battle with the cunning Joker accompanies a cluster of contemporary hotspot-themes that transform the film into "a hermeneutic treasure-trove for the post–9/11 Global War on/of Terror" (Treat 106). Regarding the staging of good and evil, *The Dark Knight* does not only depict "a more secular and less supernatural vision of evil" (Tyree 31). Neither is it limited to yet another vision of the eternal dialectic process that is indicated by the Joker himself, who tells Batman: "I think you and I are destined to do this forever." The dialectic itself becomes part of the protagonist's observation and is exhibited as scheme by the Joker. His disposition for travesty is best shown in his refusal of a meaningful background story of "how he got his scars." He tells two divergent stories and thus mocks conventionalized psychoanalytic patterns that try to establish causally determined explanations of his "insanity." Through the eyes of the other, he mirrors their distinctions that allow observing the Joker as evil and understanding his assumed reasons that made him evil. Moreover, he playfully uses intertexts. When the Joker confesses to Batman: "What would I do without you? [...] You complete me," he not only quotes a part of Tom Cruise's monologue in the romantic comedy *Jerry Maguire* (1996), but also Dr. Evil's ironic use of the now classic and frequently repeated line in *Austin Powers* (1999).

Regardless of whether the Joker is serious about these remarks or whether they are tongue-in-cheek and just bait for his observers and interpreters, he excels in rendering the public as second-order observers, too. "We should have sympathy for the devil," Treat reckons, "since the Joker's grotesqueries expose our indifferent dependency upon systemic banalities of Capitalistic evil" (107), but it is the distinction of good and evil in general and our blind spot of observing it that the Joker cunningly invites us to elevate out of "indifferent" latency. He emphasizes that he is not "a schemer," having plans and "trying to control their little worlds." After Harvey Dent becomes Twoface — another significant representation of the dialectic — the Joker tells him that he is just "doing things": "I try to show the schemers how pathetic their attempts to control things really are." In the central confrontation with Batman he rejects the schemer's observation of good and evil: "You see, their morals, their code, it's a bad joke," because "they're only as good as the world allows them to be. Since the world is the product of a scheme, it is the world of 'established order,'" and, from the Joker's point of view, Batman obeys "all these rules." Maroni (Eric Roberts), one of Gotham's leading crime bosses, also insinuates that Batman has rules, differentiating him decisively from the Joker: "You got rules. The Joker, he's got no rules," and because Batman has rules, or even if just one single rule, he has "nothing, nothing to threaten" the Joker with, "Nothing to do with all your strength."

Admittedly, in contrast to the Joker, Batman is not indifferent to killing people — even when the opportunity arises to kill the Joker easily after his car crash, Batman resists this temptation. Nevertheless, it is not as simple as Maroni states. The equation that following rules equals good (i.e., defending the established order), and having no rules equals evil (i.e., fighting for "fair" chaos), does not add up. Since the Joker's background story is not known and as he has no verifiable identity, the Joker *comes into being* only as performance and as staging. Considering that in addition he exposes his staging *as* staging (and nothing more), he indeed becomes, in the words of Jacques Derrida, "a sort of *joker*, a floating signifier, a wild card, one who puts play into play" (93).

Obviously, even the Joker follows a rule: to subversively use the established order to break rules and to overthrow the world of the schemers. Despite his deceitful self-characterization not to be a schemer, due to this one rule, he ultimately becomes a master-schemer. He always "came prepared," he always has a second plan or "an ace in the hole." The kind of anarchy the Joker intends to discharge is paradoxically grounded in plans and schemes. His means of transforming common schemers into second-order observers is basically a short-circuit: "I took your little plan and I turned it on itself," he explains to Dent. He does exactly the same with the resources the "established order" provides him: be it abstract, yet conventionalized narrative patterns to construct and playfully subvert identity; the concrete and extensive use of gunpowder, dynamite, and gasoline as favorite warfare agents because "they're cheap"; or the smart and overwhelming application and manipulation of mass media to attract attention and to theatrically construct a self as effect of the media — what would a clown be without an audience?—, the Joker continuously turns processes on themselves. This is what puts "play into the play" and alludes to blind spots of the schemers—and ourselves.

As the Joker points out to him, Batman, on his part, is also not a common schemer. "Don't talk like one of them. You're not. Even if you'd like to be. To them you're just a freak like me." Furthermore, he is a second-order observer as well, who observes the distinction of good and evil people draw. Through the eyes of the other, he installs an image of Batman, which is neither clearly good nor evil, but ambiguous. According to Todd McGowan, superheroes in general, and Batman and the Joker in particular, share an exceptional relation to the law. However, they differ in that superheroes violate the law in order to sustain it while villains are up to dissolve it:

> Though Batman tries to save Gotham and the Joker tries to destroy it, though Batman commits himself to justice and the Joker commits himself to injustice, they share a position that transcends the inadequate and calculated ethics authorized by the law itself [n. pag.].

Corresponding to Alfred's (Michael Caine) characterization, Batman "can be the outcast"— and as he violates a rule, which nearly precludes differentiation between him and the criminals he fights, he actually becomes one: a military project that facilitates total surveillance is resumed by Wayne and utilized by Batman in order to trace the Joker. Since this attributes "too much power for one person," as Lucius Fox (Morgan Freeman) remarks, "Batman has crossed a line beyond heroic exceptionality" (McGowan n. pag.). This transgression, McGowan concludes, blurs the line between criminals and non-criminals. However, Bruce Wayne is not correct when he says "Batman has no limits." He is not able to transgress every line and neither he nor the Joker cancels the distinction of good and evil by making it indifferent. Rather, as observers of a second-order and due to second-order cybernetics, the observer changes the observed — and, by means of feedback, is changed by it at the same time. *The*

*Dark Knight* relocates the focus from representations of ontological good or evil to the distinction itself. It still provides the genre's traditional patterns and narrative structures, but beyond that it also points out their function. Therefore, on the one hand, it is still possible to extract the inscribed dialectics of good and evil and designate the Joker as the evil villain and Batman as the (dark, modern or anti-) superhero fighting the evil. On the other hand, the film offers the opportunity to interpret it contrarily.

Randolph Lewis, for instance, argues that the Joker as "an anti-capitalist culture jammer [...] *is not just a devil* but also *a postmodern messiah* who inveighs against the discreetly authoritarian order of late consumer capitalism in which brands and regulations have eclipsed the soul" (n. pag., italics added). Thus, Batman, "boring" and "old," a "benevolent terrorist [...] whose vigilante tactics differ not in kind but degree" (Treat 106), "might win the day, but ultimately he *is Gotham's real villain* because his joyless victory brings nothing but another day of the unsatisfying status quo" (Lewis n. pag.). In this view, Batman's quotation of Dent's prophecy comes true and he really lives long enough to see himself become the villain. Instead of asking who actually *is* the villain or the hero, respectively, or whether either of them *is* good or evil, which would mean to merely identify fixed a priori positions, second-order cybernetics emphasize good and evil as dynamic *processes*. Thus, the difference in not transposed into indifference. As it is reflected and displayed in the figure of second-order observers, it is rendered thoroughly ambiguous. In addition, as *The Dark Knight* positions Batman and the Joker as second-order observers, the film confronts its own observers— the public and the critics— with their own blind spots, and thus rather by showing than by telling what cannot be said — i.e., the contingency of observance — designs a poetics of ambivalence.

Superhero films, which, as the ones discussed in this chapter, are narrated *qua* poetics of ambivalence, cannot avoid the constitutive dialectic. But as they exhibit the negotiations of good and evil as theatrical spectacle on the level of the films' *histoire*, they double it on the level of *discourse*. Ultimately, this means that superhero films like Nolan's *Batman*, Raimi's *Spider-Man,* and Singer and Ratner's *X-Men* additionally show that stagings of good and evil are always stagings made by the medium of film at the same time — and thus point to their own contingency.

## Notes

1. The relation between evil and disability would require more substantial research, for which this is neither the place nor the time. For a more thorough analysis, see Norden 125–143.

2. Using an epoch-making phrase by Jean-François Lyotard, we "define postmodernism as incredulity toward metanarrative" (xxiv). Having said this, postmodern superhero films are superhero films that refuse to accept a stable good/evil dichotomy as metanarrative.

3. Scheffer's essay is full of interesting hypotheses but is at times imprecise and slightly inconsistent. Among other things, it does not become clear how good and evil could be correlated to one another in the first place, if the very distinction between them did not exist. To do precisely this, however, is Scheffer's main objective.

4. In the following, we limit ourselves to representatives from a "western" tradition: On the one hand, as we will argue, the economic success of the Hollywood blockbuster representative is significant. On the other hand, these films deal with concepts of good and evil that are indebted to an occidental, Judeo-Christian tradition.

5. Concerning this sequence, two things are remarkable: First, that Christopher Nolan prefers Boito's adaptation (1868) of Goethe's *Faust* to the far more popular version by Charles Gounod (1859), and second, that Boito chose Mephistopheles as the eponymous character of his opera. A reason for this might be that the devil Mephistopheles is, of course, central to the problem of evil. Since he is "a portion of that power, whose wills are evil, but whose actions good," he points out that good and evil are always intertwined. Accordingly, the evil that Mephistopheles represents is that of inverted, if not perverted, good: the world is born out of chaos and darkness, its course leads into nothingness. Although this position is taken to its extremes in *The Dark Knight*, there are already some structural similarities between Batman and Mephistopheles, which, in turn, cast a cloud over Batman's integrity. In addition, one should always keep the theatrical frame of Goethe's *Faust* in mind.

6. As is put forward by Darius 34.

7. See McGowan n. pag.

8. See Lara 239–250.

9. See Wandtke 14.

10. The resulting repercussions are analyzed by Johnson 64–85.

11. See <www.imdb.com/boxoffice/alltimegross?region=world-wide> (11.05.2010).

12. Behavioral biologist Konrad Lorenz already put this observation forward in the 1960s. Literally translated, the original title of his study reads "The So-called Evil: On the Natural History of Aggression."

13. Wilde's veritable "comedy of errors" also focuses on dynamics of hidden, secret, and mistaken identities.

14. See Greenblatt.

15. This phrase is borrowed from Erving Goffman's seminal study.

16. "Hence, I submit in all modesty, the claim for objectivity is nonsense!" (Foerster, *Understanding*, 285).

# Power, Choice, and September 11 in *The Dark Knight*

CHRISTINE MULLER

## *Introduction: Ambivalent Heroics,* The Dark Knight, *and September 11*

After September 11, 2001, many who were not immediately affected by the attacks reported a stunned sense that "the world had changed."[1] Why? What could this mean? Psychiatrist Judith Herman characterizes traumatization as injury and disempowerment through physical and volitional violation — that is, overpowering of a person's body and will — and recovery as the struggle to integrate this experience into a meaningful world view (33–50, 133–236; Janoff-Bulman 49–61, 93–165). In other words, traumatic events subject individuals to the experience of not being able to protect themselves or others when protection is most necessary, producing horror in the recognition of this utter powerlessness. Such ordeals undermine a person's understanding of him/herself as capable of acting and willing productively, without incurring substantial harm or that which a person would most want to avoid. Accordingly, such ordeals prompt within survivors a need to recalibrate their life expectations in light of their newly intimate awareness of living in a world of risk. In effect, according to psychologist Ronnie Janoff-Bulman, trauma shatters the most fundamental assumptions that govern functional daily living, leaving survivors and witnesses questioning what they really can know about and do in this world (70–72).

I argue that this shattered assumptions model, developed in the field of psychology with its focus on an individual's mental health, poses significant cultural implications as well. After all, culture serves as a site through which shared meanings about human life — such as individuals' senses of subjectivity, agency, and responsibility — are produced, challenged, and negotiated. Indeed,

46

given that culture cultivates and supports meaningful human life, an event of sufficient scale and scope to shatter collectively-held fundamental beliefs can trigger a cultural trauma, wherein members of whole communities, whether neighborhoods or nations, must wrestle with similar meaning disruption and reconstruction. In effect, cultural trauma operates as a crisis of knowledge and power for individuals in relationship with their communities, exposing fault lines within cultural formations and, in doing so, occasioning the need for alternative possibilities. In other words, the notion of cultural trauma invokes questions of subjectivity, agency, and responsibility under conditions of imposed constraints and limited, perhaps exclusively adverse, options—questions coincident with concerns raised in the aftermath of September 11 as well as through the dilemmas driving the plot of the 2008 Warner Bros. blockbuster *The Dark Knight*.

Allusions to September 11 abound in *The Dark Knight*. A promotional poster for the film's theatrical release, which now serves as DVD cover art, featured a bat-shaped fiery crash zone penetrating the upper floors of a skyscraper's façade. The image, reminiscent of the planes crashing into the World Trade Center towers, appears nowhere in the actual film, foregrounding a provocative self-consciousness in how the film invokes September 11 (Cox; Dawson; Dudley; and Moore). In fact, settings and subplots persistently echo the crises of Manhattan on that particular day and throughout its wake, which many movie reviewers acknowledged (Stevens; Tyree), with a few considering such references somewhat heavy-handed (Cox). Specifically, some argued fervently that *The Dark Knight*'s themes transparently favored the Bush administration's War on Terror in response to September 11 (Ackerman; Klavan), and some argued just as fervently that the film exposed this response's flaws (Baker; Binh; Dray; Orr) These divergent perceptions of a single text point to the richness of a narrative that can elicit entirely opposed, yet equally committed, reactions. Importantly, for many—including myself—this richness reflects a text positioned in the unkempt middle, where patently right answers fail to reside and choices must be made without the luxury of self-righteous reassurance (Bradley; Crouse; Dargis; Eisenberg; Kerstein; Rickey; Schager; Stevens). Indeed, director and screenplay co-writer Christopher Nolan has demurred about deliberately producing an explicit September 11 text (Eisenberg).[2] Instead, he has portrayed the film as an evocative medium through which audience members can struggle with issues well-grounded in Batman's fictionalized history yet well-suited to our own historical realities (Boucher "Christopher Nolan on 'Dark Knight'"; Kerstein).[3]

Drawing on a cultural studies framework that views popular culture texts as sites for negotiating shared meaning formations, I argue that references to September 11 infuse *The Dark Knight*'s plot so the film can serve as a fraught confrontation with that event as a cultural trauma that has confounded conventional moral certainties.[4] Almost all viewers, depending on their experiences of that day, can be considered witnesses if not survivors of September 11. Accordingly, the film's numerous, direct parallels with that day's images and challenges impel viewers to bring their experiences with September 11 into their encounter with the film's fictional traumatic moments. However, *The Dark Knight* avoids offering the audience any "feel-good" or ethically satisfying resolutions to the troubles it dramatizes through this connection between the film, the viewers, and September 11. Instead, I will show how this connection incites viewers to interrogate their own moral orientations in relationship to the film's staged exigencies and, by extension, their involvement in or even contributions to counterpart real-world exigencies: the kind of complex, ambiguous choices or even lose-lose scenarios that September 11 has occasioned. In effect, I will show that the film openly alludes to September 11, links these allusions to Gotham's security concerns and moral susceptibilities as well as to "good guys" Bruce Wayne (Christian Bale), Jim Gordon (Gary Oldman), and Harvey Dent's (Aaron Eckhart) repeated struggles with The Joker's (Heath Ledger) relentless morally taxing scenarios—which are sustained, if not propelled, by the city's ambivalences—and uses these depictions of the Gotham community's risks and responsibilities to implicitly call on viewers to recognize their own risks and responsibilities in the analogous crisis of September 11. I argue that, in this way, this popular culture text explores and implicates its audience in the culturally traumatic complexities of agency and accountability in the wake of September 11.

## Staging September 11 as a Cultural Trauma

Resonances with September 11 permeate *The Dark Knight* from the start. The film begins outside of time and place with a frame-consuming, slow-motion, blue-tinted and melancholy chiaroscuro of dense, roiling fireballs. We have seen this before, in the telltale flames bursting from the sides of office towers confirming the impact of passenger planes. We could not see what we knew they obliterated: the whole bodies of human lives, vanishing in an unexpected instant. Even in that day's replayed video coverage, the planes perhaps travel too inconceivably for our minds to register what they are doing as they are doing it, with disbelief and fear inciting our mental resistance as they seem to, but surely could not, be heading for a collision with occupied skyscrapers. But the fireballs mark the undeniable and irreversible moments from which the post–September 11 world starts to unfold. They form the threshold between what possibly could have been averted and what can now never be undone. In *The Dark Knight*, balls of flame, accompanied by a faint, asynchronous, apprehensive undertone of a sustained note, introduce the subsequent action. Rather than disappearing through a straightforward fade-out or dissolve, the flames seem to push toward the audience, displaced in the montage by a dark void at the center of the frame as it expands into the familiar Bat Symbol, the gloomy emblem of a haunted hero flying forward and looming larger until viewers see only black (Nolan, *The Dark Knight*). It is a bleak beginning with its oblique reference to a September 11 context of foregone doom and foreclosed hope, with the fireballs having suspended us within the instance of awareness that sometimes we have fear and few, if any, options.

Yet such references become increasingly more direct. The film jump-cuts from the almost ethereal hushed blaze to an IMAX — and in appropriately-equipped theaters, an engulfing — aerial shot steadily zooming in on the upper floors of one among a cluster of skyscrapers in a dense cityscape. As the continuous undertone crescendos — now clearly audible and supplemented by brisk percussive beats that intensify anticipatory tension, as well as distant street noises that ground events in their contemporary urban setting — the building fills the frame, its windows reflecting the city skyline until one of them explodes outward. Indoors, from the opening of the blown window, two men soon launch and secure a cable to another building. The camera, situated behind the men as each latches onto the cable, pursues them with a swift tracking shot as they jump into the air to glide toward the neighboring rooftop. However, at the ledge, instead of following the men as they slide forward along the cable, the shot abruptly becomes a tilt-down to show the street traffic several stories below, creating a point-of-view that enables viewers to feel as though they have followed the men out the window and into their own freefall (Nolan, *The Dark Knight*). These images are also not new; we have seen people clustered at blown-open office windows, and some jumping out of them. Yet there is one difference: the IMAX filming and the camera's positioning draw audiences into a perspective they did not have on September 11, one located within the building that drives outward into a stomach-sinking plunge. Associations can be made between what we have seen on the news and what we see in the theater, with the act of witnessing in the theater intensified through the IMAX effect of immersing its audience in the staged action. We have been invited to experience ourselves as more than just passive observers, who can watch from afar without connection or consequence.[5] With this invitation, the film occasions for viewers the opportunity to recognize within the September 11–related predicaments it dramatizes our own susceptibilities, complicities, and responsibilities.

Details throughout the film promote further correlations between Gotham, New York City, and September 11.[6] When The Joker is guarded in jail by a veteran cop (Keith Szarabajka), he taunts the officer, "How many of your friends have I killed?" The question chills, coming from someone other characters have termed a "terrorist" (Nolan, *The Dark Knight*). In the aftermath of September 11, the staggeringly high casualties to close-knit communities like the New York City police and fire departments were evident in the hardships of survivors who lost multiple colleagues and friends in a single morning, who afterward would attend an almost endless progression of funerals and memorial services.

Indeed, the police commissioner's (Colin McFarlane) funeral, set in Gotham but filmed near Ground Zero in Manhattan (Tyree 32) — while other city scenes were filmed in Hong Kong, Chicago and London (*The Dark Knight* Production Notes) — features marching rows of solemn uniformed officers to the mournful sounds of bagpipes as a somber echo of real-life commemorations. Later, during the car chase among The Joker, an armored police van transporting Dent, and Batman, a burning fire engine blocks the van's route, detouring them to more dangerous streets (Nolan). The now-recognizable image, a fire truck crushed and ablaze, poses a warning far exceeding in its portentous overtones any significations independent of September 11 (Tyree 32). Additionally, when Batman returns to the site where Rachel Dawes (Maggie Gyllenhaal) was killed, he hangs his head in the foreground of a smoldering pile of debris, with firefighters in the background sending arcs of water over collapsed steel beams, a scene evocative of Ground Zero (Tyree 32). Moreover, Gotham is overtly connected to Manhattan when The Joker addresses the "bridge-and-tunnel crowd," a reference to those who commute to the island from the city's other boroughs and New Jersey (Nolan, *The Dark Knight*). Indeed, when Gordon must call the National Guard to assist throngs of people gathering at the water for ferries toward safety, memories of the unprecedented, "like a movie" evacuation of Lower Manhattan might surface. Such allusions, integrated seamlessly throughout the narrative, create a context for the story that couches interpretative possibilities for the film's staged exigencies in terms of a particular exigency, September 11, in the audience's own recent past.

Similarly, throughout *The Dark Knight*, interiors feature floor-to-ceiling windows, reminiscent of the World Trade Center's design, which permit the uninterrupted presence of Gotham (Nolan, *The Dark Knight*). These settings foster suggestively porous boundaries between a city's interiors and exteriors, which September 11 frighteningly showcased when planes rent open enclosed spaces, around which office workers crowded for air and relief. Notably, when Batman pushes The Joker over the ledge of a construction site, he uses a grappling hook to retrieve the villain (adhering to his rule never to kill) and suspend him in mid-air upside down, a precarious position from which The Joker reveals his anticipated victory in spite of his capture and his ferry plan's failure. He explains, "I took Gotham's white knight. And I brought him down to our level. It wasn't hard — see, madness, as you know, is like gravity. All it takes is a little push" (Nolan, *The Dark Knight*).[7] His characterization of Dent's devastation as a downfall while he himself hangs in the air facing downward (although the camera vertically rotates, ultimately positioning the audience with him in head-first suspended freefall) eerily summons and preserves the moments of descent of those who jumped from the World Trade Center, moments frozen in time by, among other records, the "Falling Man" photograph by AP photographer Richard Drew. They were fearful moments to witness, embodying our shared ultimate vulnerability in their evidence of utter despair and powerlessness, and in their prelude to a horrific end. And The Joker has put his finger precisely on this shared vulnerability: that madness, like gravity, takes only the right push. Cultural theorist Raymond Williams' concept of "structure of feeling" signals specificities in the variables of shared experience (128–135). For example, those of a particular generation understand the events they have lived through in ways that differ importantly from the interpretations of future generations because their respective contexts, from which each generation draws insight, differ importantly. *The Dark Knight's* historical associations with the context of September 11 evoke a structure of feeling of contemporary angst as the film's conundrums unfold before an audience immersed in its own lived experience of perceived threats and moral uncertainties.

## *Expectations, Obligations and Risks:*
## *The Community at the Center of the Fight*

Insinuations of causal connections between Gotham's populace and the city's perpetual troubles in the context of these historical associations afford viewers the opportunity to reflect on their own relationships to September 11 and its aftermath. In the film's middle pivot — unrelenting, staccato-paced action disrupts any sense of a narrative arc — Gotham's brash, idealistic District Attorney Harvey Dent reluctantly presides over a press conference he has convened at Batman's insistence. In front of a shoulder-to-shoulder crowd, he stands behind a microphone-packed podium situated in the corner of a room with wall-to-wall windows exposing the city outside, a setting that figuratively suggests through framing his cornering by Gotham's norms. The Joker has been fulfilling his promise to kill Gothamites until Batman reveals his secret identity, and the masked crime fighter has decided to meet this demand to attempt to forestall the further murder of innocents. Dent, angered by what he perceives as "giving in," proceeds with the media event, but tries to use the opportunity to boost public morale and enlist the city's support in resisting The Joker's ultimatum. However, a reporter (Sophia Hinshelwood) characterizes Dent's reluctance to expose Batman as protecting "an outlaw vigilante" over "citizens," with which the crowd agrees. Soon after, a heckler yells that because of Batman, "Things are worse than ever" (Keith Kupferer). After Dent pleads for calmer reflection about the fate of Batman and of Gotham, a police officer (Joseph Luis Caballero) shouts, "No more dead cops," an invocation of legitimated authority, supposedly endangered by Batman, which fully divests Dent of any power to win over the assembly on his behalf (Nolan, *The Dark Knight*). These voices for Gotham have clearly deemed Batman the root cause of, and certainly not the solution to, the city's worsening violence, demarcating the public as hapless sufferers and Batman as irresponsible adventurer.[8] Given this characterization of Gothamites as blameless victims uninvolved in the crises that threaten them, Dent can expect little participation from them in their city's salvation; corrective action, like the threats it strives to counteract, seemingly must occur without them. This detaching of accountability for corrective action from those for whom it is purportedly taken not only limits Dent's options, but also, given the film's allusions to September 11 and its aftermath, poses real-world challenges as well.

However, Dent's comments in this scene make clear, as he tries to dissuade public opinion from pushing the Batman into The Joker's hands, that Batman's behavior does not occur in a vacuum of reckless self-indulgence, and The Joker's cunning does not occur in a void of freewheeling aggression, from which Gotham can free itself by scapegoating someone already risking himself on their behalf. After all, as he points out, Batman's activities are not the proximate reason for the public's turn against him. He says, "We're doing it because we're scared. We've been happy to let the Batman clean up our streets for us until now." Indeed, earlier in the film, over dinner with Wayne, Dent, and their (not fully known to Dent) shared love interest Rachel Dawes, Wayne's date Natascha (Beatrice Rosen) refers to Gotham as "the kind of city that idolizes a masked vigilante," to which Dent responds, "Gotham City is proud of an ordinary citizen standing up for what's right." At this point, it would seem from their comments that the average man and woman have welcomed Batman's arrival. Yet Natascha counters, "Gotham needs heroes like you — elected officials, not a man who thinks he's above the law," with which Wayne concurs, asking, "Who appointed the Batman?" Dent's answer, "We did. All of us who stood by and let scum take control of our city," catches Wayne's attention (Nolan). For him, a new prospect unfolds: the possibility that Gotham could render Batman obsolete by accepting some answerability for — and accordingly, some risk to — itself rather than allowing a shadowy figure to shoulder the entire burden of rescuing a community gone awry. Dent's perspective fosters an alternative vision, one that encourages citizens to recognize their own responsibility for their community's well-being.[9] In this view, effective citizenship involves actively cultivating democratic principles throughout daily public life, rather than just through an occasional vote. Such a view raises useful questions about the contours and implications of explicit consent, implicit acquiescence, hesitant resistance, and firm opposition in a post–September 11 environment of hard choices, a disconcerted populace, and a federal government willing to act audaciously.

Given this scene, The Joker's and the Batman's antics seem to occur in the conditions of a community whose long-term welfare and principles yield to the short-term demands of exigency and expediency. Accordingly, plot developments depend on how expectedly the general public responds to The Joker's exploitation of a guiding dynamic to Gotham's social structure: the belief that dirty work is necessary, and that somebody else should be doing it. Such a belief forms the core enticement for The Joker's manipulations, a chance to test investments in individual interest, the common good, and the social order. Such a belief rings familiar in a post–September 11 world, in which audience members themselves have wondered what is necessary and what is right, what threatens them and how they can respond, in the aftermath of a calamity that has showcased the high stakes of these very questions.

## Escalation, or the Art of Picking a Fight

Recognizing these contradictions in Gotham's mores and reveling in their fecundity for engineering mayhem, The Joker excels at tailoring interventions that maximize dissension and hopelessness and expose the delicate perforations separating the upstanding from the prone. Repeatedly, this engagement manifests in his fabrication of no-win scenarios that test others' resourcefulness and resolve. When Dent and Rachel disappear immediately after The Joker's arrest, Batman grills him for their whereabouts in a monitored police interrogation room. The Joker goads Batman doggedly, relishing and fueling the anger that drives Batman further along the fine line of torture as he slams the prisoner into a table, the wall, and the two-way mirror, then delivers successive blows to the face. In the end, these assaults prove gratuitous, since The Joker wants to reveal the captives' locations. "That's the point," he explains, "You'll have to choose." He has told Batman, "Killing is making a choice. You choose between one life or the other. Your friend, the district attorney, or his blushing bride-to-be" (Nolan, *The Dark Knight*). With Dent and Rachel in distant parts of the city, Batman can rescue only one of them, knowing that the police, who cannot move as decisively, will likely fail to save the other. Hence, The Joker's taunt that "killing is making a choice": Batman must choose at all in order to save at least one of them, but by choosing to save one, he by default has chosen to "kill" the other. Christopher Nolan has characterized this interrogation scene as crucial (Boucher, "Christopher Nolan Revisits"). After all, the quandary it dramatizes, that even formidable power can be hamstrung and sabotaged and choice can sometimes lead only and inevitably to problematic outcomes, permeates the entire film. The Joker tells Batman, "You have nothing, nothing to threaten me with. Nothing to do with all your strength," savoring how well his design to incapacitate the dominant has worked (Nolan, *The Dark Knight*). In The Joker's terms, even as Batman uses all of his strength, he can accomplish nothing, and in fact it is specifically *by* using all of his strength that Batman generates futile results. The ability of a determined few to expose the powerful as vulnerable, and therefore to incite ever more desperate reactions, resonates with other references to the film's September 11 context.

Interestingly, then, both Dent and Wayne's butler Alfred (Michael Caine) expressly call The Joker a "terrorist," an attribution unique among cinematic incarnations of the oft-nicknamed character. Is he? He introduced his first demands for Batman's unmasking via the broadcast of a tortured, eventually murdered, copycat vigilante whose dead body he hung outside the mayor's (Nestor Carbonell) office window. He holds a city hostage by fulfilling his promise to kill until Batman surrenders, starting with a judge and the police commissioner, as well as with unsuccessful attempts on the district attorney's and the mayor's lives. He blows up a hospital when the general public fails to fulfill his request that they assassinate a lawyer (Joshua Harto) who knows Batman's identity (Nolan, *The Dark Knight*). Although formally defining "terrorism" launches a loaded task far too exhaustive for this particular paper, for most people's comfort levels, perhaps he fits the bill insofar as he targets the unsuspecting and unarmed so fear can amplify his efforts to tilt power relations in his favor.

But if so, what kind of a terrorist is he? Defining terrorism frequently stalls at the point when one person's "terrorist" is another's "insurgent," "rebel," or even government (Banks, Nevers and Wallerstein 5–9). In cases of insurgency and rebellion, the reasoning goes, on a playing field where the motives and means of the dominant players are suspect, why should the rogue contestant be singled out for reprobation (5–6)? In this sense, corrupt Gotham City could represent the kind of failed system that needs replacing, and the extremity of its opposition is the measure of its failure. Yet this approach presumes actors with political aims: even if some such actors use reprehensible methods to achieve their ends, ends still matter, actions are undertaken toward the achievement of *something*. On these terms, there is a certain logic to these actors' deeds, according to which meaningful outcomes can be imagined and effective interventions can be calibrated (8–9). On these terms, an interested public can sense some kind of stable foundation for whatever policies they endorse or reject.

However, some have contended in real-world debates over terrorism that for certain groups, there is no end in sight, neither legitimate purpose nor feasible cessation (Juergensmeyer 148–166). Indeed, regardless of what we might infer about possible motivations given the United States' political and economic involvements overseas, no messages and no demands accompanied the suicide plane crashes on September 11 taking thousands of lives. At the time, there were no strings attached. The event occurred as an end in itself, massive destruction as self-sufficient spectacle, rather than as overt advancement of a specific cause or interest. In such cases, the argument goes, modes and drives lie outside reason, refusing negotiation and confounding ordinary forms of counteraction (Juergensmeyer 148–166). If so, all the old rules of engagement, principles that might be effective and justifiable against, say, criminals or combatants with decipherable operating principles of their own, would seem no longer to apply. In their absence loom alternatives with burgeoning and disquieting practical and moral implications (Stern 288–296). Under such circumstances, for those interested in a way forward that offers both peace and justice, no clear and easy path readily presents itself. As The Joker would say, "Nothing to do with all your strength" (Nolan, *The Dark Knight*). In this sense, The Joker surpasses the threat that any individual terrorist might pose, which can be delimited within calculable estimations of goals, damage, and containment. Instead, he embodies the kind of peril terrorism writ large poses, which menaces a perpetual state of untold danger undermining the premises of any functional community by propagating profligate and exploitable uncertainties and fears, the kinds of uncertainties and fears that can amplify distrust and soften receptivity to extreme responses.

## *"Giving someone else a chance": Involving Gotham in the Battle for Its Soul*

From this posture, The Joker attempts to fully sabotage any remnant of Gotham's civic virtue. During the interrogation scene between him and Batman, The Joker tells Batman, "They need you right now. But when they don't, they'll cast you out like a leper. You see, their morals, their code — it's a bad joke. Dropped at the first sign of trouble ... I'll show you: when the chips are down, these — these civilized people, they'll eat each other." He later makes good on this threat by creating a no-win scenario involving two ferries, the Liberty and the Spirit (perhaps the Spirit of Liberty?), whereby one ship carrying prisoners and another carrying assorted others leaving the city are both rigged to explode by midnight, with passengers able to save themselves only if they detonate the other ship. When the free passengers vote to blow up the ship of prisoners, seemingly proving The Joker right, no one actually moves to activate the detonator. So a white, apparently straight (a close-up shot provides a full view of his wedding ring), middle-aged, middle-class businessman (Doug Ballard) — the figure of relative privilege in the Western world — steps up to take the detonator, irritated that "No one wants to get their hands dirty" (Nolan, *The Dark Knight*). Yet, when he holds it in his hands, he feels the weight of the decision that only direct action can convey. It is one thing to vote for others to kill on your behalf; it is another to become a killer yourself and live your life as such. The Joker has touched on a danger of democracy, the temptation for individuals to vote their own interests at the expense of others. It is this vulnerability that has permitted his escalating antics, halted only when the democratically-minded fully value the lives and the interests of others as commensurate with their own.

Critically, on both ships, individuals choose not to kill others in full awareness that such a choice would lead to their own deaths (Nolan, *The Dark Knight*). Gothamites have, for the first time in the film, accepted the predicament that Batman has shouldered on their behalf, the sometime incompatibility between ideal and action that well-meaning people should perceive as not precluding responsibility for the consequences of their behavior. In this instance, to The Joker's dismay, they opt for self-sacrifice over self-preservation, finally putting a brake to the violence that has continued to escalate when no one else had been willing to take such a stand. Their decision halts The Joker's devastating run as effectively as Batman's coincident hand-to-hand combat with the villain. The passengers and Batman prove mutually indispensable to one another, with the passengers' intervention in their own fates offering mundane, risky, but recognizable hope for stable civic virtue rather than a further call for the kinds of extraordinary measures that tend to lead to uncontainable outcomes. Although, in the end, the ships do not explode since Batman successfully defeats The Joker before he can trigger the explosives, the decisions on the ferries are made in ignorance of any way out. As a result, they serve as an unenviable but powerful model of the modes, the stakes, and the negotiations of living as a free — that is, safe, autonomous, and responsible — individual.[10]

In this context, allusions to the War on Terror, the historical but not inevitable consequence of September 11, resonate as real-world parallels to the film's staged no-win situations. Batman's abduction of Lau (Chin Han) from Hong Kong to Gotham to deliver him to law enforcement invokes the notion of extraordinary rendition, with Batman circumventing laws the police cannot. Moreover, Lau's use as the center of a RICO case against the city's mobsters calls to mind the legal means that might successfully combat ordinary crime, but perhaps falter when targeting adversaries with more complex motives, means, and resources. Similarly, Batman's construction of a city-wide surveillance system, which he enlists Lucius Fox's (Morgan Freeman) help to operate to locate The Joker, immediately appalls Fox, who sees the system as "unethical ... dangerous ... wrong." However, in this case, its one-time-only deployment, since Batman arranges its implosion once The Joker is captured, evades any resolution of ethical dilemmas. At the same time, the video-taped torture and killing of the vigilante Batman impersonator (Andy Luther) reminds us of similar tapes of ill-fated security contractors in Iraq, while The Joker's cell-phone activation of a bomb, a kind of improvised explosive device (IED), likewise draws on once alien tactics and concepts that have become, only through the War on Terror's progression, commonplace. In the concluding scenes, when both Batman and police SWAT teams seek to rescue hostages at a construction site, only Batman realizes quickly that the victims have been disguised as their victimizers, and vice versa. The ensuing tangle, with Batman trying to free the real hostages, unmask and defeat the real hostage-takers, and prevent the SWAT teams from accidentally killing the innocent, instantiates the troubles contemporary, especially non-conventional, conflict causes when distinctions between civilians and non-combatants cannot be clarified (Nolan, *The Dark Knight*). In each instance, the film evokes the terrain of contemporary dilemmas that, in their action-film setting, duck direct commentary on real-world solutions.[11] Instead, these performances of viewers' current landscape's pressures and constraints occasion our consideration of how to weigh and reconcile our own risks and duties in a post–September 11 world.

# In Conclusion: The Dark (K)night of the September 11 World

In his attempt to foster hope among frightened and disillusioned Gothamites and rally them to resist The Joker in a city where, they protest, "things are worse than ever," Dent tells his press conference audience, "the night is darkest just before the dawn. And I promise you, the dawn is coming" (Nolan, *The Dark Knight*). The 16th century Spanish, Roman Catholic Saint John of the Cross originated the term "the dark night of the soul" to characterize the fraught paradox afflicting the most committed of spiritual devotees: the closer they get to God, the more they feel his absence. This conception has emerged in present-day headlines with the revelation of Mother Teresa's decades-long crisis of faith, during which she performed world-celebrated acts of social service in the name of Jesus, all the while suffering secretly from an acute sense of his abandonment (Van Biema). According to John of the Cross and contemporary theologians, this dark night signals the sacred process by which God's love purifies souls and draws them to him, an encounter between divine infinity and human finitude of such overwhelming disproportion that the unfathomable connection is experienced as a lack. For those in the throes of such an ordeal, perseverance in benevolent action evidences the faith they doubt within themselves. According to skeptics, however, the experience of lack is, quite simply, only that: a realization that in fact nothing does lie beyond the material world to defend the belief in something more (Van Biema). Either way, the dark night of the soul marks a turning point for those who operate on the edges of human possibility. After all, who but the exceptional will stake their very souls on doing the right thing, even when doing that right thing offers no reward, neither material nor spiritual benefit, and especially at times when "the right thing" itself seems too precarious a concept to justify obligation?

In its immediate aftermath, September 11 was perceived as a social purgation, with the day's horror and its aftermath's uncertainties suddenly (and ultimately only temporarily) rendering obsolete arbitrary preoccupations, such as the preceding summer's media obsession with shark attacks and Congressman Gary Condit's illicit and, as ceaselessly surmised but later disproved, possibly criminal relationship with the missing Chandra Levy (Rutenberg). Yet as the aftermath continued to unfold, attention to serious concerns ended up raising more questions than answers, with controversial War on Terror measures at sites like Abu Ghraib and Guantanamo Bay belying any notion of the U.S. as a nation that holds itself to a higher standard. The dark night of the 9/11 world is one in which threats showcased by the attacks on New York and Washington, DC persist, but also one in which a both effective and just response seem to many at best elusive, at worst impossible. What we can do and what we should do have seemed to pose often incompatible options, obscuring the substance of perseverance through action in lieu of belief that sustains those who muscle through more traditionally spiritual crises.

In *The Dark Knight*, The Joker capitalizes on such a crisis of faith, his villainy manifesting in opportunistic leveraging of desperate moments. In *Batman Begins*, the film that launched Nolan's Batman narrative, Rachel Dawes tells her long-time friend Bruce Wayne, as he struggles as an adult to find the right response to his parents' murders in his childhood, that "it's not who you are underneath, it's what you do that defines you" (Nolan). Her admonishment focalizes Wayne's iterations of his alter ego, Batman, who combats criminals according to a moral code superseding personal interests and prohibiting killing that Wayne believes separates him from common vigilantes. In other words, he commits to the principle that his actions must speak for themselves, and they must speak for a better alternative than the forces he is battling. Even before Rachel's corrective, he articulates this conviction to the mentor, Henri Ducard, who has trained him to fight in the name of justice but then requires him to kill an untried prisoner, also in the name of justice. Ducard rebukes, "Your compassion is a weakness your enemies will not share," to which Wayne replies, "That's why it's so important. It separates us from them" (Nolan, *Batman Begins*). In this way, Wayne demarcates a dividing line, not only between hero and villain, but also between hero and vigilante. However tenuous the thread, it is the one he holds onto. Whether a weakness in fact or a survivors' sustaining strength, it is a thread of choice as well for those wearied and troubled in the wake of September 11.

As I have shown here, *The Dark Knight*'s dramatic allusions invite, and even compel, audience members to connect their own personal experiences of September 11 with their experience of viewing the film. This approach anchors within superhero fiction dilemmas analogous to the no-win scenarios occasioned by September 11 and its wake, including the subsequently equivocal efforts to formulate a coherent, effective, just response. In this way, the film permits consideration of, without prescribing or proscribing definitive conclusions about, the responsibilities of those who act on behalf of others, as well as those who allow others to act on their behalf, in matters of justice and public safety. In effect, *The Dark Knight* instantiates and leaves unresolved the kinds of moral quandaries September 11 has posed, exploring and implicating its audience in the culturally traumatic complexities of agency and responsibility under conditions of constrained choice and shattered meaning and subjectivity.

## Notes

1. In his contribution to a multi-authored piece in Scotland's *The Sunday Herald*, "Five Years On: How 9/11 Changed the World," James Cusick writes, "The symbolism of the Twin Towers was less the loss of innocent life than the truth conveyed: if such a thing could happen in Manhattan, heart and economic soul of American power, it could

happen anywhere. When they claimed the Brighton bombing and the attempt to assassinate Margaret Thatcher, the IRA expressed it best. "We only have to be lucky once, they said, you have to be lucky all the time. And who, then, are 'you'? Everyone. All of us. Whether a commuter in London or a Lebanese child hearing jets scream in the sky, the war on terror has become conscription. No-one is exempt." This excerpt offers one example of the multiple, unique ways in which September 11, 2001 was understood as "world-changing" by people globally.

2. Eisenberg also mentions that "British actor Michael Caine [who portrays Alfred in this film] has observed that Superman is how America sees itself and Batman is how the rest of the world sees America." This quote opens the door to one way of understanding the film's politics.

3. For a discussion of how comics generally have served as cultural texts, see Kaveney (267). See Turner and Palmer for discussions of how films generally have served as cultural texts. For a critical, in-depth consideration of how this film resonates with September 11, which shares many of my concerns, see Kerstein.

4. In regard to cultural memory, Sturken writes, "Crisis occurs when cultural rules are broken — when both the structures and the fractures of a culture are most visible" (258). In the aftermath process of meaning formation, she argues that cultural memory links the past with the present through the production-in-use practices of a diverse and often divergent American public (257–259). Similar to what Sturken notes about the Vietnam War and the AIDS epidemic, "America is inconceivable without" (14) September 11. In this sense, *The Dark Knight* serves as a "technology of memory," or a mechanism by which audiences can negotiate the implications of a shared experience (1, 9–10).

5. See Lovell and Sergi for an analysis of how sensual stimuli viscerally immerse audiences in the not just viewing, but more broadly sensing, experience of encountering this film.

6. For background on how and why fictional cities in comics have typically stood in for New York City, see Reynolds (18–19).

7. For a discussion of how The Joker's fascination with corrupting others has driven his behavior in other stories, see Anders (29).

8. For a discussion of similar public ambivalence about Batman in Frank Miller's *Batman: The Dark Knight Returns*, see Reynolds (105).

9. Kaveney notes that in comic books generally, "reliance on superheroes [is n]ever shown as a substitute for collective action" (20).

10. While much more could be said about Hannah Arendt's argument that violence and power are absolute opposites, the civilian response here supports her claim that "the extreme form of power is All against One" (41). She premises her position by contending that although violence provides a strength-multiplier (46), its effects are unpredictable, and therefore under violent conditions goals become almost subsidiary to the means taken to secure them (4). Accordingly, she warns, "The practice of violence, like all action, changes the world, but the most probable change is to a more violent world" (80), leading to the escalation rather than the resolution of conflict. For this reason, power, or the impact of collective "support and consent" (49) rather than of singular aggression, affords more equitable stability.

11. For a discussion of how comic book victories tend to be partial or provisional for the practical reason of needing to preserve continuity, see Reynolds (81–82) and Kaveney (140).

# The Mythos of Patriarchy in the *X-Men* Films

BETTY KAKLAMANIDOU

> *Taking power away from a man is a dangerous thing.*
> *Someone always pays.*
>
> Glenn Close as Patty Hewes, *Damages*

Even though the fictional Patty Hewes does not possess any actual super-hero powers—although that could be debatable taking into consideration her legal victories, mental capacities and her uncanny ability to survive the most dangerous situations—her quote echoes exactly the state of affairs in both her basis of operations, contemporary New York City, and the filmic superhero universe: Men are here to stay and women can only be led to believe they can fill their shoes and/or act as equals. Patriarchy works in carefully calculated ways, and the latest superhero cinematic narratives serve once again as the proof of its hegemony despite the filmic evidence that points to a newfound respect for the powerful female heroine. The new millennium did indeed bear witness to numerous examples of female superheroines taking center stage in both television and film: shows such as *Alias* (ABC, 2001–2006), *Charmed* (WB, 1998–2004), and *Buffy the Vampire Slayer* (WB, 1997–2003), and films such as *Charlie's Angels* (2000), *Lara Croft: Tomb Raider* (2001), *Lara Croft Tomb Raider: The Cradle of Life* (2003), *Charlie's Angels: Full Throttle* (2003), *Underworld* (2003), *Catwoman* (2004), *Aeon Flux* (2005), and *Elektra* (2005) were domi-nated by super female strength and ingenuity, and showed that women are just as capable as men to tackle any kind of threat and any villain with a God syn-drome and/or world domination plans.[1] Lara, Elektra, Natalie, Dylan, and Alex, among others, were the protagonists in their respective fictional worlds. Super-heroines also found a place in superhero teams, such as *The League of Extraor-dinary Gentlemen* (2003), the two *Fantastic Four* films (2005 and 2007), *Avatar*

61

(2009) and the *X-Men* franchise. The latter narratives enabled the heroines to work alongside their male partners and, in a way, proved that there is nothing a woman cannot handle.

## The Contemporary Ubiquity of the Super Heroine: Real Progress or Clever Subterfuge?

What does this ubiquity of extraordinarily super women mean? Is one of the last male-centered fictional spaces— the superhero film —finally accepting what the three feminist waves have been striving for for more than a century?[2] Are these super heroines treated and/or accepted by both their creators and the audience as equal comrades of the male heroes? Is the superhero film a new step in gender articulation? A single answer cannot easily be given since there are still superhero narratives which prefer to "use" women as the leading man's object of affection and/or "damsels in distress," such as Mary Jane (Kirsten Dunst) in *Spider-Man* (2002), Rachel (Katie Holmes) in *Batman Begins* (2005) and Lois (Kate Bosworth) in *Superman Returns* (2006). Although one could rightly argue that the new millennium Mary Jane, Lois and Rachel are nowhere near as powerless and/or dependent on male help as in their past representations, they still perpetuate the myth of the strong male and the weak female in search of love and support. Of course, a complete and thorough study of all the superhero film texts, which should also include their production side and/or a survey aiming to reveal how audiences receive, understand and interpret these sometimes subtle gender articulations, is a task which could certainly illuminate aspects not yet thoroughly examined, but, which, nevertheless, goes beyond the goals of this chapter.

These film texts all share a common mythology. From Achilles to Wolverine and from Jason and the Argonauts to Batman, it is surprising that many things have not changed in a period of thousands of years. Nevertheless, in this apparent inactivity lies the true nature of myth. "Mythology is static. We find the same mythical elements combined over and over again," wrote Claude Lévi-Strauss (17), and despite our contemporary heroes' sophisticated weaponry and/or powers, their essence — that is, their effort to uphold the law, protect the innocent, and/or save humanity — has stayed the same. Lévi-Strauss' work, along with Roland Barthes' theory on the same subject, will help us to explore the great mythos of patriarchy in the four X-Men films (*X-Men*, 2000, *X2: X-Men United*, 2003, *X-Men: The Last Stand*, 2006, and *X-Men Origins: Wolverine*, 2009). I argue that the patriarchal structure of modern society is a myth as defined by Roland Barthes, which is constructed to uphold its hegemonic interests and perpetuated via the widely popular film medium. I intend to analyze the trajectory of the main female heroines in the four films and show how those who defy patriarchal authority are subtly and progressively stripped of not only their powers, but also their cinematic presence.* The patriarchal structure of the cinematic X-Men world, defined by the paternal male figures of Xavier (Patrick Stewart) and Magneto (Ian McKellen)—who personify the poles of good and evil—may allow women to assume important positions in their world and the film narratives, but only insofar as those heroines abide by their rules and answer to them.

## Jean Grey: The Unbearable Fate of the Superheroine

In 1957, Barthes defined myth as discourse; a system of communication; a message that is not confined to oral speech but is hidden is many representations such as photography, sports, shows, and cinema. Barthes argued that although there may be ancient myths, none can last forever, because it is only human history that can regulate and decide on the life and death of mythic language, since the messages it contains are used to resolve social conflicts. Today, film has become one of the most fecund terrains for the discussion of myth, since it reflects the social status quo, while it "in some instances ... takes up direct simultaneous participation in the texts of social history and even predicts the directions that social history will ultimately take" (Palmer xi).

Superheroes have been part of societal mythology for thousands of years. The ancient Greek Hercules and Achilles are among the first superheroes on earth: part mortal and part god, they had human flaws, but they were also almost indestructible. This dichotomy between human imperfection and fantastic strength or abilities is still what defines the superhero of the 21st century. However, with rare exceptions, superheroes are male individuals who operate in a strictly patriarchal context, one of the most durable mythic environments in the western world. It is in this male-dominated universe that the women of X-Men try to act.[3] The four films of the franchise follow a somewhat backwards trajectory. The economy of the film medium dictates that a central character should emerge as the main focus of each narrative, accompanied by secondary, albeit structurally indispensable in terms of plot evolution, characters. In addition, rarely do we learn their complete backgrounds. This may lead to a reverse "guilty until proven innocent" verdict, as will be proven later on, but it also adds to the enhancement of the desired and/or anticipated emotional audience response.

The four films were written, directed, photographed, and edited by men. The only woman of the films' main production team is Lauren Shuler Donner, one of the few powerful female Hollywood producers.[4] It becomes clear that the film texts will be narrated by a male point of view, a practice that goes back to ancient Greek mythology, and in that tradition, these modern men will be "making a statement about their own society without necessarily knowing it" since the essence of their stories still remains "the stuff of men's lives and

*The author would like to thank Peggy Tally and Richard J. Gray II for their comments, and Petros Zafeiriou for his continuous support.*

fantasies" (Jane Cahill 7–9). As was noted above, contemporary cinema has long embraced female power and strength. However, the patriarchal system consistently makes sure that male supremacy will remain at the top of its hierarchy. This is accomplished through myth and its subtle and above suspicion qualities. For myth is

> *depoliticized speech*... Myth does not deny things, on the contrary, its function is to talk about them; simply, it purifies them, it makes them innocent, it gives them a natural and eternal justification, it gives them a clarity which is not that of an explanation but that of a statement of fact [Barthes, *Myth Today* 109].

In other words, the great myth of patriarchy inventively states that no matter how many things women have accomplished, they will always be less of a "hero" than their male counterparts. In the X-Men franchise, the myth follows an ingenious trajectory in that it starts by bestowing enough power on the central female characters— Jean, Storm and Mystique —and then continues by stripping them little by little of all their cinematic presence and authority.

The ingenious "trap" of patriarchy is constructed in the first two films. The first *X-Men* film revolves around Logan/Wolverine (Hugh Jackman) and Marie/Rogue (Anna Paquin) and the path towards their integration into Professor Charles Xavier's team of mutants. We see Logan struggle to survive as a fighter in a seedy Canadian bar with no memory of his past, and Marie, whose power is the ability to absorb another person's life energy just by a simple touch, run away from home after realizing she cannot ever have a boyfriend without endangering his life. After Rogue and Logan's chance encounter at the bar and the realization on her part that he is also a mutant, she hides in his trailer hoping he can help her. After they are attacked by Magneto's right-hand man, Sabretooth (Tyler Mane), they are saved by Scott Summers/Cyclops (John Marsden) and Ororo Munroe/Storm (Halle Berry) and taken to Charles Xavier's School for the Gifted where they meet Charles and Jean Grey (Famke Janssen). Meanwhile, Senator Robert Kelly (Bruce Davison), a fervent enemy of mutants, is trying to pass the "Mutant Registration Act" which will force all mutants to reveal their identities and powers. Magneto sees this as an opportunity for war and decides to abduct Rogue, use her powers and destroy all mankind.[5] *X2: X-Men United* introduces new characters, such as the teleporting Kurt Wagner/Nightcrawler (Alan Cumming), military scientist and mutant expert William Stryker (Brian Cox), his mutant son Jason (Michael Reid Mackay), and his assistant Yuriko Oyama/Lady Deathstrike (Kelly Hu), among others, and centers on Stryker's efforts to kill all the mutants through controlling the Professor and making him use Cerebro in order to locate all the mutants in the planet. When this plan fails, it is Magneto who seizes the opportunity to kill all the humans. In the end, however, Jean manages to save the X-Men and the entire world by sacrificing herself near Alkali Lake, the place used by Stryker in the past for experimentation on mutants.

We are first introduced to Jean in the sixth minute of *X-Men* while she is addressing the United States Congress, explaining slowly and in a calm tone of voice during a hearing on the subject of the possible danger mutants pose to society that mutation is the next stage of human evolution. Jean is standing at the center of an enormous conference room, dressed in a very elegant red suit. She is wearing brown rim glasses and her long, brown hair falls softly on her shoulders, creating the look of a scientist/educator who, despite obvious natural beauty and meticulous attention to external appearance, is competent and knowledgeable. However, as soon as she finishes her sentence, she is attacked by Senator Kelly, whose agenda is to turn the politicians and the public, who are also attending the hearing, against mutants in order to pass the Mutant Registration Act. At first, she answers calmly, but as the Senator keeps raising his voice and demands that mutants identify themselves, he creates an atmosphere of fear and doubt that leads to Jean's obvious unease and confusion. Alternate shots of the Senator and Jean reveal a clear dichotomy between strong man, who manages to control the audience, and a confused and unpleasantly surprised Jean, who looks around, perplexed, gives out inaudible sighs, takes her glasses off in an attempt to speak, but finally does not utter a word. When the Senator's final remark is met with enthusiastic applause, we see a long shot of Jean from Professor Xavier's perspective, who is sitting in the auditorium balcony. She is simply standing there, admitting defeat. Her failure as a persuasive public speaker is subsequently balanced in the ensuing scenes. This time Grey is in a safe place, Charles' school, her home since her adolescence. She is treating Logan in her laboratory and is in full command of her faculties while she explains his condition to the Professor, Storm and Cyclops. Although she clearly acknowledges Charles' superiority, evidenced by the respectful tone she uses when she addresses him, she exhibits an assertive, educated, and composed personality. Her limited cinematic presence (Jean appears in eight brief scenes during the 104 minutes of the first film and is also present in the extensive climactic battle scene along with Storm, Logan and Cyclops towards the end) does not provide enough information as to her character, background and strength and clearly promotes Logan as the "star" of the film. We learn that she is telekinetic and a bit telepathic, and that the Professor is teaching her to control her powers. However, two scenes prove that she has still a long way to go. When she tries to read Logan's mind, she sees a cluster of unsettling scenes of his adamantium injections and stops, troubled and obviously distressed. When she tries to use Cerebro, she almost collapses but manages to find Magneto's whereabouts. These two scenes confirm that, although she is an accomplished and confident physician, she is still unable to control her powers and is dependent on male guidance. It is of course necessary that the director and the writer withhold information and show Jean's progress gradually in order to build up audience expectation. Nevertheless, neither Scott nor Logan shows any sign of vulnerability or discomfort with their powers. Moreover, Jean "is part of a classic love-triangle with her fellow X-Men Scott and Logan — Cyclops and Wolverine. She functions as the focus of a continuing heterosexual matrix, promoting the traditional male-female relationship to the audience" (Rebecca Housel 84).

The first noticeable thing about Jean in *X2* is her appearance. Gone are her long hair and her elegant skirts. She is now wearing her hair shorter while she is always dressed in pants. The red color is equally there, in her hair and items of clothing. These seemingly superficial changes, however, are signs which semiotically lead to interesting observations. Her medium-length hairstyle and pants create an androgynous look which, combined with Famke Janssen's features and height — Janssen is six feet tall — create a strong cinematic image, which can attract both the male and female audience. Moreover, this "masculinized" image could also be interpreted as an attempt to show that, by looking more like a man, Jean can achieve the status of the ultimate superhero at the end of the narrative. After Stryker's and Magneto's respective attempts to win the war between humans and mutants, the X-Men find themselves unable to escape as a result of a malfunction of their jet. The dam is collapsing and Jean can feel that the strength of the water will kill them all. Alternate close-ups of Jean with the water emerging through the walls insinuate that not only can she sense what is wrong, but she is also capable of seeing it. She then makes her decision. She looks at all of her friends over her shoulder, her eyes filled with tears, and steps outside the jet. Xavier senses her absence, and although Scott starts shouting and asking Storm to take the ramp down, Jean controls the jet and ignites the engine. "I know what I'm doing. This is the only way," we hear her say through Xavier's mouth as they share the same power. A cinematically impressive shot shows Jean with her two arms raised, one to lift the jet and the other to stop the massive torrent of water. Just before she unleashes the water and drowns, however, her eyes turn red — a sign of her future metamorphosis into the Phoenix — and she closes her eyes, accepting her fate. Jean sacrifices herself to save humanity and the mutant community and assumes the position traditionally reserved for male heroes in most film genres, echoing the respective acts of selflessness of Robert Duvall as Spurgeon Tanner in *Deep Impact* (1998), and Bruce Willis as Harry Stamper in *Armageddon* (1998). In *X2*, it is a woman who saves the day and leaves the two men who love her (Logan and Scott) behind, crying, while her company of friends, colleagues and students feel sadness and gratitude for her sacrifice. Most importantly, however, although the first two films begin with Magneto's and Xavier's voice-overs, *X2* closes with Jean's voice-over and a repetition of the stages in human evolution which we first heard uttered by Magneto in the first film. A circle has closed, but it is now a female voice that signals the "forward leap in evolution." Although comic aficionados understand that the last helicopter shot, which shows the sign of the phoenix forming over the lake that destroyed Stryker's facilities, marks Jean's potential rebirth as the villain, the common viewer cannot help but appreciate Jean's altruism and place her in the pantheon of superheroes who deserve admiration and praise.

However, Grey's noble gesture will not be respected for long. *X-Men: The Last Stand* finds our superheroes faced with the vaccine which can "cure" them. However, it begins with Charles and Magneto's first visit to Jean's house, twenty years before we were first introduced to them. Even before they enter, Charles says, "This one is special." The Professor is perhaps acknowledging that not only is there another mutant with the same powers, but also one that might surpass him. However, the purpose of this scene is not to show how Jean's parents treated her as a sick person who had to go away or to introduce us to the character. The scene is merely a smokescreen to demonstrate that Jean's dark side (the Phoenix) was already present in her adolescence — she actually lifts all the cars and machines outside her house while talking to Charles telepathically — and that it was the Professor, a man, who managed to subdue it and show her the "right" path. The Svengali scenario, repeated in countless written and audiovisual tales, negates the possibility of knowing how Jean would decide to face the world if left to her own devices and assures that her adult self will always be marked to a great extent by male influence. After her sacrifice in *X2*, her rebirth in *The Last Stand* as the Dark Phoenix, the symbol of resurrection and eternal life, transforms her into the ultimate villain despite the positive connotations that surround the mythological bird.[6]

When Scott visits the lake where his love lost her life saving everyone else, Jean emerges from the sea in an extraordinarily blinding light. Like a beautiful, ancient Greek siren, she approaches Scott; her appearance (her long hair and black leather suit, reminiscent of the *X-Men*'s modest doctor and *X2*'s savior respectively) seems to remind both Scott and the audience of the character of the previous two films. However, after she utters her first lines, something in her tone of voice changes. She seems more confident, more sure of herself. Once she starts kissing Scott, her eyes open and red veins cover her face. We thus become sure that it is not Grey but the Phoenix who has come back to life. After she kills Scott, she is found unconscious by Storm and Logan and taken back to Xavier's school. There, Charles reveals to Logan:

> Jean Grey is the only class 5 mutant I've ever encountered, her potential practically limitless. Her mutation is seated in the unconscious part of her mind and therein lay the danger. When she was a girl, I created psychic barriers to isolate her powers from her conscious mind. And as a result Jean developed a dual personality. The conscious Jean, whose powers were always in her control, and the dormant side. A personality that, in our sessions, came to call itself the Phoenix, a purely instinctual creature, all desire and joy and rage.

In this revealing monologue, the great patriarch is exposed. It is He who created the barriers to protect her from her powers— which he admitted helped her save her life in *X2* when he could not. It is He who created Jean, the sensible and lacking in self-esteem scientist who obeyed him no matter what. And it is He who—for the first and only time in the three X-Men films—becomes upset and says that He will not explain himself to anyone, let alone Logan when the latter is expressing his doubts whether his actions should take into consideration what Jean really wants or who she wants to be. Jean never stood a chance. As soon as Charles realized that she was equally or more powerful than he, he found a way to tame the "beast." But now the "beast" has returned to reclaim her individuality and unfortunately confirm that, in a man's world, no female can claim the throne. When the Phoenix eventually arises, she goes back to her home, the nest she should have set on fire when the time of her death would approach, and in a cinematically amazing scene, she kills the Professor. She lifts up the entire house and lifts Charles from his wheelchair while Eric's and the Professor's mutants are fighting inside and outside. The alternate close-ups of the furious and determined Phoenix and of the always serene Charles—suspended in the air—convey their respective emotions: rage and sympathy. In the last seconds before his death, time stands still through a slow motion montage, and then suddenly the Phoenix actually obliterates the Professor, who manages to telepathically tell Jean not to let her dark side control her before accepting his eventual demise with a smile, which connotes the generosity of his spirit and cancels his previous aggression. Before Phoenix has a chance to calm herself, she is taken by Magneto to be used as his weapon against humans and the "cure." It is at this point that the Phoenix as villain stops being interesting, for "What then happens is that she stands around for most of the rest of the film looking sulky and forms an alliance with Magneto more or less by default" (Kaveney 261–2). Not only does she lack the edginess and eccentricity of Batman's Joker or the exuberance and shrewd ingenuity of Superman's Lex Luthor, she has to ask to be saved, in other words to die, by and in the arms of Wolverine, her unrequited true love. Thus, "*The Last Stand* becomes unalloyedly the parable about women not being able to handle power that the comics version arguably to some extent avoided being" (ibid. 261). Unfortunately, this is not the first time that women are punished simply for being superior to man. Jean had to be destroyed once she stopped being the obedient helper and became the most powerful mutant of all. Patriarchy cannot accept this gender reversal and shrewdly turned her into the villain in order to justify her death and restore order. Harriet Hawkins (54) observes that "ever since Lilith, the desire to play the star part rather than a supporting role has been deemed anathema—an accursed thing—in woman. And it still is."[7] In turning the Phoenix into the villain, *The Last Stand* succeeds in firstly, demonizing the female and secondly, in establishing Logan as the ultimate superhero, paving the way for *X-Men Origins: Wolverine*.

## Storm and Mystique: The Teacher and the Rebel

Storm and Mystique hold significant narrative positions in the cinematic X-Men universe despite their being at opposite ends of the spectrum; Storm is part of the "good guys," while Mystique is Magneto's devious right hand. They are both beautiful women, portrayed by Halle Berry and Rebecca Romijn-Stamos, respectively. However, "Storm isn't on the scene for her physique or face. And she is not the center of a traditional, patriarchal heterosexual matrix.... She is her own person, and brings considerable substance to the X-Men" (Housel 78). Storm is one of the most stable characters in the first three films. Not only is she an accomplished fighter and deliverer of witty one-liners—"Do you know what happens to a toad when it's struck by lightning?" she asks Toad in *X-Men*, and while he stares at her in confusion she calmly retorts, "The same thing that happens to everything else," just before unleashing her powers onto him — she is also one of the teachers in Xavier's school. Storm always demonstrates patience, tolerance, sensitivity and empathy, even when she faces enemies and/or danger. For instance, in *X-Men*, she is the one holding the hand of the transformed Senator Kelly before he dies, and in *X-2* she develops a genuine relationship with the odd-looking Nightcrawler, which leads to their saving the Professor from inadvertently killing all the mutants inside Cerebro. Her most important function, however, is that she is the one Charles entrusts with the future of the school for the gifted and she is the one who decides to keep it open after the professor's death at the hands of the Phoenix. One could readily argue that Xavier's decision invalidates the argument that patriarchy refuses to appoint women to top positions and he/she would be right unless they knew the context of the Professor's decision. Xavier intended to pass the torch to Scott and not to Storm. However, since Scott "took Jean's death too hard," the Professor started thinking about Storm. In other words, Storm got the job by default. Furthermore, teaching is usually connected to such feminine qualities as patience, emotional understanding, and nurture, and it has almost always been among the most common career choices for women in both the real world and its filmic representations. From Bette Davis' socially conscious Lilly Moffat in *The Corn Is Green* (1945) to Michelle Pfeiffer's tough Louanne Johnson in *Dangerous Minds* (1995), female teachers exhibit a sensitivity and emotional richness that their male colleagues seem to lack.[8] Finally, at Xavier's funeral, Storm has the honor of delivering the eulogy. Holding back her tears, she insists that they "must carry on his [the Professor's] vision, and that's a vision of a world united." A world united, indeed, with women constantly pressured to play second fiddle.

Mystique is one of the most intriguing female villains in the cinematic X-Men cosmos. Driven by rage and hostility against those humans who made her "afraid to go to school as a child," starting with her parents, who tried to kill her, she mainly does Magneto's dirty work due to her extraordinary shifting power but also her physical strength and intelligence. In *X-Men*, she abducts Senator Kelly, she encourages Rogue to leave the school for the gifted, and she tampers with Cerebro, endangering Xavier's life; while in *X2* it is thanks to her feminine charms that she manages to help Magneto free himself from his plastic prison. It is also in *X2* that we see her in her human form for the first time. In a clichéd representation of the dangerously captivating femme fatale, Mystique as Grace appears as a gorgeous blonde with incredibly long legs—accentuated by a low-angle close shot which renders them even longer—and seduces one of Magneto's prison guards, only to inject him with iron and help Eric escape. Her seduction techniques and her way of creeping into places through turning into whomever is needed for her goal is also highlighted by her snake-like mutant appearance, her yellow eyes and "her indigo skin clumped with patches of scales" (Housel 82). Housel argues that Mystique's nature is characterized by "an unstable, changing duality" due to the fact that she can change into both male and female forms, and that it is this duality that prevents her from transcending "to the singularity necessary to complete the hero cycle" (ibid.) However, most superheroes have to face this duality: Superman/Clark Kent, Iron Man/Tony Stark, Hulk/Bruce Banner—the list is long. If one accepts Housel's argument, then most superheroes are caught in a vicious circle and/or cannot fulfill their destiny. It is true that they do have problems with their "other" side, but both the audience and the fictional characters manage this duality, which is in a way part of every human being. In other words, we would all be forced to ask questions such as: Is Bruce Banner an accomplished scientist, or should we consider him a green monster and nothing else? Mystique's extraordinary shape-shifting may help her change into every male or female form she wishes, but nothing can deter the audience from understanding that the curvaceous and luscious creature they see on the screen is definitely a woman, no matter how easily she can change into a man.

And it is her female nature that patriarchy stigmatizes and ultimately punishes in *The Last Stand*. When the captured Mystique is transported with other mutants to be "cured," Magneto comes to what seems to be her rescue. However, what he really wants is information on the antibody and the recruitment of new talent. When a guard points his gun at him, it is Mystique who gets shot trying to protect her master. Lying naked on the floor of the bus, she is soon metamorphosed into a beautiful human woman. Surprised and saddened, she looks up and says Eric's name in the hope he will be there for her. Magneto simply acknowledges that she saved him but without even thanking her, he coldly states, "You are not one of us anymore." While he abandons her with the rest of the mutants, he adds, "Such a shame. She was so beautiful." Mystique is reduced to a useful weapon: a tool that broke and can be discarded with little remorse whatsoever. In addition, there is no mention of her help and/or abilities, just the superficial statement that she was beautiful: an attractive object which Eric no longer needs. Magneto's callousness leads Mystique to the U.S. government to reveal his plans and base of operations. "Hell hath no fury like a woman scorned," says the President when he sees footage of Mystique on a screen, while Magneto's heartless and cruel treatment of Mystique never does become an issue nor is it used to explain what drove her to betrayal. The President's use of William Congreve's quote is yet another example of the devious working of the hegemonic patriarchy. The ancient Greek dramatist, Menander, also wrote that the three sources of evil in the world are fire, woman and the sea thus confirming the patriarchal mechanisms that have been at work since antiquity keeping women submissive and teaching them proper behavior under male laws.

## X-Men Origins: Wolverine

After Jean's death, Mystique's ostracism, and Storm's placement in the benign role of school principal, patriarchy had successfully completed its goal in neutralizing female power and went on in establishing, once again, the much anticipated male order. Since the fourth *X-Men* was designed around Wolverine's back story, the filmmakers produced a true buddy movie as underlined by a visually astounding credit sequence, which shows Logan and Victor (Liev Schreiber) fighting side by side in the American civil war, World War I, World War II, and Vietnam, since the story centers on these two mutant brothers who were born 200 years ago. Women may be present in the story, but they are undoubtedly secondary characters, used to illuminate aspects of Logan's past and also uphold the mythos of male superiority.

A pre-opening-credit sequence reveals how James/Logan tragically kills Victor's dad using his claws for the first time, just before he finds out that he was his own father, too. After the murder, James' mother, overwhelmed by what she witnessed, looks at him and asks, "What are you?" Astonished, frightened and still angry, little James starts running in the woods only to be stopped by Victor, who promises they will always be together. This maternal rejection, which could easily be attributed to a mother's— or any human beings for that matter, regardless of sex — natural surprise when her offspring extends claws from his knuckles and kills another person, does not interest the filmic narrative. Without any further exploration of what happened to James' mother, the audience is presented with a female monster; a mother who rejects her own flesh and blood can be nothing less. Of course, it also goes without saying that the cinematic text uses her as the perfect excuse of adult Logan's hot temper and residual frustration.

Logan and Victor go through life together until they are recruited by Stryker (Danny Huston) to assist him with his devious plans. When Logan has enough of Stryker's manipulative methods and Victor's use of unnecessary violence, he quits the team and the narrative flashes forwards six years into the future. Logan is settled in the Canadian Rockies, works as a lumberjack, and is in love with his schoolteacher girlfriend, Kayla (Lynn Collins), who knows of his peculiarity and does not mind the occasional accidental scratch or buying new sheets every time Logan has a nightmare and wakes up with his claws buried into their mattress. Kayla is presented as the tender, understanding and patient woman who drives her man to work, picks him up and takes care not only of their house, but also of his past wounds. In other words, she is the perfect female patriarchal model. Kayla is narratively important insofar as she provides the key to the evolution of the plot. Just one minute after the first half hour of the film, she is murdered by Victor and is conveniently absent from the better part of the narrative. Love becomes Logan's motive, and the rest of the film focuses on his attempts to avenge her death. His anger and desperation force him to accept Stryker's offer to obtain his adamantium claws in order to be able to vanquish Kayla's murderer, unaware of the fact that Victor is also working with the military scientist who exploits mutants. Through the suffering he endures during the operation and his determination to take revenge for his lost love, Logan/Wolverine becomes the eternal hero in the tradition of thousands of stories and myths around the world; a lone wolf who lost his love and tries to take revenge and/or find peace of mind. The film is reduced to a series of fights, albeit visually striking and satisfying, until Kayla re-enters Logan's world and is proven to have been working for Stryker all along. Logan is therefore twice betrayed by a woman in the film; His mother and his first love, the one that gave him the alias Wolverine.[9] Despite Kayla's confession to Logan that she was at first forced to enter a relationship with him because Stryker was holding her mutant sister hostage, he remains suspicious until he is convinced that she truly loved him in the course of their living together. However, since the superhero narrative usually prefers its male heroes unattached, Kayla dies in the end. She is not only punished for her ruse, but she also sets Logan conveniently free for his next adventure since the adamantium bullet Wolverine received to the head before the end credits erased his memory.

## Tale as Old as Time

The preceding discussion demonstrated the understated and at first unnoticed mechanisms that maintain the myth of patriarchy in the *X-Men* films. The X-Men universe is governed by male rules, and no woman could ever hope to ascend to the top. Jean and Mystique tried in their respective ways to be the best they could be, but were eventually disempowered. Their fate shows that "the more successful and brilliant and ambitious and glamorous and famous [a woman] is in her own right, and the more she enjoys her success, the more she must be morally anathematised as a *femme fatale*, a vampire, an unnatural monster, a superbitch" (Hawkins 55). Although Hawkins is mostly interested in literature, her conclusions can also be applied to film narratives since "like virtually everything else created by human beings," film also tends "to reflect the sexual, social, psychological and theological traditions and taboos of the cultures that produced them" (ibid. 100).

Nonetheless, besides Jean and Mystique, the structure of the X-Men's fictional world swarms with male potency and prerogatives. Even leaving Xavier and Magneto aside, the two great patriarchs with God complexes, all official posts are occupied by men. Mihkail Lyubansky notes that the mutants "are intended as an allegory for oppression in general" (77). It is unfortunate that this oppression does not include women. For instance, in *The Last Stand*, the Department of Mutant Affairs with Hank McCoy/The Beast (Kelsey Grammer) serving as Secretary is indeed progress in a world which is afraid of mutants. However, the secret conference Hank attends consists exclusively of men — thirteen to be precise — with not even a token woman to soften the testosterone levels that persist when they all watch the failed attempts of an FBI investigator to get information from Mystique regarding Magneto's whereabouts. Despite her mutation and the danger she poses, in this scene, Mystique becomes an objectified female image in the second degree, as she is not only watched, admired and feared by the men in the filmic scene like a post-modern femme fatale, but is simultaneously watched by the viewers of the film. In the beginning of *X2*, Magneto's voice-over concludes: "It is an historical fact; sharing the world has never been humanity's defining attribute." He should have said, "sharing the world has never been man's defining attribute."

## Notes

1. At the same time, these narratives constitute a new cycle of the superhero or action/adventure genre, which Marc O' Day (201–218) defines as "action babe cinema." Although O' Day approaches the heroines of these films using Yvonne Tasker's term of "musculinity" which "indicates the extent to which a physical definition of masculinity in terms of a developed musculature is not limited to the male body within representation (Tasker 3), and Laura Mulvey's theory of "to-be-looked-at-ness" to prove that these female representations are a step forward in gender politics, he does acknowledge the fact that most of these films are set in a patriarchal environment.

2. For more on feminism and especially the two last feminist waves, see Joanne Hollows and Rachel Moseley (1–22).

3. Jane Cahill (7) correctly reminds us that "The stories that we call Greek myths are men's stories.... Their substance is the stuff of men's lives and fantasies victory in war, glorious death on the battlefield, heroic enterprise, the slaying of monsters, the fathering of sons.... Female characters in myth are mothers or wives or virgins, defined always in terms of men. Most of them are bad or unusual women: there is Medea who kills her children; there is Clytemnestra who, though married to the richest king in Greece, commits both adultery and murder; there is Thetis who puts her babies on the fire; there is Jocasta who marries her own son." Moreover, Greek mythology includes several examples of super powerful female monsters, such as Medusa, the Sirens, the witch Kirki, Scylla and Charybdis. Robin Hard (94) also notes that the first person Zeus sent to the world to cause trouble was a woman, Pandora. Additionally, Hard (135–138) underlines that although Hera, Zeus' wife, was firstly celebrated "As a goddess of married women," she was later portrayed and is still viewed today "as a wronged and vindictive wife who is constantly wrangling with her husband and persecuting his mistresses and their children."

4. In her long career, Lauren Shuler Donner has produced films which belong to

diverse genres, such as romantic comedies (*She's the Man*, 2006; *You've Got Mail*, 1998), dramas (*Any Given Sunday*, 1999), and action/superhero films (*Constantine*, 2005). Her success is confirmed by a staggering $3 billion gross worldwide. (imdb.com).

5. The choice of both director and screenwriter for the first film was to present the X-Men as "an established group [...] into whom our viewpoint characters are inserted and eventually treated as equals, or at least — in Rogue's case — equal foci of attention" (Roz Kaveney 258). In an interview, Bryan Singer, the director of the first two films, confirmed that "you want to be able to be accessible to all the people who don't understand or might not be familiar with the comic."

6. For more on the Phoenix and its existence in several ancient civilizations, see Sophia Fotopoulou, http://www.newsfinder.org/site/more/phoenix_the_symbol_of_re birth/.

7. Lilith was Adam's first wife, who "left the garden of Eden because she disliked being ordered around." For more on Lilith, see Vanda Zajko's "Women and Greek Myth" (2007).

8. There are, of course, many cinematic examples of brilliant male teachers (*To Sir, with Love*, 1967; *Children of a Lesser God*, 1986; *Dead Poets Society*, 1989), but the interesting thing is that what makes those men so inspirational is that they are not afraid to show their feminine side and openly be sensitive, emotional, indecisive and even scared.

9. The name Wolverine comes from an old tale Kayla narrated to Logan one night. The moon always seems so lonely because she once had a lover whose name was Kuekuatsheu (The Wolverine). They both lived in the spirit world and every night they wandered the skies. One day, Kuekuatsheu was deceived by another spirit, the Trickster, who told him that the Moon had asked for flowers. The Trickster advised Kuekuatsheu to come to earth to pick some wild roses to please the Moon, leaving out the fact that when you leave the spirit world you can never get back. Wolverine is forever forced to look up at the lonely moon all night and howl her name.

# Vivacious Vixens and Scintillating Super Hotties

*Deconstructing the Superheroine*

RICHARD J. GRAY II

The inclusion of "hot" female superheroes has been *en vogue* within the realm of comic books for decades. Not surprising, comic books were initially largely a boys' club, and with the exception of Dale Messnick's Brenda Starr, many of the leading female comic book characters were nothing more than vivacious and scintillating creations of the male imagination.[1] Even a powerful figure such as Wonder Woman carried whips, bracelets and chains, which responded in a less-than-subtle way to male sexual desires.[2] As these "vivacious vixens" and "scintillating super hotties" have migrated from comic book pages to film, they have also become increasingly more significant characters. No matter the medium in which these superheroines are found, through the images created by their designers, these women embody the intellectual and sexual power of their generations.

To evidence the fact that the "bad girl" remains an object of interest in post–9/11 superheroine comic book art, and, subsequently, in the superhero film genre as well, I cite a television interview from July 22, 2009 in which Amber Lee Ettinger ("Obama Girl") interviewed several men who were "browsing the racks" at Midtown Comics, New York City, just one day before Comicon San Diego, the largest comic book convention in the United States. "Who do you think is the sexiest superhero?" Obama Girl asked. One thirty-something man replied, "It's Power Girl. She's awesome, ya' know. 'Cause she's all hot and everything, but she can kick your ass ... so you respect her."[3] Another replied, "Yeah, [Catwoman] she's good and everything, but she is BAD on the inside." Finally, a third man answered: "I guess Rogue would be a sexy superhero. She's got that whole, uh, flirtatious attitude, as well as the fact that you can't really touch her. She is irresistible in that way, because you want her, but you obviously can't touch her."[4] Such statements serve as a point of departure toward developing an even greater understanding of what makes superheroines truly "hot," and they also serve as a springboard to an investigation of how these superheroines are visualized in film. Therefore, these statements underscore some of the complexities related to an evaluation of what constitutes superheroine "hotness."

Whether good or evil, the drawings of these women constitute what has been called "bad girl art," a term that originated in the 1990s, which referred most specifically to comic book women who were both violent and sexually-provocative in nature."[5] In her work entitled *Busting Out All Over: The Portrayal of Superheroines in American Superhero Comics from the 1940s to the 2000s* (2002), Brandi Florence analyses such "bad girl art" in (anti-)superheroines who have "super-sized" breasts, strong thighs, and thin waists, and who are often depicted in uncomfortable, erotic positions. Florence believed that this trend would fade in the 21st century, but as we leave the first decade of the new millennium, "bad girl art" continues to gain momentum in comic books, as well as in the filmic representations of these superheroines. Though a host of authors have written about the depiction of superheroines in comic books, there has yet to be a significant study that evaluates the portrayal of superheroines as "bad girls" in the new millennium within the medium of film. Therefore, this chapter deconstructs superheroine identity as "bad girl art" by examining the physical representation of the superheroine in the new millennium against a theoretical backdrop informed by theorists such as Betty Friedan, Judith Butler, Julia Kristeva, Laura Mulvey, Jacques Lacan, and Sigmund Freud. On our path toward developing an even greater understanding of how superheroines are portrayed in the 21st century, this essay examines a range of characters taken from several popular films, including Lara Croft, Rogue, Jean Grey, Storm, Kitty Pryde, Catwoman, Elektra, Invisible Woman, Æon Flux, through an application of Laura Mulvey's notion of the "male gaze."[6] In the end, this chapter will more fully illustrate how selected "hot" film superheroines of the new millennium continue to fill the male need for sexual distraction and escape.

## *Understanding "Hotness" in the Superhero Film Genre: The Feminine Mystique from Lara Croft to Æon Flux and Beyond*

The quest to understand the significance of the "hotness" of superheroines in the new millennium is, in part, the quest to understand the construction of the female identity itself. In an American context, one could argue that this quest began during the feminist movement of the 1960s. Referred to largely as the "second wave" of the Women's Movement in the United States, the movement addressed issues including both unofficial and official legal inequalities, sexuality, family, the workplace, and, reproductive rights. Published at the same time was the controversial New York Times bestseller, Betty Friedan's *The Feminine Mystique* (1963), which "ignited the contemporary women's movement in 1963 and as a result permanently transformed the social fabric of the United States and countries around the world" and "is widely regarded as one of the most influential nonfiction books of the 20th century."[7] Friedan hypothesized that American women were victims of a false belief system which required them to find identity and meaning in their lives through the domestic sphere, which caused them to lose their individual identity (332). Though many criticisms of Friedan's work remain, the evolution of the female superheroine against the backdrop of this particular feminist context is relevant within the present study.[8]

Suffice it to say, the ascension of the female superheroine has come about largely through the help of male dominancy. Her rise to prominence has occurred, in part, as a result of her ability to capture — indeed, to harness — the sexual attractiveness/power, or "hotness" that she possesses. Further, for the most part, the vivacious vixens and scintillating super hottie superheroines of the new millennium have become masterful adherents to traditional gender, sexual, racial, ethnic, and class stereotypes (Inness 8). Like their male counterparts, superheroines are typically white, middle or upper class, and have strong heterosexual appeal.[9] As Stephanie Mencimer explains, however, men do not want women who are too violent, too tough, or too masculine in films. "To achieve box office success," she adds, "the new action babes have to celebrate women's power without being so threatening that men would be afraid to sleep with the leading lady" (18).[10] Thus, women are no longer depicted exclusively as dependent upon the male of the species—victims that need to be rescued at the last minute by the male hero. Mencimer's statement also brings to light several questions regarding the significance of superheroine sexual power. First, are they sex symbols created exclusively for the male audience? Second, do their hypersexualized appearances, in fact, add to their super power(s) or do they detract from them? Finally, does their sexuality as portrayed through their physical representations somehow "pigeonhole" women into self-perpetuating pre-sexual revolution stereotypes?

The transformation of the film superheroine began in the last decade of the 20th century in what could be called (with respect to the superheroine) a nascent Third Wave Feminism, which has come to full fruition over the last several years.[11] By 1995, Marvel comics had published a four-issue miniseries starring the popular character Rogue, who would ultimately become the sexy unattainable film superheroine of *X-Men* fame. Trina Robbins writes that by the arrival of the new millennium, "comic books had become not merely a boy's club, but a Playboy Club" (166). Thus, at the turn of the 21st century, male readers and viewers were looking for filmic "pin-up" girls. When it comes to the male superhero in particular, artists stress the athletic abilities of the character. When it concerns the superheroine, in contrast, it is the depiction of physical perfection that is emphasized. The sex-object heroines that appeal to a largely male audience must be depicted as hypersexual pinups; drawn with skinny waists, ginormous breasts, and slutty outfits (Sara Pezzini, Elektra, Huntress, Supergirl).[12] Superheroines must exemplify perfect physical specimens in the form of their sexual appeal in the same way that the superheroes must embody physical strength. Superman is "faster than a speeding bullet, more powerful than a locomotive, and able to leap tall buildings in a single bound," and Flash, the Scarlet Speedster, has the ability to run and move extremely fast, and he uses superhuman reflexes which appear to violate the laws of physics.[13] We would all agree that the fastest woman in the world, although she would be able to defeat most men in a footrace, still remains incapable of defeating the fastest man in the world.[14] This does not devalue her in any sense, though it does reveal that her authentic "talents" may be found, at least from a male perspective, in something of an entirely different nature: her sexual allure. When the superheroine is brought to film, if the creators are going to truly tap into that male sexual desire that will bring men to watch such films, she must be portrayed in a way that the male of the species (and parts of the female audience, for that matter) finds sexually appealing: lots of flesh, or in leather jumpsuits, fishnet stockings, spiked heels, etc. We must continue to point out, however, that men do not want to feel physically threatened by women, or by superheroines, for that matter. Whether attainable or not, women must remain approachable.

This chapter certainly acknowledges the fact that the vivacious vixen and scintillating super hottie superheroine is not a 21st century construct, but it is rather a "stopping point" on the path toward her future evolution. Images of women with large bust sizes, slim figures, bare legs, and half-naked appearances became enormously popular after the success of Wonder Woman in the early 1940s. In the post–World War II era, superheroines ultimately became "the stuff of male sexual fantasy: a push-up bustier, panties, and high-heel boots, all in white."[15] Today, both in Western society as well as within the superhero "kingdom," women are becoming increasingly more sexualized. As described by Jones and Jacobs: "Females, perpetually bending over, arching their backs, and heaving their anti-gravity breasts into readers' faces, defied all laws of physics ... the Victoria's Secret catalogue became the Bible of every super-hero artist...."[16] While some critiques may argue that depicting women in a vivacious and scintillating manner is a symbol of their strength and power, others argue that, in these superheroine representations, women are being (s)exploited.

From a theoretical perspective, however, what is at work here in the construction of superheroine representation is the concept known as the "male gaze." This theory was first introduced by film theorist Laura Mulvey in her essay entitled "Visual Pleasure and Narrative Cinema" (1975). In her work, Mulvey described the concept of the gaze as "a symptom of power asymmetry."[17]

In principle, the male gaze "denies women agency, relegating them to the status of objects." This perspective is certainly informed by the psychoanalytic theories of Jacques Lacan, and, of particular relevance here, is the notion which he called the "mirror stage." Lacan described his "mirror stage" as the moment that a child begins to recognize his own reflection in the mirror, which is a crucial moment in the development of the ego. In the world outside of the superhero scenario, this means that women are (re)presented as men would want to see them.[18] Thus, women become an aberrant reflection of male desire. These same images are presented to women as something they should aspire to be if they want to attract men. In other words, on one hand, we can perceive the power and control that characters like Wonder Woman possess as a woman's control over a man. On the other hand, we can also perceive such control as an artificial construction which is initially attributed to woman by man himself. In this self-perpetuating dichotomy, the female is entirely powerless, for it is mostly male writers and artists (within the genre of superhero films) who develop the popular and acceptable representations of the idealized woman. Consider the *X-Men* films (2000, 2003, and 2006), *Batman Begins* (2005), *Superman Returns* (2006), and the *Spider-Man* films (2002, 2004, and 2007). They are all not only financially successful, but critically acclaimed as well. This is perhaps true because of the presence of a strong male superhero character at the heart of each of these films. In contrast, superhero films with female protagonists, such as *Catwoman* (2004), *Elektra* (2005), and *Æon Flux* (2005), were both box-office and critical failures. The *X-Men* films, for example, include powerful female characters capable of moving objects with their minds, controlling the weather, and running through walls, among other things, but the male characters, such as Wolverine (Hugh Jackman), Professor Xavier (Patrick Stewart), and Magneto (Ian McKellen), still remain the prime character focus. This strongly suggests that there is a gap between the power of female sexuality to lure men to watch these films and the power of female sexuality to create good plot and story.

There is, therefore, no doubt that the concept of the "male gaze" applies both to the development and the perception of film superheroines. Film theorists have used the term more generally to describe the way that mainstream culture forms the vision of the viewer (Childers 173). To interest the spectator, films must employ one of two principles: narrative or spectacle. In popular film in particular, representations of women have traditionally operated in the form of spectacles, with dance and showgirls being the most obvious and blatant example. On film, representations of women appear in ubiquitous displays of the female body, which sometimes occur in the form of gratuitous sex scenes which do little, if anything, to strengthen the story or the plot. Women are objectified — put on parade — with the sole purpose that they might be viewed by men. In terms of narrative, when the woman is seen as an object, the film viewer "feels a sense of control, a command over the world of the ... story..."

(Childers 174). Further, there is an applied notion of scopophilia or voyeurism. Though Freudian ideas with regard to filmic interpretation are certainly not new, such analyses remain relevant and appropriate within the context of this chapter. For Freud, scopophilia referred to the relationship that exists between sexual motivation and visual stimuli. In short, the gaze alone can provide satisfactions that are independent of physical touching that border on masturbatory (22). In film, watching these female characters engages the scopophilic drive.[19] Thus, as the heterosexual male spectator finds pleasure in looking at women, he subjects them to a potentially manipulative gaze. Film creates the ideal environment for encouraging the male gaze, for it promotes the spectator's ability to "peek in" at the private worlds of others while, at the same time, film does not allow the actors to tell the spectators, "You can't look at me like that!" The binary opposition created between the male gaze and his manipulated female subject is omnipresent, self-evident, and difficult to break.

In "Visual Pleasure and Narrative Cinema," Mulvey further underscores how, ultimately, "the meaning of women is sexual difference, the absence of the penis as visually ascertainable, the material evidence on which is based the castration complex essential for the organization of entrance to the symbolic order and the law of the father" (35). In film representations, women are the "bearers of the bleeding wound of castration, the signification of the lack of penis/phallus" (35). In what has become one of the most quoted passages in feminist film theory, Mulvey argues that "in a world ordered by sexual imbalance, pleasure in looking has been split between active/male and passive/female. The determining male gaze projects its fantasy onto the female figure, which is styled accordingly" (33). By extension, film becomes the stage on which female desire is simultaneously constructed and revealed as constructed. Furthermore, according to Julia Kristeva, Western culture's obsessive male gaze seems to have always outlined the female body antagonistically: "object of scopophilic desire and enigmatic vessel of life and death, sublime essence of beauty and abjectified, uncanny other against which the speaking subject can define himself" (9).[20]

In the first decade of the new millennium, representations of technology, pleasure, and sexuality have intersected in films with female superheroines, such as the *X-Men* series, *Lara Croft: Tomb Raider* (2001), *Lara Croft Tomb Raider: The Cradle of Life* (2003), *Daredevil* (2003), *Catwoman* (2004), *Elektra* (2005), *The Fantastic Four* (2005), and *Æon Flux* (2005). In 2000, the *X-Men* film trilogy began. That following spring, *Lara Croft: Tomb Raider* (2001) broke box-office records.[21] At this juncture, we certainly wonder if these films were progressive or feminist, or were they simple (s)exploitation? Further, what do these representations say about the heterosexual men who view them? It is clear that in no case does it suffice that the superheroine simply "kick ass." She must also be "smokin' hot." Certainly, there are some who argue that men will watch "attractive" women do just about anything, be it mud-wrestling or lingerie football. But while simple sex appeal might initially attract men to Lara Croft and other superheroines, it seems that this represents only half of the equation. The other half takes us back to Obama Girl's 2009 interview at Midtown Comics, New York City: "It's Power Girl. She's awesome, ya' know. 'Cause she's all hot and everything, but she can kick your ass ... so you respect her."[22] Further, it is said that men want what they cannot have: "I guess Rogue would be a sexy superhero. She's got that whole, uh, flirtatious attitude, as well as the fact that you can't really touch her. She is irresistible in that way, because you want her, but you obviously can't touch her."[23] Thus, as Mencimer also points out: "today, women seem to be kicking ass, and men don't seem to mind, within reason" (17). "Within reason" becomes the key phrase. If the superheroine is too tough, men will turn away from her (this is what we see when Jean Grey becomes the Phoenix in *X-Men: The Last Stand*). "Hotness," therefore, as it applies within the context of the representation of the new millennial superheroine, is a delicate balance between sex appeal and physical strength. Nonetheless, does the sexual element still give men *some* control over women? Initially, it may seem difficult to understand why men are not threatened by the arrival of powerful superheroines — these women who truly "kick ass." When balanced, I would suggest that in the last decade, the superheroine offers men a "best of both worlds" scenario: they possess both the physical ass-kicking strength and strong sex appeal that men need in order to satisfy their "scopophilic drive."

If we think about the notion of gender as a societal construction, we can then understand why artists continue to depict women's gender within highly sexed bodies: "You have to be careful not to draw them bloopy or dumpy, but at the same time, if you draw them too hard and chiseled, they start to look masculine, which is definitely not good" (Bart Sears 38). "Vivacious" and "scintillating" have become the standard by which superheroines are measured, but making them look "juiced up" is avoided at all costs because muscled female bodies "can drift out of difference, ceasing to be a radically different female body, into an unsettling sameness, a body that seems no different from a 'male' body" (Schulze 78). As Judith Butler underscores in her essay entitled "Performative Acts and Gender Constitution," "The more sexualized the exaggerated female anatomies become, the more the factitiousness of their origins is revealed" (405). We should, then, perhaps consider the superheroine body as "masquerade": "flaunting femininity holds it at a distance.... The masquerade's resistance to patriarchal positioning lie[s] in its denial of the production of femininity as closeness, as presence-to-itself, as, precisely, imagistic" (Doane 49). What is most important to note in this discussion is that, although the male viewer tends to consider the superheroine as "putty in his hand," the entire physical representation of the superheroine is illusory.

This realization is evident in the character of Lara Croft, who appears in the film *Lara Croft: Tomb Raider* (2001), based on the already popular *Tomb Raider* video game series. Lara Croft, portrayed by Angelina Jolie, embodies the "scopophilic" representation of the superheroine. The film's opening sequence introduces Lara Croft with no dialogue. Like in the video game from which she was incarnated, Croft is dressed in all black with a form-fitting top (accentuating her large, firm breasts) and tight shorts, guns strapped to each thigh. Lara's physical design is inherently and overtly sexual, and she is also a fairly violent character. To a certain extent, her physical form reflects the masculine desires of her intended audience. Less exaggerated in the film than in the video game, Lara's hourglass figure signifies supreme control over the human body. She stands upright, her legs apart, pointing her "D-cup" breasts at her male audience.[24] She initially fights a large robot, and after immobilizing it, she then moves to a computer terminal/laptop and removes a disc, revealing she actually owns/controls the robot which is used in her "tomb raider" training. By training via a robot (rather than humans), she requires machines to refine her "machine-like" skills, which implies that she could also be programmed by her male viewer (and some female viewers). Immediately after the battle, Lara is shown in the shower, her naked body gazed upon by the camera. She then removes her towel in front of the butler (Chris Barrie) allowing the audience to voyeuristically gaze upon her naked torso (in a PG-13 shot from the rear), briefly revealing her breasts. Her butler says: "A lady should be modest," and she replies sarcastically: "Yes, a lady *should* be modest," thus implying that she, in fact, is not quite a "lady." The opening scene of the film is quite reminiscent of the video game in which Lara Croft first appeared, a game which took the "male gaze" to an entirely new level by introducing a female protagonist who could be easily manipulated by the video game player. After this opening scene in which the viewer gets a glimpse of her naked body, the male viewer cannot help but wonder, "What else can I get her to do?"

More than any film series of the beginning of the new millennium, the X-Men films contain several powerful superheroines (Rogue, Jean Grey, Storm, and Kitty Pryde) who bring the boundaries of female physical strength and sexual appeal to an entirely new level. The first X-Men film showcases genetically-gifted mutants, who have become the world's newest, most persecuted minority group. In the case of the superheroines of the X-Men trilogy, as they increasingly become more able to control their superpowers, they also become sexier: to master one's superpower is to master one's sexuality. In *Matters of Gravity: Special Effects and Supermen in the 20th Century*, Scott Bukatman suggests that superheroines in comic books do not just have "wimpy powers" like invisibility and telekinesis anymore; they are more powerful and dangerous, and they now fight alongside their male companions, as seen in the X-Men films (65). However, when these superheroines are brought to film, although they might fight alongside their male counterparts, they tend to have decidedly inferior powers than those of male superheroes. Further, when compared to the original comic book texts from which they originated, "the cross-medium migration from comic book to live action blockbuster film can be charted and read for how the superheroine bodies are mapped with respect to femininity"

(65). The powers attributed to female superhero bodies are linked to traditional notions of female power, including manipulation, sexuality, and masquerade, such as wearing leather jumpsuits, wigs, etc. (Lindsey 288). Accentuation of "physical" elements largely involves stylized positioning of the body in order to capture certain voyeuristic "shots" (emphasis of the breasts, for example), in order to depict an idealized female form. This somehow diminishes the super-heroine's superpower.[25]

Female "mutant" superheroes have also become a ubiquitous character type within 21st-century superhero films. In the *X-Men* films, we see character transformations like that of Rogue (Anna Paquin) who, in the comic books, is confident and capable, but is cinematically depicted as a scared and helpless teenager who has great difficulty understanding and controlling her superpower. Jeffrey A. Brown argues that, in her comic book incarnation, Rogue's ability to steal a man's power with a touch or a kiss is fetishistic, drawing on the iconic powers of the dominatrix (66). In the film trilogy, however, Rogue's youth and inexperience are emphasized, and although it does appear that she undergoes some sort of (sexual) maturity, for the most part, she remains the seventeen-year-old girl to which we are introduced during the initial film. By *X-Men: The Last Stand*, there is a vaccine to "cure" mutants of their afflictions with which Rogue is inoculated. Nonetheless, it seems that the very storyline of the film works not only to limit Rogue's powers, but also to victimize her. Her innate "female strength" is diminished and we are left with little more than a character who, as Professor Xavier states, is "incapable of physical human contact, probably for the rest of her life." In terms of Mulvey's notion of the "male gaze," however, Rogue is quite mysterious. She wears a cloak which makes one wonder what she is hiding beneath. We know that she longs for physical contact, but that she is unable to realize her physical desires, which further underscores the adolescent sexual repression that she experiences. In *X2: X-Men United* (2003), Rogue has now gained the ability to absorb any person's memories and abilities just by touching them. Still unable to wield this power, Rogue could easily kill anyone and, thus, she must stay away from others. By the time she appears in *X-Men: The Last Stand* (2006), part of her hair has turned white and she begins to don a leather jumpsuit. Although Rogue has neared the point of becoming "hot," she will be forever weak in her ability to manipulate her superpower and, therefore she will never truly achieve "super hottie" status.

Another mutant superheroine, Jean Grey (Famke Janssen), finds herself in a similar situation to that of Rogue. In *X-Men*, Dr. Jean Grey serves as the physician of the X-Mansion. Grey is a low-level telekinetic, and she also has mild telepathic abilities. In *X-Men*, there is something inherently "sexy" about her character, due perhaps to her initial awkwardness as she learns to master her supernatural abilities. The development of her powers seems to suggest, like Rogue, a parallel evolution in her journey of sexual self-discovery, as, through the films, her character moves from a near helpless woman who wears glasses (reflecting her nearsightedness/naïveté) and who exhibits a sex-ually-repressed "librarian look" to one who exudes greater self-confidence. When the viewer is first introduced to Jean, she is wearing red, a color which "is inherently exciting and [whose] amount ... is directly related to the level of energy perceived. Red draws attention and a keen use of red as an accent can immediately focus attention on a particular element."[26] The "particular ele-ment" on which the camera initially focuses our attention is her breasts. The second scene in which we see her, she is wearing a white lab coat over a tight red shirt, which also emphasizes her breasts. When she walks into Xavier's office for the first time, the camera also focuses on her chest. The male viewer is initially drawn to her because she represents both physical beauty and intel-ligence, though as we will see in the later films, Jean becomes so wickedly pow-erful, that no man in his right mind would dare involved himself romantically with her.

Therefore, though a relatively weak character in the initial *X-Men* film, as she develops in *X2: X-Men United* and in *X-Men: The Last Stand*, Dr. Jean Grey becomes increasingly more powerful. In *X-Men: The Last Stand*, she possesses limitless telepathic powers as well as limitless telekinetic powers, which even surpass those of Magneto's and Xavier's. The Jean Grey/Phoenix character emerges in the X-Men comics when the Phoenix, a mighty alien entity, merges with Jean Grey, attracted to her powerful mind. In *X-Men: The Last Stand*, Phoenix represents the evil side of Jean Grey's personality. The storyline rein-forces Jean Grey's unstable emotional and mental state as significantly con-tributing to the manifestation of her powers. For example, when she gets angry or upset, she accidentally levitates objects in the room. In the final battle of the film, Jean Grey/Phoenix saves all the mutants by stopping needles fired at them containing the mutant vaccine. However, unable to control her powers, Jean Grey/Phoenix begins to systematically destroy the entire island of Alcatraz.

Dr. Jean Grey completes the "smokin' hot" part of the equation, but she remains unable to become a true sexy superheroine until she is able to "kick ass," which she succeeds in doing in *X-Men: The Last Stand*. What limits her "hotness," however, is that she crosses the line when she attempts to "get it on" with Wolverine, who senses that it is actually the evil side of her that wants him. Further, Professor Xavier reminds her that it is her weakness of character which has led to her inability to control her powers, placing those around her in grave danger: "Look what happened to Scott (James Marsden). You killed the man you love because you couldn't control your power" (*X-Men: The Last Stand*).

Storm, or Ororo Munroe, who is played by Halle Berry, has a similar char-acter development on the path toward scintillating super hottie. Storm works as a teacher at the X-Mansion and has the ability to manipulate the weather. Like Dr. Jean Grey, the character of Storm was, initially, also quite weak as a sexy superheroine. In *X-Men*, she wears a white wig, which creates a stimulating contrast with Berry's light brown skin. Storm wears low-cut white undershirts, a necklace, and in several scenes, she even wears a "collar," which suggests something that can be controlled, like an animal. The white undershirts emphasize Berry's breasts. Toward the end of the first film, Grey and Storm both don black leather jumpsuits, which follow the contours of their femininities. Both here and in the several other superheroines who wear jumpsuits, whether made of leather or of spandex, the jumpsuit serves a dual function. First, it serves as a "second skin," which from the perspective of the viewer, allows all of the nooks and crannies of the female body to be displayed. Secondly, the wearing of the jumpsuit suggests sexual repression, as if there is a physical barrier preventing consummation. With jumpsuit on, Storm begins to float in the air; she controls the wind, and lightning. As Storm learns to harness and control the power of the weather, her eyes glow and her hair turns gold, flowing, and electrified, which underscores a hidden hyper-sexuality. However, it appears that she does, indeed, reach a delicate balance between sex appeal and physical strength. Her "hotness," therefore is confirmed. Nonetheless, in *X-Men: The Last Stand*, during an intense battle scene, Wolverine says to her: "Don't get your panties in a bunch." His response carries more than a simple, "Don't get so upset." Sexual innuendo resonates in his words. No matter what power Storm possesses, no matter how capable she becomes of controlling that power, no matter how sexually appealing she becomes, will she ever be perceived as anything more than "hot"?

The last *X-Men* superheroine examined here, Katherine "Kitty" Pride is introduced in the original *X-Men* film in nothing more than a cameo played by Sumela Kay. Initially a rather insignificant character, Senator Kelly (Bruce Davison) refers to her as "the girl who can walk through walls." Kitty is first seen in Professor Xavier's class at X-Mansion; she returns for her books which she had left behind, grabs them, and passes through the door on her way out. Professor Xavier responds with a jovial "Bye, Kitty," while Wolverine looks on in amazement at her ability to pass through solid objects. In *X2: X-Men United*, Kitty is played by Katie Stuart in what could, at best, be called a brief appearance. In this film (like in the first), Kitty has the ability to "phase through matter." She passes through walls and people to escape the military forces of William Stryker (Brian Cox) during an attack on the X-Mansion. In another scene, Kitty falls through her bed to avoid an assault (an implied rape, perhaps). In *X-Men: The Last Stand*, Kitty is portrayed by the actress Ellen Page. It is this particular representation that will be considered in this essay. Like Dr. Jean Grey and Storm, Kitty has a more important role, in contrast to her cameo appearances in the two previous films, which were played by relatively unknown actresses. Kitty serves as a rival to Rogue for the romantic attentions of Iceman (Shawn Ashmore), since their close friendship and their kiss (available on the DVD under "Deleted Scene") makes Rogue increasingly jealous and frustrated. Kitty also joins the X-Men in the battle on Alcatraz Island, breaking off from the battle to save Jimmy/Leech (Cameron Bright) from the Juggernaut (Vinnie Jones). Leech is a mutant boy whose power neutralizes the powers of nearby mutants and his DNA is used to form the "cure." In *X-Men: The Last Stand*, it is also suggested that Kitty had a romantic relationship with Colossus (Daniel Cudmore). Although most viewers would scarcely even remember Kitty from the initial *X*-Men film, it is hard to ignore Ellen Page's transformation from an innocent girl who trades in her brown, frumpy parka for a black leather jump-suit. In what is arguably her sexiest scene, the petite Kitty races through walls as she is pursued by the Juggernaut. "Don't you know who I am? I'm the Jug-gernaut, bitch," he says to her as Kitty eludes him. Juggernaut is defeated when Kitty uses Leech's nullification power against him. When he thinks that he has finally caught them, he says, "I'm the wrong guy to play hide-and-seek with." Kitty responds: "Who's hiding, [brief pause] dickhead?" Kitty and Jimmy then escape the building through the holes that Juggernaut smashed on his way into the building.

Though Kitty has limited screen time in *X-Men: The Last Stand*, she still emerges as a character to be noticed. Unlike the other mutant superheroines, there is something "sexy" about her. When she is in the classroom, she challenges Professor Xavier. From that minor confrontation, we learn that she is intelligent and self-confident. Her language has a fresh quality as well, for none of the other mutant superheroines would have pulled out so witty a retort as "dick-head." Further, when Juggernaut calls her a "bitch," her ability to physically elude him is almost a tease. Finally, her name "Kitty" is mildly suggestive of something naughty. Her hair is always tousled as well, which looks like she has just emerged from the throes of passion. She is a tiny little thing who seems to be on the precipice between adolescence and womanhood. It appears that her journey of self-discovery is complete, for, like Storm, she reaches a delicate bal-ance between sex appeal and physical strength. Like Storm, Kitty's "hotness," is validated as well.

Without a doubt, the sexiest superheroine "kitten" of the new millennium appeared in *Catwoman* (2004), which found Halle Berry in the lead role. Owen Gleiberman described Catwoman as "a good-time bad girl whose kinky strength — her banishment of all that's passive and fearful — is also her crazi-ness" (47). Wearing red lipstick, a dominatrix leather jumpsuit, and a pointy-eared black mask, Berry looks "hot" and bad, while she totally embodies the whole cat role with her posturing. When the film begins, Berry's character is called Patience Philips, an artist who works for a cosmetics company called Hedare. When Phillips learns that company's forthcoming skin cream is toxic, she is thrown into a river and is reborn, thanks to a cat called Mau. Lacking the character "strength" because of her "bad girl" side, Catwoman is really noth-ing more than a hypersexualized superheroine. "If people go see the movie," said Berry, "'they'll see I'm projecting a lot more than sex. It's about being empowered, being O.K. in your skin. Sure, it's sexy. To me a certain amount of being sexy, that's O.K. It's where I've evolved to as a woman. And as a result, I'm more O.K. with expressing that in my work'" (Waxman E1). "When you talk about Halle Berry, it's all about her sexuality," said Todd Boyd, a professor of critical studies at the University of Southern California School of Cinema-Television. Boyd added, "Her popularity as of late is curious because of the overriding sexual component that, in my mind, takes attention away from what would normally be conversations about acting skill." One Hollywood studio executive, who would only speak under the condition of anonymity, noted that the actress's perfect features were intimidating to women, and that her emphasis on sexuality had objectified her to men. Such a statement once again underscores the fact that there is a very fine line between mastering one's sexuality and subjecting one's self to the objectifying male gaze.

Further, *Catwoman* producer Denise Di Novieven stated that "while male-driven comic-book movies have a number of successful models to draw from — Richard Donner's *Superman*, Tim Burton's *Batman*, Bryan Singer's *X-Men*— the heroines have, well, none. America is not ready for a female superhero" [in a lead role] (Schwartz 20). Perhaps men do not wish to see it, either. And although new millennial superheroines have been fairly well-received as supporting characters (let's face it, Kitty Pryde was hardly a central figure in *X-Men: The Last Stand*), the fact that America does not appear to be ready for a female superhero in a lead role could perhaps be explained by the words of screenwriter John August: "Studios think all teenage boys are horny, and therefore want to see a beautiful girl kicking ass. But teenage boys are also kind of terrified of women, so the sexuality drives them away" (20). Further, as Marvel CEO Avi Arad told *Entertainment Weekly*, "It's more challenging to make a female superhero," acknowledging, in part, that audiences generally appear more willing to accept men in superhero roles (20). As previously stated and now confirmed by people "in the business," it is important to balance superheroine sexuality with superheroine superpower so that the superheroine does not dominate her male counterpart or her male viewer. When the superheroine becomes the central role of the film, this suggestion takes on even greater importance, as witnessed both in *Catwoman* and in *Elektra* (2005).

Of ABC's *Alias* (2001–2006) fame, Jennifer Garner's Elektra character was, perhaps, the only thing to salvage from the otherwise poor *Daredevil*, which starred Ben Affleck in the title role. Trained as a ninja warrior after her mother's murder, in the spinoff *Elektra*, the character is introduced in a smooth sequence which illustrates her sexy and dangerous nature as she overcomes multiple guards en route to her quarry. Lightning-quick and in red-leather pants and a top with an exposed midriff, she wields a pair of phallic three-pronged knives called "sais." In several brief flashbacks, we learn about Elektra's troubled childhood, which included a domineering father who forced her to reach total perfection in everything that she did, which has now transformed her into an obsessive-compulsive personality. She is ultimately hired to kill both a 13-year-old girl and her father, who have become targets of the Hand, a sinister organization. Now determined to save the girl, Elektra faces great opposition.

Elektra's primary ability is a strong knowledge of martial arts and weaponry, which is accurately portrayed in both *Daredevil* and *Elektra*. In the comic book version, however, she also has the ability to make people see illusions as well low-level telekinetic abilities, like those seen in the Dr. Jean Grey character in the original *X-Men* film. These "supernatural" powers, which are quite characteristic of the mutant superheroes/superheroines which appear in the *X-Men* series, are severely downplayed here, as the film, for the most part, depicts her more as an action heroine (gadget heroine) than as a "superheroine." Another ability that she has lost in the filmic version is her ability to "mind jump." Like telepathy, this ability allows Elektra to know exactly where others are going to be found. In a sense, this ability is her capacity to leap into the mind and not only read thoughts, but also the processes behind those thoughts. In the film, however, her contribution to the otherwise flat dialogue creates nothing more than the images of a sexy woman in a bright, red suit. Elektra fails to move beyond the stereotypical "comic book," flesh-popping portrayal which likely made her character popular in *Daredevil*, for which she won the 2004 FLEXY award, which is given to the sexiest actor/actress of the silver screen. This also suggests that her character masters nothing beyond the sex-imbued phallic sword, which she wields with great talent and precision. Thus, this defines the "hotness" of her character. In a sense, Elektra is not a threat to the male viewer. He does not really expect her to do anything more than "kick ass" and look good. In this respect, Elektra does, indeed, reach that delicate balance between sex appeal and physical strength.

That same year that *Elektra* was released in theaters, Jessica Alba portrayed Susan Storm Richards (Invisible Woman) in the film *Fantastic Four* (2005).[27] Initially, Sue's passive invisibility power turned her into a "damsel in distress" with the other member of the Fantastic Four team. In the 2005 film, Sue is a scientist who leads Victor Von Doom's (Julian McMahon) Department of Genetic Research. Upon the arrival of the cosmic storm, she is given the ability to manipulate light, which permits her to disappear and generate force-fields which are difficult to detect. Unlike in the comic version, Sue is unable to render her normal clothes invisible, which leads to an embarrassing moment when she tries to disrobe in order to sneak her way through a crowd, only to reappear while still in her underwear. Though Sue's powers are definitely influenced by her emotions as well as her sexuality, as the film progresses, she manages to control her abilities, which are particularly evident during the team's battle with Von Doom. At the end of the film, Sue accepts a proposal of marriage, which subjugates her legally to male domination, thereby maintaining the patriarchal status quo. In the film, Alba wears a blue, tight-fitting jumpsuit, which accentuates the natural curves of her body. In some scenes, her character wears glasses, which, although they might initially reflect a childlike innocence, place her on the verge of the sexually-repressed "librarian look" that we witnessed in Dr. Jean Grey. Like the black leather jumpsuits worn by her superheroine colleagues, the tightness of her costume reflects an inherent duality: On one hand, it reveals the most intimate details of her body's topography; on the other hand, her costume reflects the needs of the character to keep her sexuality "under wraps." The transformation of Sue Storm came about through the work of artist John Byrne, who brought to the screen a character who is more assertive and confident, as one who has become a leader of the team. Byrne summarized his adaption of this character from the comic book to the film as follows:

> It was during this period that fanboys started to notice that not only were Sue's powers quite formidable (when she worked up the will to use them), but also that she ... was something of a hottie. This was a shocking twist, since she'd always been Marvel's Madonna — a Super-Mom/Super-Wife, more in the tradition of Donna Reed or Florence Henderson — but it went hand-in-hand with her newfound strength of personality.[28]

I would add that we can interpret the word "personality" as "sexuality," as this chapter maintained throughout its course that there is a direct relationship between the ability of the superheroine to master both her superpower and her sexuality. They are, arguably, one in the same.

First famous in *Dark Angel* (Fox, 2000–2002), the *Fantastic Four* brings to film Alba's photogenic qualities, which we had already experienced on television. But, as we soon learn in the film, Alba brings much more to the Sue Storm character than beauty and sex appeal. When the team is forming before the TV cameras and a reporter asks which member is the leader of the group, we already know that it is going to be either Sue or Reed (Ioan Gruffudd). In the comic version, however, Sue Storm has already been the team's leader, and she has done a good job at it. Her deference in the filmic version once again underscores the recurrent theme that superheroine power (be it superhero abilities or authority), for whatever reason, seems to be diminished in their cinematic representations. Nonetheless, the filmic Invisible Woman never becomes a "damsel in distress." Without a doubt, Sue shows herself to be quite strong. Jessica Alba herself "has a kindness and a strength that are suitable to a superheroine and a role model for young people, and these movies give her a chance to show that."[29] Like Storm and Kitty Pryde, Sue reaches a delicate balance between sex appeal and physical strength. In this way, like these two particular superheroines, her "hotness" is validated as well.

At the end of the same year in which *Elektra* and *Fantastic Four* were released in theaters, MTV films released *Æon Flux* (2005), which starred Charlize Theron in the title role. In 25th-century totalitarian city-state Bregna, *Æon Flux* is an assassin-member of the "Monicans," an underground rebel organization led by The Handler. One day, Æon returns home to find that her sister, Una (Amelia Warner), has been killed. When Æon is sent on a mission to kill the government's leader, Trevor Goodchild (Marton Csokas), she discovers that she is unknowingly playing a part in a secret coup. In a plot that seems a bit convoluted, the rebel ninja Æon Flux does slow-motion flips and jumps that show off her sexy physique in black leather. In the opening scene of the film, she passes through the scene in a black dress with a long slit on her left side, revealing her naked thigh and black garters. She is wearing a head covering which looks like something out of an S&M video. She walks under a gable where she meets a man, himself also decked out in black. The two kiss, but it is a kiss through which the man passes a pill into Æon's mouth; a pill which is used to send messages telepathically. In a later scene, her slicked-back black hair and the purple collar that she wears are reminiscent of Catwoman, or a 25th-century dominatrix. On another occasion, when Æon is confined within a white marble cell, her black open-front, open-back bodysuit-combined with the fact that she is being monitored through glass, give the feel that she is a performer in a "peep show." There are several scenes in the film in which she is nearly naked. Since the film is rated PG-13, however, the camera only shows the contours of her breasts. In one such scene, Æon awakens and it is evident that, during the course of the night, she had made love to Trevor. When she ultimately makes love to Trevor, therefore, her yielding to him evidences, once again, woman's succumbing to patriarchal authority.[30]

Thus, unlike Storm, Kitty Pryde, and Sue (Invisible Woman), Æon appears to have little control of her sexuality, and for that matter, her "superpowers" remain nothing more than a future version of those which we had already seen in the Elektra character. Further, in contrast to the character development of superheroines such as Storm, Kitty Pryde, and Sue (Invisible Woman), Æon never moves beyond the superficial qualities of her character: "As for Theron, she holds the screen as capably as ever, and is called on to perform an impressive array of acrobatic stunts and still manage to keep her bangs dangling seductively in her face; like Angelina Jolie before her in the *Tomb Raider* movies, she turns combat into the ultimate fashion statement" (Chang 48). Further, though Theron is attractive in her interpretation of the title role, like everything else in the film, she is caught in the overall "campy" nature of the representation.[31] Entertainment writer George Epaminondas described the character as "an insurgent with a penchant for clingy ensembles, leather corsets and a louche Louise Brooks bob" (367). Therefore, a futuristic dominatrix at best, Æon's overall "hotness" never reaches that of some of her comrades, for she does not balance sex appeal and physical strength.

## Conclusion

The argument presented in the preceding pages served to develop an understanding of what constitutes superheroine "hotness" in the new millennium. In the end, this analysis has brought to light the following general assessment as it applies to how to evaluate the "hotness" of film superheroines in the current age. When it concerns the development and representation of the superheroine, it is all about establishing a delicate balance between sex appeal and physical strength. If the character becomes too sexy, she is probably a dominatrix (Catwoman, Æon Flux), a shallow character who may initially lure spectators, but who ultimately will fail to keep them. If the superheroine is too powerful (Rogue, Dr. Jean Grey), this reveals a failure to establish the necessary balance between sex appeal and physical strength. Too much sex, too much "ass kicking" may chase away the male audience. If one of the central functions of the "male gaze" is to deny women agency, then the gaze must continually perpetuate that characteristic. With agency, women are no longer under the "puppeteering" control of men. They become a Jean Grey/Phoenix, dangerous and unpredictable, who places the lives of those around them in jeopardy.

A host of superhero films is slated for release from 2011–2012. Among these films are *Green Hornet, Thor, X-Men: First Class, Green Lantern, Captain America: The First Avenger, The Dark Knight Rises, The Wolverine, Spider-Man Reboot, The Avengers*, and *Kick-Ass 2*. This trend suggests both that superhero films continue to remain popular at the box office and that they are here to stay. Although it is uncertain which superheroines these new films will showcase, we cannot help but wonder how the portrayal of these female characters will continue to evolve. Will they establish the necessary balance between sex appeal and physical strength and become truly "hot"? In *Thor* (2011), for example, will Jane Foster (Natalie Portman) have the power of immortality? How will Emma Frost's (January Jones) ability to change her body into diamond form translate to the silver screen in *X-Men: First Class* (2011)? Will Carol Ferris (Blake Lively) as Star Sapphire in *Green Lantern* (2011) have a gem of power to fly and to hurl blasts of force which parallels the power of Green Lantern's ring and which also allows her to survive in space? Finally, rumor has it that *The Dark Knight Rises* (2012) will include both a female love interest for Bruce Wayne and a female supervillain.[32] Will she be a Catwoman-like figure? Will there be any female superpowers involved? To find out the answers to these and other related questions, we turn no further than to the refrain that closed cliffhanger episodes of the *Batman* television series (ABC, 1966–1968): "Tune in tomorrow — same Bat-time, same Bat-channel!"

# Notes

1. For the purposes of this chapter, the term "superheroine" will be used broadly. As evidenced by Batman, who is sometimes referred to as a "gadget hero," it is evident that superheroes are not obliged to have innate superpowers to be considered a superhero.

2. "Twisted Sisters: A Collection of Bad Girl Art." *Whole Earth* Spring 1998: 29. Web. 22 Sep. 2010.

3. "Who is the Hottest Comic Book Girl?." YouTube.com. 24 July 2009. 18 July 2010. <http://www.youtube.com/watch?v=F2K5slGadDQ>.

4. Ibid.

5. For a more in-depth description of "bad girl art," see <http://www.comicvine.com/bad-girl-art/12-43535/>.

6. These superheroines were chosen specifically because they emerged from comic book characters which were migrated to film from the year 2000 and beyond. They reflect female superheroes who served as supporting characters and as main characters of their respective films. This sample is by no means exhaustive. I would like to thank Betty Kaklamanidou for her help in preparing this chapter. Any shortcomings are those of the author.

7. "Betty Friedan, Who Ignited Cause in 'Feminine Mystique,' Dies at 85." *The New York Times*, February 5, 2006.

8. This discussion would be weakened if it did not acknowledge the French feminist writer, Simone de Beauvoir, and her influential *Le Deuxième sexe*. In her book, de Beauvoir argues that women throughout history have been defined as the "other" sex, an aberration from the "normal" male sex. She further suggests that "One is not born, but rather becomes, a woman." (331).

9. Lara Croft, for example, comes from an extremely rich family.

10. Jordan Titus (77–99) explores the world of the "dangerous-feminine" in the "bad girl" comics. Created to revive sagging comic book sales, these bad girls were angels and devils who wore little more than a smile and spike-heeled boots.

11. See Mavic Cabrera-Balleza's "Grrl Power and Third Wave Feminism," *Women in Action* Aug. 2003: 1.

12. It would be an error to fail to acknowledge a female readership of comic books as well as a female viewership of superhero films.

13. For an analysis of the role of physics as it applies to superheroes, see James Kakalios' *The Physics of Superheroes* (New York, Gotham Books, 2005).

14. The fastest man in the world, Usain Bolt (Jamaica), ran the 100 meter sprint in 9.58 seconds (2008). The fastest women in the world, Florence Griffith-Joyner (USA), ran the 100 meter sprint in 10.49 seconds (1988), a time which would not have placed her among the ten fastest men in the world. <http://www.olympic.org/en/content/Olympic-Athletes/>.

15. All citations from this paragraph are taken from the web site of *Fantasy Magazine* at <http://www.fantasy-magazine.com/2008/08/the-objectification-of-women-in-graphic-novels/>.

16. Ibid.

17. See "Gaze," *Art & Popular Culture*. <http://www.artandpopularculture.com/Gaze>.

18. See Jacques Lacan's "Le stade du miroir. Théorie d'un moment structurant et génétique de la constitution de la réalité, conçu en relation avec l'expérience et la doctrine psychanalytique," Communication au 14e Congrès psychanalytique international, Marienbad, International Journal of Psychoanalysis, 1937.

19. For a more complete explanation of scopofilia as it applies to film, in particular, see Sudeep Dasgupta's article "Multiple Symptoms and the Visible Real: Culture, Media, and the Displacements of Vision" in *Invisible Culture* 10, 2006: 1–16.

20. Although Mulvey's theory represents one of the most significant feminist theories of the second wave, this study would be weakened without recognizing the fact that recent feminist film theorists (including Mulvey) have extended the notion of the "male gaze" to show that it is not exclusively male. The notion of a "female gaze" certainly exists, though it is, perhaps, not as universally accepted in film studies as its male counterpart. For more on notions of the "female gaze," see Hollows, Joanne and Rachel

Moseley (eds.) *Feminism in Popular Culture*. Oxford & N.Y.: Berg, 2006, and Tasker, Yvonne and Diane Negra (eds.). *Interrogating Postfeminism: Gender and the Politics of Popular Culture*. Durham and London: Duke University Press, 2007.

21. *Lara Croft: Tomb Raider* (2001) grossed $274,703,340 worldwide. <http://box officemojo.com/movies/?id=tombraider.htm>

22. "Who Is the Hottest Comic Book Girl?" YouTube.com. 24 July 2009. 18 July 2010. <http://www.youtube.com/watch?v=F2K5slGadDQ>.

23. Ibid.

24. Angelina Jolie, in fact, normally wears a C-cup, but the director felt that in order to preserve this element of the character's sexuality, it was necessary for Jolie to wear a bra that would further emphasize her bust. <http://www.nyrock.com/interviews/2001/jolie_int.asp>

25. Alyssa Rosenberg states that "rather than drawing on extant rich stories about female superheroes, contemporary comic-based movies either downplay their powers and their personalities or rewrite them as trashy high camp" (39).

26. http://www.squidoo.com/colorexpert.

27. Alba is considered a sex symbol. She appears frequently on the "Hot 100" section of *Maxim* and was voted number one on AskMen.com's list of "99 Most Desirable Women" in 2006, as well as "Sexiest Woman in the World" by *FHM* in 2007. See also Maxim's "2007 Hot 100." <http://www.maximonline.com/Girls/Jessicaalba/slideshow/1126/47.aspx?src=GM7070:MD>.

28. Cited in <http://fantasticfour.ugo.com/?cur=jessica-alba&gallery=true>.

29. Ibid.

30. It seems relevant to recognize that the superhero world essentially functions in the same way as the world of mortals. Men are heralded for their sexual conquests, whereas women are labeled as "tramps" or "sluts." Why should Æon be any different?

31. Since the early days of comic book adaptation, film writers have struggled to not make superhero films campy. For more on this see Brian Lowry's "Getting Serious about Comic Book Adaptations: Superhero Pics and Series Have Found a Middle Ground between Camp and Pretentiousness." *Daily Variety* 284.2 (2004): 4.

32. Mike Fleming (2010-11-11). "Chris Nolan to Meet Actresses for Batman 3." *Deadline*. <http://www.deadline.com/2010/11/chris-nolan-lines-up-actresses-for-bat film/.>.

# Evolving Portrayals of Masculinity in Superhero Films
## *Hancock*

CHRISTINA ADAMOU

Although much attention has recently been paid to action films, which have flourished again from the 1990s onwards, the academic study of superhero/superheroine films is still a very new field of research. Even if we take into account that the rebirth of the superhero genre is more recent, the delay in academic study is quite notable and it may be due either to the interdisciplinarity inherent in the genre—comics and film — or to "quality" issues, with which academia is still struggling, even though the barrier between popular culture and high culture has supposedly been eliminated in a postmodern era (Jameson 35).

The recent rise in the production of superhero/superheroine films calls for attention to the genre's ideology, in the wider sense of the term, as a hierarchy of values and beliefs about how the world is or should be. The very idea of the superhuman, struggling with great power, opens up questions of ethics and politics. The increasing number of superheroines as protagonists, e.g., *Catwoman* (2004), *Elektra* (2005), or their prominent place in sequels, the very titles of which seem to exclude them, such as the *X-Men* films (2000–2009), raises questions of gender. However, the majority of the genre's protagonists are still male, rendering masculinity the "structuring norm" of the genre. Masculinity also functions as the structuring norm of femininity, since heterosexual gender stereotypes are based on binary oppositions and are thus defined through the exclusion of each other's characteristics and their antithesis, as I will later argue.

Superhero films, like most films— with the exception perhaps of experimental abstract films that do not use actors form discourses around gendered identities. This chapter looks into engendering masculinity in superhero films and traces the possible evolution of masculine heterosexual identities, using *Hancock* (2008) as a case study. Hancock (Will Smith) is a superhero who lives in a trailer and often sleeps on benches, gets drunk and becomes rude. Although he uses his superpowers, flying and extraordinary strength, to fight crime, he ends up destroying public and private property and being hated. When he saves Ray's (Jason Bateman) life, Ray uses his PR experience to change his image, focusing on Hancock's clothes, the use of his superpowers and behavior. In an unexpected turn, Hancock, who suffers from amnesia, discovers that Ray's wife, Mary (Charlize Theron), is also superheroine who used to be his partner. At the end of the film, Hancock becomes a respected superhero while Mary decides to stay with Ray and his son.

As far as the concept of the evolution of masculinity is concerned, it has a dual meaning. While it mainly refers to the evolution of male heterosexual identities with regard to cultural stereotypes, it also refers to the male heterosexual identities of superheroes. I will thus make occasional references to two of the most popular superheroes: Superman and Spider-Man. Apart from the intriguing inclusion of the word "man" in their superhero names and the obvious similarity of flight (or swinging in Spider-Man's case — no pun intended), all three are marginalized, fatherless and platonic heterosexuals, as I will later argue. As we are focusing on images of this millennium, references will be made to *Spider-Man* (2002) and *Superman Returns* (2006).

As far as methodology is concerned, it is helpful to use a synthesis of gender theory, close analysis and semiotics, in order to illuminate the cultural mythology of masculinity in superhero films. The use of semiotics in particular may be considered anachronistic or rigid by some film scholars. However, terms such as connotation, denotation and myth are useful shorthand references and do not necessarily require the strict categorization of every sign and process of signification. Close analysis has been successfully used in studying film since the beginning of film studies and similarly to semiotics allows for a reading of all cinematic codes that affect gender identity. These codes include sound, music and dialogue as well as acting, which is crucial to analysis, as it performs gender. Last but not least, gender theory provides an array of theoretical contexts. These wider theoretical contexts usually have a complex dialogic relation to the films, which do not tend to fall neatly into theoretical boxes, so semiotic and/or close analysis can illuminate the complexities of the dialogue between theory and the audiovisual text.

Superhero/superheroine films are stimulating objects of study with regard to gender representation and their use of audiovisual codes. Apart from the rebirth of the genre and its evolution through the inclusion of both heterosexual genders to which I have already referred, I was mainly motivated by the intrinsic characteristics of the genre with regard to gender. The study of fantasy narratives, such as sci-fi fiction and superhero/superheroine films in particular, offers an array of case studies of cultural myths that define gendered bodies placed beyond biology. Although superheroes and superheroines are clearly gendered, the main characters' bodies are certainly not limited by human biology and are defined solely by fantasy. Of course, the same claim could be made for any cinematic character, but in some genres the conventions reinforce it by asking the viewers for a bigger suspension of disbelief. Apart from science fiction, which is the obvious example, in action films such as *Crouching Tiger, Hidden Dragon* (2000), we witness action heroes and heroines flying, while in the *Harry Potter* films (2001–2011) humans perform magic. Therefore, bodies with superpowers seem to move far beyond any cultural stereotypes around sex and gender.

This is particularly important, as cultural gender theory has often faced alleged limitations by biology. Biological sex has either been seen/claimed as the basis for gender or posed beneath and beyond it (Butler, *Bodies That Matter* vii–23).[1] Of course, questions of biology vs. culture will keep emerging and become even more pressing as conservative ideologies regain ground. In spite or maybe because of that pressure, it is also important to look into gendered cultural myths, particularly when they are inherently independent of biology. Although the construction of cultural myths is inherently complex and intertextual, superheroes are placed beyond biology and, theoretically, they need not be bound by it. They are firmly grounded in popular culture and thus offer a unique opportunity to study the evolution of gendered mythology in western culture. In a parallel self-reflexive effort to forego any claims to "the truth," based on biology or personal empirical experience and being a white heterosexual woman, I have chosen to focus on black masculinity. In order to keep my arguments more focused, I will be analyzing gender and make occasional references to race when needed, since racial and gender stereotypes are often inextricably linked.

There are different views on masculinity, but I will refer to the ones that the respective film supports or undermines. Judith Butler summarizes the essence of different theoretical perspectives; for Wittig "To be male is not to be 'sexed'; to be 'sexed' is always a way of becoming particular and relative, and males within this system participate in the form of the universal person" while for Foucault "the body is not 'sexed' in any significant sense prior to its determination within a discourse through which it becomes invested with an 'idea' of natural or essential sex. The body gains meaning within discourse only in the context of power relations" (Butler, *Gender Trouble*, 113, 92).

Although these views may seem contradictory in that the first one argues that the males are not sexed, while the second one argues that males are also sexed within a particular discourse, they need not be. Males are portrayed as "universal" within particular discourses of contemporary western culture, while women are "sexed" as different. Neale's views can further illuminate this argument. As he argues, "[h]eterosexual masculinity has been identified as a structuring norm in relation both to images of women and gay men. It has to that extent been profoundly problematized, rendered visible. But it has rarely been discussed as such" (Neale 9). Masculinity becomes the structuring norm of other genders, as it is the universal that defines difference.

Acting also plays an important role in constructing such power relations, structuring norms, the "normality" of the universal person or — in other words— gendered mythologies. The necessity and the importance of analyzing screen performance have been demonstrated in Baron and Carnicke (2008). There is also a pressing need to analyze acting as a creation of gender. For Butler, sex is produced on the surface of the body through everyday behavior and movement. What Butler proposes contradicts Christian ideas of the body as a vessel and is also differentiated from the rather static psychoanalytic view of the body as a representation of a unified ego. The dynamic idea of the body as a constant creator of gendered identity can be particularly useful for the analysis of performance. This idea was applied by Butler to everyday life as well as acting, but it has not been adequately explored in film and performance analysis (*Gender Trouble*). Acting produces sex or gender in the creation of the character. The process of creating sex or gender can become more conscious, both for the artists involved and for viewers, than it is in everyday life. It is notable that the difference between each superhero and his alter ego is constructed mainly through costume and acting. Acting is also crucial in producing gender for a particular character as well as reinforcing, undermining or altering cultural stereotypes around genders. However, its role in creating the meaning, ideology and aesthetics of the cinematic text has been largely overlooked.

Analyzing the creation of gender through acting involves, of course, the same challenges as examining acting. Acting constitutes a work of art that is often seen as inseparable from the artist and/or "internal," as it involves the actor's body. However, the time of the performance in theatre and both the time and space of viewing the film in cinema place acting in a defined context, thus separating it from the artist to a certain extent. Moreover, recent ethnographic studies have demonstrated that actors do not feel the emotions of the character to the same degree and that acting — independently of the method or style used is actually a conscious process (Schoenmakers 2008). Another difficulty in analyzing acting is the huge variety of facial expressions, gestures and movements that actors offer. Therefore, it is easier and more objective to define, for instance, a particular shade of red in the set or costume or a movement of the camera than to define a particular smile. A close-up or medium close-up, or a dark or light red are elements of the audiovisual text that can be identified and then interpreted, whereas a broad smile or a cynical or crooked smile are notions "suspect" of containing subjectivity or already connoting a particular reading. The solution could lie with the use of the Laban Movement Analysis System proposed by Cynthia Baron and Sharon Marie Carnicke (2008). However, I will venture a semiotic reading, trying to describe/identify before interpreting. An important reason for favoring semiotics is that it can be applied to the whole audiovisual text and include acting, even when it is not the main focus of research.

Acting and other audiovisual codes, such as tone of voice, costume and special effects, perform the binary oppositions that have culturally defined masculinity and femininity and have rendered the masculine gender much more visible in the public domain. "Femininity (as defined by patriarchy) is usually associated with being small, quiet, passive, emotional, nurturing, non-aggressive, dependent, and weak. Masculinity (as defined by patriarchy) is usually associated with being large, loud, and active, with non-emotional aggression and strong leadership qualities" (Benshoff & Griffin 205). Femininity is also traditionally linked to the private sector: home and family; while masculinity is linked to the public sector: work, politics, etc. Power and aggressiveness as well as control of one's body and space are attributes stereotypically associated with the male heterosexual gender (Easthope 48–51). This link with the public sector strengthens the equation of masculinity to universality, as being in public means being visible and acting visibly, while femininity in the private sector remains "hidden."

Control of voyeurism (Mulvey) can be applied to male genres, as the male hero and villain "are subject to voyeuristic looking, both on the part of the spectator and on the part of other male characters" (Neale 16). If that is true for classical Hollywood, it becomes rather excessive when it comes to superheroes, as the spectacle is organized around their bodies and their abilities. When Ray shows Hancock covers of superhero comics, in an effort to illuminate what a successful superhero should look like, the bodies on display have excessive muscles. Their exaggerated muscular system is also accentuated by the movements depicted. In superhero films, the camera, the cinematography, the costumes, special effects and editing as well as the costumes emphasize the spectacle of their bodies, as I will argue.

Although voyeurism links superheroes to femininity, it has been noted that their characteristics are rather hyper-masculine. Superheroes' powers are excessive and so are the traits of their gendered identities, which are usually stereotypical. It has also been noted that women become more masculine as they become stronger and braver (Johnson et. al. 229–230). However, Hancock, an extremely strong, brave male, needs to acquire feminine characteristics in order to be successful. During his transformation, Hancock learns how to be kinder and more sensitive to other people. This learning curve is completed when Hancock eventually accepts and expresses his own vulnerability. After his first successful intermission during a bank robbery, where he shows concern and respect for other people and public property, he goes to dinner with the couple helping him and reveals his own identity crisis. His movements also become more controlled and restrained. Although they could not be characterized as feminine, they display feminine attributes.

Interestingly enough, it is from the public sector and extreme visibility in public places and in the media that the city and citizens of L.A. want to ostracize Hancock for being too "masculine." At the beginning of the film, Hancock is certainly large, loud, active and aggressive, to such an excess that, far from being a leader, he becomes marginalized. It is conventional for superheroes to be initially marginalized and later to be transformed into leaders. Peter Parker is bullied at school, while Clark Kent is marginalized at home and to a certain extent in the newspaper where he works. However, both become leaders via their alter egos as superheroes. Their everyday identity links them to everyday people that may feel disempowered within Western social structures and invites sympathy, while their superhero identity embodies desires for power and changing the world.

This convention is altered in more recent films such as the *X-Men* franchise or *The Incredibles* (2004). Marginalization is caused by society's fear of their superhero powers, their Otherness. Although there are implications of fear of great power in Superman's myth as well, there is a shift of focus to fear of the Incredibles' and the mutants' powers. This fear can be interpreted both in psychoanalytic and political terms. Fear of Otherness, in Kristeva's sense, is the projection of one's own unconscious onto others, as the discovery of the unconscious is the first discovery of the Other in the Self (181). Fear of the Other and/or the Other in the Self as the unconscious does not contradict the emphasis on cultural symbols, roles and stereotypes, for it is in relation and accordance with those that identity and desire are formed. The child enters the symbolic through the mediation of the "name of the father"; the cultural norms, conventions and stereotypes that inform our identity and sexuality. In social terms, the uses of great power that might not have social consensus problematize democracy.

There is no space here to analyze further the ideological implications of this shift in marginalizing superheroes and superheroines because of their powers, but I am noting it in order to highlight a further shift in Hancock. At the beginning of the film, Hancock is homeless, drunk and rude. Furthermore, he crushes a car on a skyscraper, showing no concern for the difficulties and expenses that the crash would bring to the city of L.A. Significantly enough, it is not the fact that he has superpowers nor a secret identity that marginalize him, but the way in which he uses his powers. Thus, the concern here is not focused on the fear of the Other in Kristeva's sense, or even the threat of a great power functioning independently of democracy. The main concerns are the financial damage and the havoc he causes, epitomized by the word "asshole," addressed to Hancock by a young boy at the very first sequence of the film and repeated at various sequences afterwards. His marginalization is not primarily based on fear of Otherness, but on his uncontrolled aggression, the effects of which are measured in financial terms. Although this shift may be linked to genre, since *Hancock* begins as a self-reflexive superhero comedy, it nevertheless foregrounds the effects of excessive aggressiveness, which is considered a masculine characteristic.

Hancock has no alter ego, so the representation of masculinity is more unified in this film. Superman and Spider-Man become leaders as superheroes and peaceful citizens as their alter egos. Their superhero identity is more masculine: it is stronger and more active in the public domain and thus embodies a masculinity that they cannot represent in their everyday lives. Hancock only has his superhero identity and its masculinity is even more excessive than that of most superheroes.

In the first sequence of the film, we see Hancock sleeping on a bench, drinking alcohol, being rude to a young boy who wakes him up and alerts him to the presence of "bad guys" who are sexually harassing a female passer-by. He is thus established as a "bad boy," too. While his aggression towards the young white boy and his aggressive sexuality towards the white female passer-by could possibly be read as echoes of the Black Buck, the stereotype of the aggressive and sexually active black male, the intertextual association promoted by the film seems to be with hip hop mythology. Hancock's loose fitting clothes and hat seem to be references to the look of most hip hop singers as well as Will Smith's own music career. Will Smith has linked his careers as an actor and as a singer before, when he wrote and performed the hits "Men in Black and "Black Suits Coming" for *Men in Black* (1998) and *Men in Black II* (2002) respectively. It is also worth noting that Will Smith's career and star image have been based on a complex relation between personification and impersonation (McDonald 141–153).[2] While he has been associated with building memorable characters (impersonation) from *The Fresh Prince of Bel-Air* (NBC, 1990–1996) to *Hancock*, rather than assimilating characters to his star persona, there is also a consistency of certain elements. Most of his characters have a loose body language and are "cool." Will Smith seems to bring this element of coolness, often associated with black masculinity. As he lends common characteristics to a lot of the characters he portrays, Smith's acting and star image seem to be based on personification, as well.

The element of coolness is also key in Hancock. After having been alerted to the presence of bad guys, Hancock flies off towards the action while still being drunk and crushes into birds. His spread legs and arms during his flight reflect a relaxed attitude and lack of control, accentuated by the loose movements of his arms. Furthermore, both the broad yet quick movements of his arms and his large loose-fitting clothes, assisted by the hip hop soundtrack, reflect an image of black masculinity closely linked with hip hop music and reinforcing the "bad boy" image associated with hip hop mythology. This link is also reinforced by his comment to the "bad guys:" "Three guys in a car, no girls, rave music... I'm not gonna judge."

The "bad boy" attitude is additionally reinforced by his aggression towards the criminals. The language that he uses links him both to stereotypes of aggressive and hostile black masculinity and to the working class and of course the stereotypical link between African-Americans and the working class. He warns them that: "your head is going up the driver's ass, his head is going up your ass and you do the short stick because your head is going up my ass." This is uttered in a very relaxed, confident way that shows that he is in control. The extreme tension of his eyebrows and sideways open mouth at the end of the extract though, offer a different image of masculinity. His aggression towards the criminals is expressed in a rather troubled, self-conscious manner, as his face loses its symmetry offering an image of masculinity "in trouble."

His gendered identity is highly significant with regard to his social "banishment" as it is the excess of masculine characteristics that leads to his being marginalized, as I have argued. The story focuses on his transformation from an anti-hero to a hero, from an outcast person to an esteemed member of society. This transformation undermines gender in two interlinked ways: Hancock sheds light on the inherent contradictions of such stereotypes through this excessive masquerade. Although he is extremely powerful and his ability to fly gives him the potential of ultimate control over space, he is unable to control such a power and destroys the space around him. Furthermore, it is the adoption of female characteristics, such as compassion, sensitivity, quietness and consideration for others' feelings, that eventually allows him to become a leader. Masculinity becomes visible, more active and more powerful in the public domain and fulfills a universal myth of transforming an individual from a "black sheep" into a leader by becoming more feminine.

Hancock's feminine characteristics at the end of the film follow a parallel genre change that has been noted by critics. *Hancock* begins as a self-reflexive superhero comedy and transforms into a superhero melodrama. Although the film is a hybrid of genres from the beginning, the shift is so noticeable that Ansen writes in *Newsweek*: "It's as if an entire new movie starts up." This apparent generic change occurs when the main character gets in touch with himself and transforms into a leader. The humor in the first half of the film includes both slapstick and verbal wit. Both kinds of humor, however, emanate mainly from Hancock's drunkenness, aggression and use of crude language. His aggression and violent behavior in particular are inextricably linked to stereotypes of black masculinity. So, the fact that humor emanates from the character being too aggressive performs a masquerade of black masculinity that can undermine such stereotypes.

Superheroes are conventionally displaced from society and from nuclear families. Hancock does not remember his past and we learn that he has always been around. Superman is adopted by humans but has lost his biological parents and so has Peter Parker, who is adopted by his aunt and uncle. Scarce information is given about their past lives, and the same convention is maintained as far as Hancock' biological parents and/or past are concerned. The latter two superheroes are displaced from their biological families only to be placed in model families, where the adoptive parents seek ideal, loving relationships both between them and with their adopted sons. Yet once again Spider-Man and Superman are distanced from their families: Superman moves far away and

Peter Parker has a secret identity as Spider-Man. The loss of their past distances them from everyday people, which makes them less "concrete" and more symbolic. At the same time, the distance creates space for exploring their relations to patriarchy. Superman (Brandon Routh) in *Superman Returns*, eager to be defined by his father and prove himself worthy of him, has flown as far away as another universe in search of his roots/identity. Spider-Man (Tobey Maguire), in the homonymous film (2002), kills his friend's father and thus becomes a lonely superhero, a figure that assumes the place of the father himself in terms of defining ethics, law and justice. What these respective acts demonstrate is that they have both already adhered to the ideology of their adoptive parents. Superman in *Superman Returns* tries to then pass his principles and values on to his and Lois's (Kate Bosworth) son as he discovers that he is now a father, and he assumes this new role both metaphorically, as a father of a nation, and literally as his son's father.

Hancock finds a man to dress him properly, help him accept punishment for bad behavior, and teach him good manners, so his relationship to Ray resembles to an extent that of father and son. Again, it is a relationship with a father figure that allows him to grow as a person and assume the same patriarchal place as Spider-Man and Superman. He also becomes a father figure for Ray's son — unsuccessfully at first, since he helps him deal with bullying by bullying a young boy himself. By the end of the film though, they develop a loving and respectful relationship. Ray and Hancock's relationship also becomes much friendlier. Hancock, unlike Superman, is not guided by a dead father figure and unlike Spider-Man does not kill one. At the end of the film, there is room in the world for both, and although their coalition does not include a woman, their friendship undermines the antagonism stereotypically associated with masculinity.

With regard to antagonism, it is also worth noting that there is also no super-bad-guy in Hancock. His fight with Mary substitutes for the conventional fight between the superhero and his super-opponent, but it is not a fight between good and evil. In more conventional films, such as *Spider-Man* and *Superman Returns*, great good and great evil are both represented by male figures, similarly to the Judeo-Christian tradition. In fact, Lex Luthor (Kevin Spacey) equates Superman to a god, while Superman and Lois Lane later discuss whether the world needs a savior. Lois's statement that neither the world nor she needs one is immediately challenged visually by her flying into Superman's arms. Shots alternate between medium close-ups emphasizing their proximity and happiness and bird's eye views of the city, focusing on Superman's permanent and Lois's temporary voyeuristic pleasure and superior knowledge. Just before the flight's end, Superman reassures her that he constantly hears people crying for a savior. His god-like status and his role as a lover are once again inextricably linked in a myth of superior masculinity that has great power, ultimate control of body and space, superior knowledge and godly justice.

As with most superheroes, Hancock's sexual interests remain platonic and his sexuality is therefore underdeveloped through the plot of the film; yet we are "reassured" that he is both ethical and heterosexual. The platonic love interests of superheroes have a double function: they aid the plot and development of the main characters. The girls usually need to be rescued and they offer themselves to the heroes at the end of the film as prizes for their bravery and skills. Superheroes' love interests thus still fulfill the traditional female role as an object that has been analyzed by Mulvey with regard to classical Hollywood films (10–40). At the same time, they help the development of the character who traditionally refuses to be their partner, in order to keep them safe or because they "belong" to someone else, and it is this choice that seals the highly ethical stances of Superman and Spider-Man, for instance. It is quite telling as to the girls' importance as a crucial structuring element of the plot that *Spider-Man* begins with the introduction of Mary Jane Watson (Kirsten Dunst), while the voice-over comments that Spider-Man's story, "like any story worth telling, is all about a girl." The sequence just before the end of the film contains a kiss and a dialogue between Mary Jane Watson and Peter Parker, where he tells her that his friendship is all he has to give. On an ideological level, superheroes' female objects of desire also serve as a "reassurance" of their heterosexuality, particularly since the excess in their costumes and muscles could connote homosexuality.

Hancock calls attention to this connotation through Ray's effort to change his image, which offers plenty of opportunities for self-reflexivity. During a comic sequence in Ray's house, he shows Hancock some covers of superhero comic books and Hancock reacts with the comments "homo," "homo in red" and "Norwegian homo." The implication is that Hancock has to conform to the stereotypes of popular mythology in order to become accepted as a superhero. At the same time, the film's self-reflexively comments on superheroes' conventional sexuality and implicitly calls attention to its own choices. The spandex costumes on the comic book covers that accentuate the superheroes' muscles seem to take this to an extreme that could cross the boundaries of sexuality. The movements depicted in the comics are also stronger, either fully extending or fully bending arms and legs. They offer images of "musculinity," a term used to connote the strong link in our culture between masculinity and muscles (Williams 174) on display and contrast Hancock's loose movements in the beginning of the film. His composed movement after the transformation also lacks the exaggeration of displaying muscle and is instead focused on skill. Thus, when we watch him fly off at the end of the film, the movement away from the camera is swift and we watch the flight from a distance. In addition, Hancock's costume is black, a color that does not add volume and therefore does not emphasize the character's muscles.

His heterosexuality is also confirmed by the introduction of a female love interest, in this case an ex-partner and his friend's wife, who is still happy with Ray at the end of the film. Although not getting the girl is quite usual for superheroes, as I have demonstrated, that possibility is usually left open. We rarely see Lois with someone else as in *Superman Returns* and even in those rare occasions the flirt between the girl and the superhero continues, since Superman promises Lois Lane that he will always be around.

However, the love story between Hancock and Mary evolves differently. The ultimate battle between characters with superpowers is not a battle between good and evil but seems to be a battle of the sexes. Mary appears clad in leather and with heavy make-up, particularly around her eyes. Her appearance in this scene comes in stark contrast with her motherly, girl-next door appearance throughout the rest of the film. The dynamic active superheroine thus becomes an alter ego that is opposed to her everyday life. Her choice to live solely as a stay-at-home mom is contrasted to choices made by mainly male superheroes who have a double life: a quiet one as their alter egos and a very active one. Mary seems not only to have abandoned her superheroine identity but, also to have repressed her dynamic elements.

Hancock and Mary's romance destroys the city, rather than enjoying and controlling it like Superman and Lois. Neither of them has control over his/her aggression, as feelings take over logic. They both control their bodies as well as space through destruction, as they demolish a truck, streets and buildings. They are both extremely powerful and active. In fact, Mary flies holding a truck in one hand. This shot mirrors shots of Hancock flying while holding cars, both at the beginning of the film and when he saves Ray. Their collision in the air immediately afterwards shatters the windows of a skyscraper. This equal sharing of masculine values and one feminine value—feelings over logic—could be read as undermining the stereotypes of masculinity and femininity, which attribute strength and aggression solely to masculinity and pathos solely to femininity.

However, even though Mary has told Hancock that she is stronger than him and hits him with a truck to prove it, she ends up under him at the end of the battle and he holds her down while she is crying. The end of the sequence thus contests her initial statement and shows that she is either physically or emotionally weaker. Hancock also calls her crazy, which sets her off. The dialogue between them also mirrors Hancock's repeated dialogue with villains. Hancock says: "Call me asshole, one more time" and Mary says: "Call me crazy one more time," as the utterance of each word helps them gather up enough aggression to do something extreme. Even though they both use the line to give in to feelings rather than logic, it is still worth noting that Mary's button, craziness, is stereotypically linked to femininity.

It is also worth pointing out that they both weaken each other, so it seems that in *Hancock*'s world powerful couples cannot exist. Mary's withdrawal from the public domain seems to support yet another backlash of patriarchy against feminism. Yet Mary does indeed find happiness in her private life with Ray, a literally weaker man, and Ray is happy with her, even before Hancock boosts his effort to change the world.[3] Just before the end of the film, there is a sequence where Ray, Mary and his son eat ice-cream and happily chat about her past life and people she has met, including Queen Elizabeth. This sequence, strategically placed just before they see that Hancock has painted the "All-Heart" symbol on the moon, boosting Ray's effort to change the world through more charity, establishes the family's acceptance of her superheroine identity and their happiness. This narrative choice could imply that stronger women can have successful relationships or that they can have successful relationships as long as they choose to stay at home.

Although the plots of superhero films, including the superpowers attributed to each superhero, the evolution of the love story, and the obstacles they have to overcome, are obviously important, the costumes and special effects constantly create the gendered and ethnic identity of each superhero, as these two characteristics may be inextricably linked. The control of one's body and space are again exemplified by Spider-Man and Superman, who learn how to use and control their powers. This control however is not just linked to gender but also to ethnicity. Superman and Spider-Man seem to embody American ideals. They use great power ethically and become necessary for the safety of the world. The colors of the U.S. flag on their respective uniforms strengthen the implication of embodying American ideals. Interestingly enough, Spider-Man's famous quote, "With great power comes great responsibility," precedes his last flight, which includes him landing on a pole of the flag. The film ends with a shot of this national symbol and Spider-Man right next to it, so the audiovisual text further supports the association between Spider-Man and the nation. The white male characters and masculine stereotypes are not equated to the "universal" in this case, yet they represent a wider ideology that is inextricably linked to white patriarchal capitalism. Great power and great responsibility lie with American citizens. Similarly, Superman in *Superman Returns* saves the United States, while the narrative ignores the rest of the world.

In Hancock's case, the superhero's initial uncertainty and clumsiness disable him from controlling his body and space and becoming the necessary and ethical superhero. The question that is implicitly posed here is whether he becomes "whiter" or "more American" at the end of the film. The film ends with a vision that extends beyond the United States, unlike *Spider-Man* and *Superman Returns*. It is a supposedly revolutionary vision of large corporations undertaking social responsibility worldwide. Its importance is reinstated throughout the film and at the very end, when Hancock says: "You're gonna change the world. Good job, Ray!" Although Ray's proposition to large corporations to give one of their products for free to people in need is treated with disbelief and fear by secondary characters in the film, it is still based on charity. Ray does not start a revolution nor does he propose the end of economic globalization or even fair-trade. The change that he proposes is more help to the Third World, a slight shift in balance that would still support a clear demarcation between the developed and the developing world as well as the existing class system and power structure.

Maintaining the power structure is also echoed in other choices. An effort within the plot, also apparent in audiovisual choices, is made to connect Hancock to everyday people and especially to police officers. When Hancock returns to action after his "voluntary" incarceration, he helps capture bank robbers and resolve a hostage situation. When he lands on the scene, it is apparent that both his costume and his movements resemble those of police officers. Although they are far from identical, they are both fitted in dark colors, and the leather of Hancock's costume is similar to the material of their bullet-proof jackets. His costume mirrors their uniform and his walk and tone of voice mirror that of the officer in charge. This close similarity is also apparent towards the end of the scene. When he gives the hand and trigger to the police officer, they mirror each other's slight movements of the head and hands and they say "good job" to each other, connoting both sympathy and close similarity. His movements are minimal and controlled. Although his arms and legs have some distance from his body and thus add volume to it, it is a volume that connotes authority, rather than muscularity. The transformation is not radical at his point. Although the villain threatens to blow up the hostages, Hancock seems to react mostly to his calling him an "asshole." He dares the villain to call him that "one more time" before cutting off his hand, so he does not operate entirely rationally. On the one hand, this is a reminder of his "bad boy" attitude. On the other hand, it is a well-established convention in film and television that the main characters have emotional problems and often operate outside the law in order to establish social order.

His acting is also different with regard to the opening sequence, where his aggressiveness is established. The only extreme tension we see is that of his facial muscles. When the villain asks him to help him, the raising of the eyebrows denotes perplexity but the extremity of the movement also denotes that the character is acting this out. When the villain calls him an asshole, though, the embarrassment seems grotesque yet real for the character. One of my main problems when analyzing the excerpt was determining what differentiates it from the previous reaction. The caught breath and the tension of the muscles around the eyes seem to mirror the previous reaction. However, the two sighs are deeper, his voice becomes slightly deeper and more importantly the crookedness of the mouth matches the tension of the eyes— all slight changes implying that his self-image is still a real problem for the character.

Hancock seems more peaceful at the end of the film, when he becomes a lonely superhero who helps the world. The end of the film has conflicting connotations which may initially seem rather conservative with regard to gender stereotypes. The superheroine finds happiness in becoming a supportive housewife and caring mother; her husband will try to change the world with Hancock's help, while Hancock assumes his "rightful" place in the public domain.

However, other elements of the text open it up to a different reading. As mentioned above, it is not just stated that the female superhero is stronger than her male counterpart; there is also an extended battle scene between them that reinforces her superiority and undermines the stereotypical link of strength to masculinity.

At the end of the film, it is mostly Hancock's visible transformation that undermines stereotypes. The costume clings to Will Smith's body, yet is far from images of extreme muscularity, connoting heterosexuality but also less need for excessive force. His decisions to help others not just with superpower but also through charity, and to share publicity with Ray so they can change the world move him away from patriarchal antagonistic relations.

However, it is mostly Will Smith's relaxed acting that offers a different image of the male superhero. The final sequence of Hancock flying off is preceded by a phone call to Ray. Although Hancock is sentimental in this extract, Will Smith's facial muscles are more relaxed, denoting that the character is in peace with himself. The small smile is also relaxed, which connotes effortlessness. The flight of the character is more controlled, although to a certain extent it mirrors the first flight. In addition, Hancock's legs are again slightly spread, but they are now kept straight and his spread arms are kept at each side of his body. The tension of the muscles and the expression of his face, however, do not reveal any excess effort, connoting easy control and harmony with his environment and with nature — such as the eagle that he follows.

Although Hancock's last flight resembles Superman's flights, it begins differently. Superman takes off from the ground and shows vertical control of space from the beginning. Hancock's flight also begins with verticality but we see him flying from the roof of a skyscraper and parallel to the building towards the ground. This choice may cause initial suspense and the flight could be seen as a metaphor for the character and the plot of the film: Hancock's initial fall, his subsequent gain of control, and his rise.

An obvious yet critical question when analyzing such extracts is who creates meaning and aesthetics: the actor? Special effects? The stuntman? When it comes to acting in general, the direction, photography and editing are obviously also involved. Although other creators' mediation may be more critical in action or superhero films, I think that we should examine the text, where the character is meant to be a unified whole. Another obvious question that springs to mind after having analyzed the end of the film is whether, by reinstating Hancock's masculine values, such as "masculinity"[4] and control of body and space, the film reinstates gendered values and stereotypes. The plot of the film, however, also reveals Hancock's newly found sensitivity and commitment to helping others. It is not a matter of him saving the world and being a hero, but of his friend transforming it into a fairer place. Although the film seems to support this idea for a universal person, gender is central to it. Supporting someone else's dreams and life's work has traditionally been considered a female role. Will Smith's acting, connoting uncomplicated control, peacefulness and harmony, denotes that he is happy with this role.

Strong male and female characters bring closer the transcendence of dualities such as male-female, self-other, and familiar-foreign (Housel 88). Keeping in mind all the shifts in gender stereotypes and roles that the film performs, one has to wonder if it goes as far as undermining gender stereotypes. The gender stereotypes that served as a basis for second-wave feminism are deeply rooted in our culture, as they structured dominant ideology for centuries. However, we also need to take into account the effects of feminism, particularly with regard to "the new man" and third-wave feminism. Hancock at the end of the film seems defined by the idea of the new man: he is sensitive and considerate and respects his (ex)partner's power and intelligence. Third-wave feminism seems to argue for personal choices and thus against the devaluation of being a stay-at-home mom. The "new man" seems to be making a comeback within the context of third-wave feminism.

The lack of displaying excessive force and muscularity, the connotations of calm control, and, more importantly the peace derived from taking on the supporting role in changing the world, create the myth of a gathered masculinity, of a universal person — still signified by a man, but now an African-American — content with using his powers to "do his bit." Although retaining some of its central characteristics, masculinity in *Hancock* becomes less hysterical with power and control. Will Smith's acting exemplifies the problematics of the alpha-male myth and connotes happiness when he is in touch with his own emotions. The focus on the acquisition of feminine characteristics — a given in *Spider-Man* and *Superman Returns* — also foregrounds that they are necessary for a superhero. Skoble mentions that Batman does not possess any superpowers, yet he is considered a superhero. The costume, car and gadgets he uses "make up" for his lack of superpowers. His costume in particular displays an excessively muscular body. Yet, his consideration for others and the devotion of his life to helping them make him a superhero (Skoble 35). This "feminine" motivation is central in superhero myths and is coupled with their visible excessive masculinity.[5] Its lack in *Hancock* only serves to draw attention to its importance.

The final conclusions with regard to the evolution of gender stereotypes in *Hancock* could be mixed, unless we accept third-wave feminism's ideal of valuing personal choices. Even so, the implications that Mary may be weaker and crazy may link the character to feminine stereotypes. However, it also has to be acknowledged that these stereotypical associations are not confirmed in the film. Masculine stereotypes, on the other hand, and especially those around superheroes and black masculinity, certainly evolve in *Hancock*. Aggressiveness, excessive muscularity and force as heterosexual masculine stereotypes become the source of comedy. At the same time, the necessity of adopting feminine values for heterosexual superheroes and since everyday men is stressed, there seems to be a rebirth of the "new man." Hancock also adopts a patriarchal capitalist position at the end of the film. On the other hand, he does not get the girl and he brings fame to Ray, thus "sharing" the alpha-male status. Furthermore, his devotion to his friend's cause highlights capitalism's exploitation of developing countries. Of course, the film does not revolutionize the mythologies around genders and sexualities, particularly since such an effort is made to evade connotations of homosexuality. However, as Butler notes, "If the rules governing signification not only restrict, but enable the assertion of alternative domains of cultural intelligibility, i.e., new possibilities for gender that contest the rigid codes of hierarchical binarisms, then it is only *within* the practices of repetitive signifying that a subversion of identity becomes possible" (Butler, *Gender Trouble,* 145).

## Notes

1. Judith Butler notes that by considering gender as constructed, feminist discourses imply that sex is not constructed and treat it as pre-discursive. She goes on to argue that since discourse either excludes sex through the assumption that it lies beyond it or implicitly considers it as a passive surface upon which culture then acts to produce gender, discourse thus constructs sex through these presuppositions.

2. Paul McDonald defines personification as foregrounding the performer through continuities in acting different parts and impersonation as foregrounding the characters instead of the performer, through discontinuities in acting.

3. Ray tries to persuade companies to give one of their products away to people in need. He proposes that they use the "all heart" symbol and argues that the symbol will become so recognizable that it will help other sales.

4. I am using the term coined by Williams to refer both to masculinity and muscles, as explained above.

5. Self-sacrifice and devotion to other people have traditionally been associated with women. However, they are often kept within their families and private lives and thus remain "invisible."

# Genre and Super-Heroism

## *Batman in the New Millennium*

### VINCENT M. GAINE

The superhero film can appear to be a genre in its own right, with identifiable tropes, conventions and iconography. These tropes include tragic loss, learning to use one's new powers, villains whose trajectory mirrors that of the hero, action sequences and conclusions that leave narrative points open for development in sequels to continue the franchise. However, the superhero film can also fit within the broader genres of the action film, science fiction, the blockbuster, and the revenge narrative. This paper argues that the most recent installments of the Batman franchise, *Batman Begins* (2005) and *The Dark Knight* (2008), both directed by Christopher Nolan, problematize ideas of genre through their uses of generic tropes and attention to the actual role of the "hero." Of particular concern are issues of liminality, as both the films and the character of Batman cross a number of thresholds. Batman himself crosses social thresholds such as those between legality and criminality, authority and anarchy, justice and oppression. These thresholds constitute a social and physical space that is liminal, a liminal space that Batman occupies and which features various tensions and contradictions. This essay uses evidence from the two films to support the claim that Batman's heroism is *dependent* upon his liminality. It is through the exploration of the tensions and contradictions that these films perform expansions beyond the notion of a genre that can (arguably) be identified by the presence of a costumed hero. Within the politically and ideologically charged contexts of the last decade, Batman in the new millennium explores borders both within the context of the films' diegesis and the placement of the films within contemporary production and consumption.

## *What Is a Hero?*

One might expect that defining the superhero genre would be easier than genres such as the thriller or horror: a superhero film is a film that includes a superhero. This assumption however creates the immediate problem of how to define such a character. Is the term "hero" more significant than the term "super"? Any lead protagonist can and often is referred to as a hero, and such protagonists are often heroic, in the sense of being courageous, self-sacrificing, noble and romantic. Yet while Judah Ben-Hur (Charlton Heston), John McClane (Bruce Willis), and Indiana Jones (Harrison Ford) are clearly presented as heroes, it would be odd to refer to any of them as a "*super*hero." How then do we identify what constitutes a "*superhero*"?

As is often the case in genre studies, a dilemma appears. As pointed out by Andrew Tudor (96), "[A]lmost all writers ... are defining a [insert genre title] on the basis of analyzing a body of films which cannot possibly be said to be [insert genre title] until after the analysis." In the current case, the dilemma applies not only to the superhero genre but the genre's seemingly defining feature. If we are to perform an analysis of "superheroes"—let alone the superhero genre—we must first define what a superhero is; but how can we define a subject when we have not performed an analysis?

In practice, this dilemma can be solved with knowledge of "a common set of meanings in our culture," (ibid.) meanings that instill the understanding of a superhero, and more broadly of comic books. The same cultural knowledge informs us that these two phenomena are often linked—the majority of comic books feature superheroes and most superhero characters have their origins in the comic book form. Historically, this link is practical: the realm of super-heroics involves superhuman abilities such as spinning webs, morphing the body and flight—feats that are complex, difficult and expensive to produce practically, whereas in pictorial form the only limit is the artist's imagination. Only within recent decades have film and TV special effects progressed to the stage where such abilities can be represented on screen through the use of digital imaging and animation.

The comic books themselves therefore point to a straightforward, common sense way of defining the superhero genre. The common denominator among such texts as *Superman* (1978), *Daredevil* (2003), *The Dark Knight* and *Hellboy* (2004) is, simply, that they are based upon intellectual properties licensed by comic book publishing houses such as Marvel, DC and Dark Horse. It would be hard to argue that these are *not* comic book films, based as they are upon comic books. Therefore, one way to define the genre is simply by source material.

Such a definition has precedent, as source material is a common term for film genres, be that literary adaptation, true life story, or more specific sources such as Biblical epic or Shakespearean drama. Yet comic books are distinct from other forms of literature, both in terms of cultural capital but also narrative form, especially due to their serialization and distinct practice of narrative through pictorial rather than verbal representation. It is notable that few films based upon comic books actually perform direct adaptation of individual texts, not even compressing a particular story that ran over many issues into a single narrative text. Notable exceptions would be adaptations such as *Watchmen* (2008), *From Hell* (2001), *Sin City* (2005) and *V for Vendetta* (2006), films whose source texts are stand-alone graphic novels, a form and term that only emerged in the 1980s. Nonetheless, regardless of their narrative form, the source text serves to unite all these films under a common banner. From *Superman* to *Sin City*, and from *American Splendor* (2003) to *Spider-Man* (2002), the comic book film is a recognizable type of film.

There is, however, a glaring problem with this film type — quite simply, not all comic books are about superheroes; indeed some of those mentioned above lack any superheroes or even super heroics. *American Splendor* and *From Hell* are both based on graphic novels, but they are distinctly different in theme, narrative and style to *Fantastic Four* (2005) and *The Incredible Hulk* (2008). While source material is useful for identifying the comic book film, it is not sufficient to identify the superhero film.

It could be suggested that the superhero film (or comic book or TV show) requires an individual with superpowers, be they unlimited strength and speed like Superman, abilities of an animal such as Spider-Man, or specific individual abilities such as telepathy, regeneration and teleportation, as demonstrated by the X-Men and the characters of *Heroes* (NBC, 2006–2010). Nevertheless, even though Batman, V and others possess no super powers, it would be hard if not impossible to argue that they are not superheroes. All superheroes, whether possessed of powers or not, share a number of features, tropes that serve to define both the individual characters, and the generic borders that are perceived and understood as being built around them. Richard Reynolds provides a useful summary of these tropes in relation to superheroes in comic books, some of which can be applied to film and TV superheroes as well:

- The hero is marked out from society. He often reaches maturity without having a relationship with his parents.
  ...
- The hero's devotion to justice overrides even his devotion to the law.
- The extraordinary nature of the superhero will be contrasted with the ordinariness of his surroundings.
- Likewise, the extraordinary nature of the hero will be contrasted with the mundane nature of his alter-ego. Certain taboos will govern the actions of these alter-egos.
- Although ultimately above the law, superheroes can be capable of considerable patriotism and moral loyalty to the state, though not necessarily to the letter of its laws [16].

Reynolds' summary indicates clearly that the superhero is an outsider, both from other people and from other people's adherence to social conventions. Even if he (or she) does not have superpowers, there is nonetheless an *extraor-*

*dinary nature* which sets the superhero apart from society. This essay argues that a key element to this nature is that the superhero is not a complete societal outsider, but rather that he must operate on the *borders* of society, as it is this liminal state that maintains his extraordinary nature.

## Influences and Borrowings

Two significant concerns are apparent in the understanding of the generic borders here under discussion. The first is what can be termed *borrowings*, the genres which feed into the superhero film, identified by tropes that have been incorporated into various superhero films to constitute a generic framework. The second concern is *expansions*: if the superhero genre is accepted as an identifiable cinematic mode, what elements problematize the genre's stability by going beyond the borders of the genre? In the case of *Batman Begins* and *The Dark Knight*, borrowings are multiple and expansions distinct, and these patterns indicate the existence of an identifiable genre, yet one that can stretch and mutate.

As noted, Batman has no superpowers. Nonetheless, he clearly performs tasks beyond the ability of "normal" people, but these tasks are facilitated through three major resources. The first is Bruce Wayne's immense wealth, which could be classed as a superpower since it grants him greater ability than others around him. Throughout *Batman Begins* and *The Dark Knight*, there are references to Bruce's (Christian Bale) wealth which mark him out from the other inhabitants of Gotham. In *Batman Begins*, Alfred (Michael Caine) remarks that billionaires "buy things that are not for sale," and in a later scene Bruce calmly purchases a hotel. In *The Dark Knight*, upon meeting Rachel Dawes (Maggie Gyllenhaal) and Harvey Dent (Aaron Eckhart) in a restaurant, he suggests that a couple of tables are put together, which will be allowed because: "I own the place." Bruce's wealth and, crucially, his *flaunting* of this wealth, serve to mark him out as having an extraordinary nature. Interestingly, though, he uses his flamboyant spending to present himself as a playboy, devoid of responsibility and anything but heroic. This forms a development of Reynolds' definition, who views the non-super identity as mundane. Bruce Wayne, like Batman, *is* unusual, but in a manner that is the opposite of the Caped Crusader. More significantly for the purposes of the current essay, his wealth serves to facilitate his other key resources: his skills and his devices. These resources form some of the generic borrowings that constitute the superhero film.

As the only film to devote in-depth attention to the origin of Batman, *Batman Begins* draws on a number of generic tropes and features. The resources employed by Batman noted above are a major part of this. The first act of *Batman Begins* concerns Bruce Wayne's training in an unnamed Eastern country with the League of Shadows, a self-styled group of vigilante ninjas who punish crime and corruption around the world. The training montage echoes sports and martial arts films, in which a young apprentice must learn the skills necessary to become a warrior. While Bruce demonstrates initial skill and ability, his training transforms him into a combatant worthy of the League of Shadows, much as the Bride (Uma Thurman) in the highly referential *Kill Bill* (2004) learns from a great martial arts master. Within superhero films, a montage featuring the superhero practicing his (or her) new abilities is common, such as the sequence of practice web-spinning in *Spider-Man* (2002). *Batman Begins'* training sequence, however, echoes the famous training montage in *Rocky* (1976), as well as martial arts sequences in such films as *Snake in Eagle's Shadow* (1978), *Drunken Master* (1978), *Prodigal Son* (1981) and *Young Master* (1980), or American films like *The Karate Kid* (1984) and *Kill Bill*.

Another trope of the martial arts film is that a highly trained individual can overcome many lesser or poorly trained opponents, with one-man-assaults upon entire gangs appearing in films from *Enter the Dragon* (1973) to *Oldboy* (2003). This is also a common trope of the Hollywood action film, particularly the "hard body" films of the 1980s such as *Rambo: First Blood Part II* (1985) and *Commando* (1985),[1] in which a single highly-trained individual is able to eradicate a gang or even a small army. Similarly in *Batman Begins* and *The Dark Knight* (as well as earlier Batman films and other superhero films like *Daredevil*), Batman's superior skills in unarmed combat enable him to triumph over superior numbers. Much like the action films mentioned above, action sequences are a key trope and pleasure of the superhero film, so this subgenre is another influence on the superhero genre. In the films under discussion here, Hollywood action cinema and martial arts films are combined in the formation of the (super) heroic figure of Batman.

Another key feature of Batman is the various devices and gadgets that he uses as part of his arsenal. Throughout the character's history, inventions and gadgets have been central to his secret identity.[2] Once again, *Batman Begins* provides considerable detail about the invention of these weapons, such as explosive pellets, body armor, gliding equipment and the Batmobile. This aspect of Batman borrows from the spy thriller, such as James Bond and the *Mission: Impossible* film franchise, as the equipment allows Batman to perform remarkable feats such as mapping entire buildings through sonar in *The Dark Knight*. The source for these various devices is the Applied Sciences division of Wayne Enterprises, a series of prototypes that Bruce procures for his own use, none of which are presented as especially far-fetched. Batman's body armor is protective, but not impregnable. The Batmobile is a tumbler designed for military operations, hence its heavy armor and tank-like appearance. More significant is the creative intelligence behind these devices: rather than being the brain children of Bruce and Alfred, the various devices that Batman uses are a result of the technical engineering skills of Lucius Fox (Morgan Freeman). Although Fox is a character from the comic books, his narrative role as equipment master and armorer to the Caped Crusader is unique to these recent films. The tools Fox prepares for Batman are strongly reminiscent of the gadgets prepared in the James Bond franchise by Q for agent 007. Across the Bond saga, from *Goldfinger* (1964) to *Die Another Day* (2002), a staple of the series is a scene in which Q instructs Bond on the use of various devices, from a wrist-mounted dart launcher in *Moonraker* (1979) to a souped-up BMW in *Goldeneye* (1995).[3] Similarly, Fox guides Bruce through the use of the tumbler in *Batman Begins*, and devises a sky-hook to enable him to get aboard an in-flight plane in *The Dark Knight*.[4] So arguably, this superhero franchise borrows heavily from the spy film genre and the action film, as well as the sports and martial arts film, to create a character with multiple reference points and even homages.

The capabilities of Batman are part of the character, but as Henri Ducard (Liam Neeson) tells Bruce Wayne, "The training is nothing! The will is everything!" Batman's desire, and indeed that of many superheroes, to right great wrongs is a common generic trope, as is the tragic loss of parents. In Bruce's case, he saw his parents murdered in front of him. Spider-Man/Peter Parker is present for the death of his uncle and blames himself for the event, while Superman's entire race and planet are destroyed. In the case of Batman especially, revenge is a motivating factor, revenge being a generic trope that stretches back through media at least as far as Ancient Greece. Within film, it is especially common in the Western, as an individual removes the evil influence of murderous cowboys and corrupt landowners. Often this figure is motivated by revenge, such as in *Stagecoach* (1939), *Winchester '73* (1950) and *The Tall T* (1957). The conceit of the lone avenger, driven by revenge and with no fear of death, percolates from the Old West into the similarly lawless land of the city with an inadequate or corrupt police force.

The symbol is another trope that can be linked to the Western genre. In his distinctive cowl and cape, Batman is not so much a man as a representation: upon his return to Gotham City, Bruce comments that he intends to become an "incorruptible" symbol. Much as the Western hero sports a hat and (often) a distinctive weapon that makes him a symbol of the Wild West, Batman's unique attire creates a symbol that opposes evil and injustice. A badge is of no more use in Gotham than in the frontier towns of *High Noon* (1952) or *The Man Who Shot Liberty Valance* (1962), but Batman lays down his own kind of law with the fear that the Batsuit creates, a fear similar to the intimidation created by the Western hero's slow and deliberate stalk into the saloon. In addition, a common trope of the Western is that the hero enters the town from the great untamed wilderness, able to embody and channel the law of the wild in a town where the law of man has failed. Similarly, Bruce spends time in a wilderness, where he learns to master skills and his own fear, so that he can apply these in a place where the law is inadequate.

Not that the Western is the only genre to feature a solitary hero in a morally corrupt environment. The protagonist of the *film noir* is a similar figure, often a private eye or small-time criminal who finds that the only one he can trust is himself. More overtly, the environment of *film noir* is a clear influence upon Batman with overwhelming structures, shadowy streets and social amorality. Christopher Nolan's preferred cinematographer, Wally Pfister, makes good use of the location shooting in Chicago, drawing out deep shades of color and shadow while production designer Nathan Crowley creates both ultra-modern, yet emotionally barren offices, as well as a sinister docklands known as the Narrows. This environment is particularly *noir*-ish, as Paul Schrader (229–242) identifies docks as a frequented space in the *film noir*. Much as Humphrey Bogart's Sam Spade and Philip Marlowe adhere to their own codes of honor despite the untrustworthy environments of, respectively, *The Maltese Falcon* (1941) and *The Big Sleep* (1944), so Batman adheres to his own quest for justice, restricted only by the rule that he will not kill.

The *film noir* has been classed as "a type of crime film" (Jason Holt 24). Crime is clearly a major influence in the Batman world, otherwise the caped crusader would not be necessary. The crime film is less of an influence upon Batman than some of the genres noted above, because the main focus of gangster films like *The Asphalt Jungle* (1950), *The Godfather* (1972), *Goodfellas* (1990) and *The Departed* (2006) is the inner workings of criminal institutions. Nonetheless, criminal organizations are present in Batman. While hyperbolic villains such as the Scarecrow (Cillian Murphy) and the Joker (Heath Ledger) exert major influences in *Batman Begins* and *The Dark Knight*, organized crime syndicates are also important, as the Scarecrow works for Carmine Falcone (Tom Wilkinson) and the Joker surpasses the syndicate of Salvatore Maroni (Eric Roberts). Interestingly, the language used in reference to Maroni's organization by District Attorney Harvey Dent is "the Maroni family," playing upon audience understanding of mob films in which a criminal organization is also a family business.

The police procedural such as *Heat* (1995), *Mystic River* (2003) and *Chinatown* (1974) also shows its influence, as do detective TV shows such as *CSI: Crime Scene Investigation* (CBS, 2000–present) and *Without a Trace* (CBS, 2002–2009), as Batman's detective abilities and forensic equipment receive attention especially in *The Dark Knight*. *CSI*-esque close-ups of Batman's equipment for uncovering fingerprints and testing ballistics once again play upon audience understanding and expectations for crime fighters—in the new millennium, simply busting heads is not enough; the hero needs the credibility of science and technology to be legitimate.

Interestingly, *The Dark Knight* has been compared to a "serious" crime film, having more in common with *Heat* than *Spider-Man* or *Iron Man* (2008). Indeed, more than any other film with comic book inspiration, *The Dark Knight* has been described as *something more than a superhero film*. Roger Ebert (2008) of the *Chicago Sun-Times* refers to the film as "an engrossing tragedy," Peter Travers (2008) of *Rolling Stone* describes it as "a potent provocation decked out as a comic-book movie" and Kenneth Turan (2008) of the *Los Angeles Times* hails it as "A chance to disturb us in the ways these kinds of movies rarely do." The areas identified by these critics which give the film its seemingly "non-superhero" qualities complicate the idea of the superhero film as a genre with sealed borders.

A significant feature of both *The Dark Knight* and *Batman Begins* is an engagement with political issues that might be expected in "serious" films like *Syriana* (2005) and *Munich* (2005), but would be out of place in a light-hearted summer blockbuster. The Batman films of the 1980s and 1990s had no such engagement, nor is it apparent in other recent superhero films such as those of the Spider-Man and Fantastic Four franchises. The presence of these issues are in contrast to predictions made about Batman at the turn of the millennium. In his comprehensive history *Batman Unmasked*, published in 2000, Will Brooker speculates on what form Batman might take in the 21st century. With reference to developments in DC's comic book line, Brooker suggests that Batman will be less "lonely avenger and more like the boss of a well-honed outfit" (319), and that the Caped Crusader's adventures would incorporate the light touch of the 1960s television series into its mythos. Brooker could not have predicted the terrible events of September 11, 2001, the responses to those events, the debates that would follow, and the presence of those debates within popular culture. Prominent among those debates is the tension between national security and civil liberties. The Batman films of the new millennium both participate in this debate.

However, this participation is not overt. Unlike other contemporary blockbusters like *The Kingdom* (2006) and *Transformers* (2007), neither *Batman Begins* nor *The Dark Knight* make direct reference to 9/11 or the conflicts in Afghanistan and Iraq, but they do make oblique references to the War on Terror through the America that is represented by Gotham City. These references can be found in the films' narrative and stylistic devices. In *Batman Begins*, Gotham is threatened and almost destroyed by the foreign enemy Ra's Al Ghul. Ra's Al Ghul has a fanatical belief in his righteousness, and uses a form of public transportation, Gotham's elevated train, to perform his act of terrorization. Similarly, in *The Dark Knight*, the Joker instills mass panic through assassinations and bombing. Neither of these supervillains actually creates Gotham's fear; they simply capitalize upon a state of fear that already exists. The fearful state of the city "hails" the viewer and inserts us into its symbolic design (Flanagan 139–140). In this way, Gotham City serves as a metaphor for post–9/11 America, reeling from a severe trauma. Far from being an escapist fantasy, *Batman Begins* and *The Dark Knight* identify and capitalize on contemporary fears about terrorism, exploiting and manipulating the (perceived) fear of the audience. Popular and critical responses indicate that, in some cases, this perception was correct.[5]

This engagement with contemporary socio-political events is unusual for

Batman, whose character has remained largely apolitical throughout his history. Brooker notes that in the early 1940s, while other comic book superheroes like Superman and Captain America were fighting the Nazis, Batman remained committed to his domestic war on crime. Similarly, during the Vietnam conflict, problems in Asia did not appear in either the TV series or the comic books. But much as the "patriotic icon" (Reynolds 75) Captain America was adjusted in the 1970s following the Watergate scandal into a non-nationalist figure, so did Nolan and his co-writers David S. Goyer and Jonathan Nolan respond to popular debate about responses to terrorist attacks, and presented the cinematic Batman of the 21st century as a *post-traumatic hero*. Gotham itself is portrayed as a city overcome with crime, corruption and apathy. Whereas in Tim Burton's *Batman* (1989), Gotham's administration is presented as corrupt through individual police officers such as Lieutenant Eckhardt (William Hootkins), the Gotham of *Batman Begins* is far worse, described by Ra's Al Ghul as "a breeding ground for suffering and injustice. It is beyond saving and must be allowed to die." The inhabitants of Gotham do not quell the suffering and injustice because of their apathy — apathy that they have been traumatized into by the mass corruption and injustice of organized crime. There may not have been a direct terrorist attack, but the citizens are so overwhelmed that the seemingly one good cop in the city comments that in "a town this bad, [there's no one] left to rat to."

## Liminal Heroism

Gotham's favorite son is the epitome of this traumatized community. Throughout the character's history, the motivation to create Batman has always been the murder of his parents when he was a child, but in *Batman Begins*, an earlier trauma is shown. In the opening scene of the film, the young Bruce falls into a cavern, where he is attacked by a swarm of bats. At an opera, the performers' costumes remind him of the bats and he begs to leave, and it is in the alley outside that his parents are murdered. The guilt exacerbates Bruce's trauma and his fear of bats remains until he decides to use it to his own advantage. An outright quest for vengeance would be anarchic, and indeed Bruce resolves to kill the man responsible for his parents' death in an act of revenge outside any notion of the law. Yet when his act of revenge is thwarted by the killer being murdered by someone else, Bruce maintains his desire, but shapes it into something that does not disregard the criminal justice system. Batman, therefore, is created in the *liminal* space between justice and anarchy. His crusade, however, does not end the state of fear; indeed Gotham's fear is escalated. As he tries to combat the terror tactics of the Joker, Batman becomes increasingly *oppressive* as he also escalates his methods. He becomes part of the establishment and, as part of it, problematizes the superhero role and the genre.

Over the history of comic books, the role of the superhero has been well-developed. Martin Flanagan (138) discusses heroism as "following a classic arc within American culture where the attainment of agency is linked to the assumption of power, self-mastery, and the acceptance of a singular heroic destiny." The "heroic destiny" can also be read as a form of civic duty; superheroes doing what they can for their country. Although Batman began as a vicious punisher of criminals, Brooker (65) notes that in the 1940s Batman's war was amended from personal vendetta to "patriotic duty." The crusade of the superhero is in the service of "a natural, unquestionable justice" (op. cit. 142), which the hero recognizes as "the right thing to do." The simplicity of this ideology is questioned in postmodern interpretations of the superhero mythos, such as *Watchmen* and *Heroes*, but it has also been re-evaluated in relation to Batman.

Graphic novels such as Frank Miller's *The Dark Knight Returns* and Alan Moore's *The Killing Joke* served as references for *Batman Begins* and *The Dark Knight*, and these texts question the straightforward righteousness of the Caped Crusader. In particular, *The Killing Joke* suggests that Batman and the Joker are not dissimilar, while in *The Dark Knight Returns*, Batman looks upon Harvey Two-Face and sees "a reflection" (Miller 47). Similarly, the Batman portrayed by Christian Bale occupies an interesting liminal space between heroic idealism and a disturbing reality.

The reality that Batman comes to face is one of his own making. Reynolds argues that the superhero is largely passive within individual adventures, and that the propulsion of the narrative in a comic book, as well as Tim Burton's earlier *Batman* (1989), is the villain: "The common outcome, as far as the structure of the plot is concerned, is that the villains are concerned with change and the heroes with the maintenance of the status quo" (Reynolds 51). However, the status quo of Gotham City is one of crime, corruption and injustice, which Batman seeks to change. It is Batman himself who propels the narrative of *Batman Begins* through his opposition of criminals like Carmine Falcone and Doctor Jonathan Crane (Cillian Murphy). This interventionist approach is a form of political centrism, combining individual efforts with public institutions. Bruce Wayne is an individual who contributes to public welfare, for the purpose of building faith in institutions like the criminal justice system. He demonstrates a belief in community, as he determines to "show people their city doesn't belong to the criminal and the corrupt." In this way, the political dimension of the superhero comes into relief, and shows a problematization of the revenge narrative that is played out in Batman's arc.

Tim Burton's *Batman* utilized a straightforward revenge narrative by linking Bruce Wayne/Batman (Michael Keaton) and Jack Napier/the Joker (Jack Nicholson) together: as a young man, Napier killed Bruce Wayne's parents; Bruce created the persona of Batman to fight crime, he dropped Napier into a vat of acid which bleached Napier's skin white and drove him insane; Batman subsequently discovers that the Joker was behind his parents' murder and eventually kills him. Revenge serves therefore as a overt narrative in Burton's film.

Nolan does not allow such tit-for-tat. In *Batman Begins*, the street criminal who kills Bruce's parents, Joe Chill (Richard Brake), is arrested and convicted, then years later is eligible for parole. Bruce resolves to kill him but is beaten to it by an operative of crime boss Carmine Falcone. During his training with Henri Ducard, Bruce mentions that revenge is of no use to him, though it is hard not to read a vengeful desire into his wish to combat criminals. But throughout *Batman Begins*, Bruce demonstrates that Batman is to *assist* the criminal justice system rather than replace it.

Bruce's liberal interventionism is shown to have precedent. Upon inspecting the cavern beneath Wayne Manor, Bruce learns that his great-great grandfather assisted in transporting slaves to the north during the Civil War. So Bruce's engagement with public service, in an illegal capacity, continues his family's commitment to a "natural, unquestionable justice" beyond laws. But while Batman acts outside the law, he does not place himself above it. He may interfere with crime, but criminals are then left for the justice system. This suggests that, in the films, laws are not ineffectual, but inadequately enforced. Bruce's centrist position is also part of Batman's liminality — he performs illegal acts of vigilante violence and surveillance, but does so in order to assist rather than replace the justice system. The liberal interventionism of Batman however is problematized by his notion of overarching justice, which could be seen as dictatorial. Batman's liminal state places him as both performing a public service and dictating morality. *Batman Begins* emphasizes Batman's public service, in contrast to the dictatorial position of Ra's Al Ghul and the League of Shadows.

Bruce is trained and schooled by the League of Shadows, specifically Ducard, but rebels when instructed to execute a murderer. He declares he will not be an executioner, but more significantly he will not be a judge, as Ra's Al Ghul has declared himself. The League of Shadows determines to destroy Gotham City by unleashing a panic-inducing toxin that will drive its citizens to a mass panic. This terrorization, which will lead to anarchy, is a dictatorial perspective on morality and condemnation of a place that does not reach a standard set by a self-defined elite, and the measure taken by the League of Shadows is a form of mass execution. Despite his crusade against injustice, Bruce maintains his belief in intervention and assistance rather than condemnation and judgment

It is through his liminal status that Batman is able to thwart the League of Shadows. He has fought against injustice and corruption in Gotham, but only to give the police and the District Attorney's office a helping hand. He bends the law in order to help it, demonstrating individual intervention with faith in public services. Similarly, he can use the training he learned from the League of Shadows to fight them, but needs the help of Sergeant Jim Gordon

(Gary Oldman) in order to defeat them. Batman opposes injustice, but not to eradicate those associated with it. The League of Shadows operate on a fanatical level that punishes everyone. Gotham's justice system is either corrupted or ineffectual. Alone, Batman would either be just "some asshole in a costume," as Commissioner Loeb (Colin McFarlane) describes him, or a fanatic like Ra's Al Ghul. It is through *liminality* that Batman is able to save Gotham: he must use his ninja training *and* work with the police. Despite his appearance as a lone hero, Batman is only effective in a cooperative capacity. Once again, this draws upon Westerns, as the lone hero often cleans up the town, and then lets the police and the other public officers worry about how to run it. Like these lone heroes, Batman is not a part of the institutions of law and order, and his separation is crucial to his heroism. Once Batman becomes more closely involved with the state, his heroism is compromised.

In addition, Bruce's locations reinforce his liminality; Wayne Manor is within the jurisdiction of Gotham but on the outskirts of the city as Batman is on the borders of society. Flanagan comments on liminal spaces in the comic book films *Spider-Man* and *Ghost World*, in which bedrooms appear as liminal spaces that are significant in the development of the characters. In *Batman Begins*, the liminal space is broader than the bedroom, as Wayne Manor serves as a space in which Bruce can be renewed. Upon his return to Gotham after his time with the League of Shadows, Bruce visits the cave that he fell into as a child. Far underground, he disturbs a swarm of bats, and in a primal scene, he stands surrounded by the flying mammals, embracing the fear that has haunted him. The cave is a "threshold" in the Bakhtinian sense: a space where "one is renewed or perishes" (Flanagan 290). Bruce is renewed as he subsequently builds and stores the Batsuit and his other equipment in the cave.

When the League of Shadows invades Wayne Manor and burns it to the ground, Bruce and Alfred escape via an elevator into the cave as the house collapses above them. Bruce loses hope, blaming himself for the destruction, but Alfred persuades him to endure. Once again, Bruce is renewed in the cave. On several occasions during the film, he is shown donning the Batsuit and gathering his equipment. These scenes emphasize the transition that must be made, with a sequence of shots of the cowl, gloves, utility belt, batarangs and explosive pellets, as well as the Batmobile. In addition, the cave is never brightly lit, even though Bruce rigs lights. Batman is created in a place of shadow, neither dark nor light but the twilight between them.

The film presents Batman's construction between the home and the city, the liminal physical space that is the source of Batman, an identity that is itself created in a liminal space between justice and anarchy. The significance of the cave can be discussed in philosophical terms, such as a version of Socrates' cave, and psychoanalytically as a return to a womb-like state. For these purposes, the actual physical space of the cave is important, as it is where Bruce re-creates himself as Batman. In Gotham itself, Batman is always transient, moving through alleyways, rooftops and docks. His final confrontation with Ducard takes place aboard Gotham's elevated train, a space of transition that must not reach its destination. It is from exclusively liminal spaces that Batman performs his heroic duty.

Generically, the scenes in the liminal space express a key feature of the superhero film. By putting on a costume, especially in a liminal space, the superhero becomes somebody else. In this respect, the superhero film establishes something distinctive. An obvious piece of iconography here is the costume, as the hero must don it in order to be heroic, literally assuming the mantle of the hero. Even superheroes who do not have secret identities, such as the Fantastic Four, still wear their costumes for their heroics. Amusingly, in *Hancock*  (2008), when the eponymous alcoholic anti-hero (Will Smith) tries to become more of a hero, a key aspect to his being accepted as such is when he puts on a costume! Moreover, the importance of a "headquarters" space to Batman is a common feature of superheroes— the bedrooms mentioned by Flanagan, Daredevil's hidden lockers, the Fantastic Four's Baxter Building, Iron Man's workshop — all constitute special spaces for these heroes, where the characters are both their "normal" and "super" identities. Outside these spaces, they can only be one or the other, but within the space, the "regular" and "super" identities can both exist. This makes the HQ space liminal, a space between ordinary and extraordinary in which the person who is Bruce Wayne *and* Batman *can be both*, since it is unnecessary for him to wear his costume here, yet he still does the work of a crimefighter.

The significance of such a space points to another key feature of the superhero. All superheroes must occupy both the "normal" world and the "super" world; indeed a common source of tension within superhero narratives is exactly the clash between these two worlds. Bruce Banner seeks to be a normal scientist due to the terrifying and dangerous nature of the Hulk. Peter Parker must balance the exploits of Spider-Man with his own need to support himself as a jobbing photographer and university student. And while Bruce Wayne may yearn to hang up the Batsuit so as to be with the woman he loves, Rachel Dawes, Rachel warns Bruce not to regard her as his "last hope for a normal life." Bruce's desire for normalcy is in direct conflict with what he regards as his duty to help Gotham, and it is in the liminal space of the Batcave in *Batman Begins* and an underground bunker in *The Dark Knight*, that he can actually vent this conflict.

*The Dark Knight* features other spaces, however, which compromise Batman's liminality and, consequently, his heroism. While Wayne Manor is under repair, Bruce inhabits a penthouse apartment in the center of Gotham, but barely uses his bedroom. This may indicate Bruce's maturation — he no longer lives in a family home but has established his own space. Similarly, Bruce participates in the running of Wayne Enterprises. These changes in space and environment express Bruce Wayne's movement to a position within the establishment, and the same is true of Batman.

While Batman is officially listed by the Gotham Police Department as an outlaw who is to be "arrested on sight," he actually works with the law officers of Gotham, particularly Jim Gordon and Harvey Dent. The longevity of the Batman comic book line has necessitated an engagement between the vigilante figure and the forces of law and order in Gotham City. Tony Spanakos (65–69) argues that the "The Real Dynamic Duo [are] Batman and Gordon," and indeed this relationship has not only remained key throughout Batman's history, but receives close attention in the films under discussion here. After recruiting Gordon as an ally, Batman meets with the police officer to discuss strategy, and in *The Dark Knight*, Harvey Dent joins their meeting. The rooftop sequence featuring the three of them is characterized by a circular pan, which captures the three figures of crime fighting, as well as the tensions between them. Dent is presented as an idealist, demanding that everything should be done perfectly. Gordon is a pragmatist, working with what he has. And Batman, the "hero," is an extremist, doing whatever is necessary. By presenting Batman as part of this group, and the deal that is struck between them, Batman has become part of the establishment. Despite the official policy towards him, in this scene he is effectively deputized by the state.

The deal itself, however, is questionable. The three men discuss Chin Lau (Chin Han), a Chinese banker who is the accountant for the crime syndicates of Gotham. Lau has retreated to Hong Kong, outside Dent's jurisdiction, and Batman agrees to bring him back. The clandestine nature of the rooftop meeting, the lack of questions from Dent and Gordon, and Batman's violent kidnapping of Lau in Hong Kong present state acquiescence to illegal activities. Recent studies by Stephen Eric Bronner (2005), Alan Wolfe (2006) and Wheeler Winston Dixon (2004) discuss in detail the "constricting of civil liberties under the guise of security" (Bronner 11). The justification for the curtailment of liberties is security against the threat of terrorism, as the rights of "U.S. citizens [were] seriously eroded by the Patriot Act, signed into law a mere six weeks after the attacks of September 11" (Dixon 2). Similarly, Batman commits further questionable acts as an unofficial part of the criminal justice system of Gotham.

Lau is part of organized crime, enemies of the state that Batman opposes and weakens. In a literal sense, Batman is a terrorist, performing acts of violence and intimidation which provoke fear among the crime syndicates. When the Batmobile first appears in *The Dark Knight*, it is set on an automatic mode designated as "intimidate." The Joker observes that the crime bosses of Gotham are afraid to meet in daylight, and he calls their council of war "group therapy meetings." The fear toxin spread by the League of Shadows would create mass panic and anarchy, but although Batman prevents this occurrence and uses his methods more sparingly, he has created a mood of fear among the criminal community. While Batman is a force of anarchy that is carefully channeled, the far more anarchic figure of the Joker arises in response to this mood of fear.

Previous studies of the Joker have discussed him in psychological or philosophical terms (Robichaud 70–81). In terms of political ideology, the Joker of *The Dark Knight* is coded as a manifestation of chaos, anarchy and terrorism in several ways. Unlike previous incarnations of the character, such as in the comic books and Jack Nicholson's 1989 portrayal, Heath Ledger's Joker does not have white-bleached skin — he simply wears make-up, or "war paint" as one henchman describes him. Therefore, he is a social product rather than an accidental victim of science. Nor does he have any identity beyond "The Joker" — no name or identifying features exist. He is described by Alfred as a man who "wants to watch the world burn," and the Joker declares himself to be "an agent of chaos." Harvey Dent defines the Joker as a "terrorist" during a press conference, and insists that terrorist demands should not be acquiesced to.

Unlike the fanatical Ra's Al Ghul, however, the Joker is not a threat from outside. He explains that his presence in Gotham is due to the Batman. Batman has traumatized the criminal fraternity just as a criminal act traumatized him, and from this traumatized community has emerged a chaotic and anarchic figure. The Joker states that Gotham deserves "a better class of criminal" — an ideological criminal to complement the ideological hero of Batman. Both are extremists — Batman in terms of law enforcement, the Joker in terms of chaos. The Joker is initially liminal — able to work with the mob bosses as well as robbing them, but eventually takes over organized crime completely and provokes panic throughout Gotham simply through suggestion. Both these characters are post-traumatic figures that perpetuate fear through terrorization. They begin as liminal figures, but as events escalate they become the establishment. Unlike the "tabula rasa" concept of the superhero (Flanagan 149), Batman's actions are not simply applied and then withdrawn — this War on Terror creates further terror, and, in response, Batman becomes more oppressive.

When the Joker is arrested and brought into a police interview room, he is initially questioned by Gordon, but this proves ineffective, so Batman takes over the interrogation, which includes torture. Once again, the space of the confrontation between Batman and the Joker is significant. The police interview room is within the establishment, and Batman is doing what the police will not, yet with Gordon's approval. As the lights in the room are turned on, Batman literally appears out of the shadows. In *Batman Begins* he appeared in the shadowed location of the Batcave, but here he is in a brightly lit room within a police station. Therefore, the torture that he performs on the Joker is part of the establishment as well. When the Joker does reveal the location of his prisoners, there is no attempt to apprehend Batman, as the police immediately act on the information that has been obtained. Torture, it seems, is a legitimate form of questioning, as suggested by reports from Abu Ghraib, Guantanamo, and "'rendered' detainees" (Wolfe 160).

Batman's presence in the establishment that includes Gordon and Dent has led to the disregard of civil liberties. While it could be argued that torture is legitimate when lives are at stake and that the Joker deserves what he gets, torture in *The Dark Knight* is not presented in a positive light. Batman loses his usual tight control and his effectiveness as he roars and strikes his prisoner in frustrated impotence. Meanwhile, the Joker laughs mockingly, cackling at Batman "You have *nothing* to threaten me with!" The torture is also useless, as Batman and Gordon both do exactly as the Joker has manipulated them. As a result, Rachel Dawes is killed, Harvey Dent is hideously disfigured and the Joker escapes to wreak further havoc on Gotham.

The Joker's violence begets yet more, as Batman escalates his war on him. In order to find the Joker and Harvey, Batman uses a form of sonar omni-surveillance, which Lucius describes as "unethical," "dangerous" and "wrong." Once again, it seems, desperate times call for desperate measures, and spying on 30 million people is legitimate when fighting terrorism. From a liminal and centrist position, Batman has helped create a right-wing dictatorship that compromises liberties. The film's attitude to the sonar is ambivalent: it does allow Batman to stop the Joker from blowing up two passenger ferries, but even Batman acknowledges that the surveillance device must not continue. As a tool, it would be useful for further crime fighting, but its perpetuation will maintain the dictatorship. Batman entrusts Lucius to destroy the device, ensuring that freedom is restored.

The usefulness of the sonar surveillance is questionable, however, as Harvey Two-Face murders five people and kidnaps Gordon's family. Violence in Gotham breeds more violence from within, as over the course of the two films, the threat to the city becomes more internalized. The foreign threat of the League of Shadows is replaced with the domestic threat of the Joker, who is a response to the domestic defense that is Batman. When Batman becomes part of the establishment, the Joker responds by driving Harvey mad — and the dictatorship takes on a murderous quest for revenge. The film demonstrates that the extreme tactics of Batman and Two-Face in the pursuit of injustice are themselves injustices. The Other becomes familiar and the familiar becomes grotesque, as demonstrated by Harvey's mutilated face. Batman himself has also become ethically grotesque through his actions of torture and omni-surveillance: by joining the establishment he has compromised his heroism.

The perversion of Batman in this case points to what may be the most important element of superheroism: *Batman is only heroic when he is liminal.* This concern appears in other superhero films. When Spider-Man is accepted by New York in *Spider-Man 3* (2007), he becomes insensitive and arrogant and subsequently brutal and cruel. In *Iron Man 2* (2010), Tony Stark (Robert Downey, Jr.) refuses to allow military access to the Iron Man suit as (in his eyes) it is too dangerous for the state to have control of, while in *The Incredible Hulk* (2008), Bruce Banner (Edward Norton) fears that the military will use the Hulk as a weapon. Superheroism necessitates *distance* from others, an at-best *transient* connection to the society which the heroes protect. This is distinct for the *super*hero; — John McClane can go home with his wife after saving her from the terrorists, Indiana Jones goes back to the university where he teaches, leading to the conclusion that their heroic adventures are an aberration — at least until the next film in the franchise. But for Batman, Spider-Man, and Superman, among others, heroics are the norm. It is therefore essential that they are "super" or, as Bruce Wayne puts it, "Batman has no limits" — the regime of crime fighting and disaster prevention would be too much for a "normal" person.

Here again *The Dark Knight* expands the boundaries of the superhero film by problematizing the essential liminality of the hero. By becoming part of the establishment, Batman has ceased to be a hero, as indeed he observes: "You either die a hero, or you live long enough to see yourself become the villain." Heroism, it seems, needs to be brief, perhaps as it occupies liminal spaces that become incorporated into the establishment. The extreme becomes normal, and in the case of *The Dark Knight*, an oppressive dictatorship is formed.

Batman cannot win his battle through force, but he can through a return to liminality. Rather than delivering the final judgment of execution, he defeats and captures the Joker *so that the police can arrest him*. While he was willing to resort to torture and omni-surveillance, execution would be the final act of the Batman dictatorship. Instead, Batman returns to his original endeavor — helping the police through the super abilities facilitated by his training and equipment. The Joker's assessment of Batman as "incorruptible" may be going too far: as part of the establishment he became corrupted by desperation. Rather than acting as a panacea to Batman's transgressions, saving the Joker signals his return to a liminal state, which is completed when he tells Gordon to report that Batman committed the crimes of Harvey Two-Face. Batman acknowledges that his actions have gone too far: as part of the establishment with Harvey and Gordon, the justice system became brutal and oppressive. Consequently, rather than remaining a hero who facilitates brutality, Batman takes the blame for Harvey's crimes, and in doing so takes responsibility for his own *actions*. Batman created the dictatorship, and by taking the blame, he allows it to collapse, so that the ideal of justice can survive. He, Gordon and Harvey all serve this ideal, but Batman compromised it by joining the establishment. To become a hero again, he must return to the borders.

## Conclusion

Borders are the place for superheroes, who by virtue of what is different about them do not fit into the societies that they protect. Their greater capabilities make them too different, hence the "normal" lives that writers and filmmakers devise for them. From the borders of society, they can watch and protect, but never truly share it. When they do, heroism becomes compromised. More than superpowers, costumes and equipment, the defining feature of the superhero and the superhero genre is the liminal state: superheroes *must* remain on the borders. The various generic borrowings from the spy film, the martial arts adventure and the action film, the Western and the *film noir*, are also combined in a liminal space. These borders are the subject of scrutiny in *Batman Begins* and *The Dark Knight*, as the liminal spaces appear as places of birth, re-birth and maintenance, and a loss of liminality leads to a loss of heroism. Only in a liminal state can super-heroics be maintained — once the hero joins the establishment, he may still be super, but he is no longer a hero.

At the conclusion of *The Dark Knight*, Batman returns to the liminal space of heroism. The right-wing dictatorship dies so that the people of Gotham can have their faith in justice and decency restored, even though the faith is based upon the untruth of Harvey Dent's nobility. Such compromise problematizes the "natural, unquestionable justice" favored by superhero narratives. Justice has been politicized and problematized, and neither the idealism of Dent nor the dictatorship of Batman can continue. What is left is the moderate position of Commissioner Gordon. He will uphold the ideals of Harvey Dent, pursue the renegade Batman, and do the best he can. A moderate position is where the film concludes, with Harvey eulogized as Gotham's "knight, shining," and Batman consigned to the shadows as "a watchful protector, a silent guardian." Indeed, it is Batman's return to the liminal borders that ensures Gotham does not enter an even darker night.

## Notes

1. For much more on this genre, see Yvonne Tasker. *Spectacular Bodies: Gender, Genre, and the Action Cinema*. London: Routledge, 1993.

2. See Will Brooker. *Batman Unmasked*. New York, London: Continuum, 2000. 37–39.

3. Q does not make an appearance in the most recent Bond films, *Casino Royale* (2006) and *Quantum of Solace* (2008), as these recent films have a greater emphasis on "realism" than gadgetry. Despite the approach of Nolan to keep the Batman films grounded in reality, there is a greater element of the fantastic in these films than the recent direction of the Bond franchise.

4. Interestingly, Christopher Nolan's post–*The Dark Knight* project, *Inception* (2010), heavily references the Bond film *On Her Majesty's Secret Service* (1969), and in the promotion of that film, Nolan indicated an interest in directing a Bond film. See Tim Masters. "*Inception* influenced by 007, says Christopher Nolan." *bbc.co.uk*. 9 July 2010. Web. 3 Oct. 2010. <www.bbc.co.uk/news/10562808>.

5. The majority of the reviews posted by imdb users did not view *The Dark Knight* as another superhero blockbuster, but acknowledged the film's realistic depictions, its examination of anarchy and fear and finally considered Nolan's effort a true masterpiece. For instance, user de191 believes that *The Dark Knight* is a phenomenal piece of art, "an epic crime saga," which "deserves to be mentioned in the same sentence with "Good-Fells," "Heat," "The Untouchables" and even "The Godfather," while "Chilenazo" points out that it is a "spectacular and chaotically-brilliant movie." "Imdb User Reviews." (2008): n. pag. Web. 15 May 2010. <http://www.imdb.com/title/tt0468569/usercomments>.

# Super-Intertextuality and 21st Century Individualized Social Advocacy in *Spider-Man* and *Kick-Ass*

JUSTIN S. SCHUMAKER

Super-intertextuality represents a self-reflexive theoretical model evolving from the unique text-to-text relationships that start the intertextual discourse. What sets this model apart from the intertextual is its focus on and ability to evaluate elements of genre/narrative/mythic structures—a metalevel conversation evaluating structural elements of the text and its classification.[1] The model begins with an exploration into the text-to-text relationship that builds the intertext. This intertextual relationship enacts a number of conversations, and this chapter will explore the thematic intertextual line concerning the development of an individualized social advocacy within the superhero. Individualized social advocacy represents a unique desire within the superhero to willingly speak for a citizenry that cannot or will not protect themselves. What makes this conversation super-intertextual occurs as these texts take a self-reflexive approach to the thematic line followed throughout this chapter.

This theoretical model can unveil itself in a number of film genres, but its potential dominance within superhero cinema shapes significant themes and narrative moments within the texts. At the crux of the exploration within this chapter, the super-intertextual conversation enacts an examination into the development of the superhero's/superheroine's individualized social advocacy and the gendered efforts of the text to construct the coming-of-age narrative. Current scholarship rarely explores the notions of advocacy that are so entwined in the development of the superhero. Even more rare are texts that study the development of the teenage boy and girl and their acceptance of responsibilities of superheroism. In this chapter, we will examine a single significant example of super-intertextual conversation that occurs between the *Spider-Man* franchise (2002–2007) and *Kick-Ass* (2010). The *Spider-Man* franchise offers the foundational narrative which explores the masculine coming-of-age narrative and the development of individualized social advocacy — and, notably, villains alongside the heroes who try to circumvent the development of this advocacy. *Kick-Ass* offers a number of direct responses to *Spider-Man*'s narrative progression, beginning the intertextual discourse but transcending generic, mythic or structural patterns of heroic development in a self-reflexive and metafictive call. What follows this initial conversation is the super-intertextual discourse evaluating the merits of narrative and genre elements implemented across the four texts and a critical insight into the notions of superhero identity, rites of passage, and acceptance of responsibility.

There exist a number of narrative elements for super-intertextuality to decode or unravel: costuming, alternate identities, moments of super-empowerment, voiceovers, personal sacrifices, and heroic motivation. Many of these have been discussed and categorized into a taxonomy of the genre in current scholarship. The narrative patterns enacted in superhero cinema are fairly consistent, and for this chapter's exploration into the super-intertextual conversation, identity branding and the techniques contributing to gendered narration of the coming-of-age subgenre are the mythic/genre motifs, or tropes, investigated. Through these motifs, the super-intertextual conversation among the *Spider-Man* film franchise and *Kick-Ass* explores the development of the hero's individualized social advocacy. The narrative lines within the texts of the *Spider-Man* franchise offer a concrete foundational narrative where the coming-of-age narrative is central to the development of individualized social advocacy, but elements of *Kick-Ass* respond directly to the former narrative. What follows is a clarion call: a challenge to some of the inherent values being forced into the development of the individualized social advocacy.

The interactions between the films construct the concept of super-intertextuality. The foundation of this concept is rooted in Barthes' argument that all texts are "intertexts, other texts are present in it, at varying levels, in more or less recognizable forms" (39).[2] However, this chapter seeks to show that when intertextuality offers metatextual commentary on genre and mythic structures, it operates as and constructs super-intertextuality. This chapter will uncover the significant levels of a text where intertextuality occurs and what implications it can have on superhero cinema. As this application of Barthes becomes more involved, these "varying levels" of narrative will act as the "interlacing codes" of the fabric of the text, as there exist important intersections influencing the constructions of the superhero which lead the analysis toward different lines based on the sources found within the text (39). Superhero cinema repurposes these motifs in an effort to comprehend the genre's historical narrative that Barthes suggests is present in every aspect of society ("Introduction"). Since Barthes supports the pervasive nature of narratives throughout

culture and genre, it is possible that the struggle of superhero cinema to establish narrative norms may have resulted in these repeated visual weights and
spawned a metalevel commentary coursing through the body of films exhibiting
elements of super-intertextuality revealing this search for the superhero's individualized social advocacy in the new millennium.

The films' narrative strategies explore media specificity and its relationship
to Barthes' intertextuality. Jay David Bolter and Richard Grusin depict the
inclusion of media and its relationship to intertextuality in a specialized manner
with *Remediation: Understanding New Media.* As intertextuality was conceptualized and grew, it came to encompass anything around and potentially inside
of a text. However, Bolter and Grusin construct a specialized type of intertextuality with their concept of remediation, which they define as the "formal logic
by which new media refashion prior media forms" or when new encounters old
(273).[3] For Bolter and Grusin, the process outlined as remediation predominantly manifests itself as immediacy, a style determined to make the viewer
forget the media, and hypermediacy, an aesthetic effort to remind the viewer
of the various media at work within the text. However, their theories become
problematic as they slip into binary opposition, setting "old" media against
"new" media and allowing the connotations of the adjectives "old" and "new"
to influence their thought process.[4] Unfortunately, Bolter and Grusin do not
acknowledge the possibility that media can effectively incorporate another
media for the purpose of manipulating conventions for narrative and rhetorical
purposes.[5] However, in superhero cinema, "remediation" contributes to a metalevel commentary by showing how the texts borrow narrative moments from
other texts and allowing for altered methods of narration that fight against
claims of media specificity.

In an effort to come to terms with the implications of the superhero film
genre, this chapter will follow Jacques Derrida's theoretical understanding of
genre. Derrida argues for the participation of a text within a given genre as
ascribing to the parameters of the genre as set forth by others (66). For these
superhero films, the costuming of the superheroes and providing the individuals
with extraordinary — genetic or trained — abilities function as inherent textual
efforts to participate in superhero cinema. Rick Altman's *Film/Genre* explores
the complexity of genre and film. He begins to explore superhero cinema in
other genres and how it mixes with other film genres. Superhero cinema further
compounds other genres into their texts, and this chapter explores the coming-of-age subgenre within these films. Additionally, this chapter depicts the
development of the individualized social advocate as a super-intertextual component of superhero cinema's coming-of-age subgenre.

The following sections investigate the motifs appearing among the films
and building the super-intertextual discourse about the development of the
individualized social advocacy of the superhero. These motifs operate in a
similar way to the grammars that Northrop Frye suggests construct the mythic

narrative, but in this essay, these "grammars" will be repositioned within the context of super-intertextuality (135). Their implications in building advocacy are questioned as they become repurposed for different narrative effects. With super-intertextuality, these mythic readings of the genre become the subject of metalevel commentary as super-intertextuality seeks to unravel the inherent value of these mythic moments in searching for the advocacy of the individual and their relationship to the citizenry. The branding and training of the hero and the masculine narration of the text are the centerpieces for the super-intertextual discourse constructing the development of the superhero's individualized social advocacy.

## Branding and Training in the Spider-Man Films and Kick-Ass

*Spider-Man* offers a classical construction of the superhero coming-of-age film narrative by depicting the emergence of a teenage Peter Parker into adulthood throughout the course of the film franchise. The texts confront Peter's maturation with the unique ability to protect a citizenry through the use of his superpowers. By pairing these two narrative lines of boy to man and human to superhero, the coming-of-age subgenre of superhero cinema — in which the *Spider-Man* franchise participates— offers a genre space initiating the super-intertextual discourse by implementing several motifs, or tropes, building parallel narrative lines in the depiction of Peter's quest for individualized social advocacy. This super-intertextual relationship helps to uncover the handling of the mythic and generic constructs at work within the diegesis and being constructed at the shot level of the text.

Peter Parker's (Tobey Maguire) instigator for branding his alternate identity stems from a selfish motivation: he needs money to buy a car to impress Mary Jane (Kirsten Dunst) and sees an advertisement offering $3,000 for amateur wrestlers. The identity creation montage depicts a slight high-angle mid-close shot of Peter in the right half of the image with a black marker scribbling ideas on the left. The letters captured within the image remediate prototypical comic book lettering, and the images fading in and out throughout the montage are inexplicable — that is, they have unexplained diegetic origins. When the text depicts the graph paper, the image which emerge from Peter's right hand features a radioactive spider crawling across the screen from right to left. Additionally, the montage depicts dual Peters: one smiling down upon his creation through a high-angle shot in the upper left, and the other dominating the image in a state of consternation, with both appearing through high angle shots to empower the character. These shots function to justify the overstretched artistic abilities of Peter. In narrative time, the text shows Peter at different moments of identity construction. The resulting costume feels ripped from the pages of a typical *The Amazing Spider-Man* comic book, and not created by an eighteen-year-old. The text elevates Peter beyond expected notions of his own abilities to give a point of reference to his first costume. With the text exceeding the diegetic constructions of Peter Parker, the identity is less earned through his advocacy and becomes a gift from the text; the gifts of the text reappear when the costume is actually revealed through the emergence of his alternate identity. His first attempt at a costume fortuitously avoids this sense of artistic mastery, as it is a cobbled mess of a ski mask, gloves, long sleeved shirt and sweat pants, but when he dresses up to begin fighting crime and advocate for his citizenry, the text provides Peter with Spider-Man's expected attire without any sort of montage depicting its construction. This narrative builds a superhero beyond what has been present within the character to properly afford Peter with tools requisite to obtain social advocacy, and *Spider-Man* borrows a version of this identity toggling from Clark Kent and Superman.[6] This mythic/narrative trope of an alternate identity and the process of gaining it becomes a topic of conversation in *Kick-Ass* as part of the intertextual discourse that then evolves into metalevel commentary in terms of textual awareness.

*Kick-Ass* presents a recent entry into superhero cinema exploring the possibilities of superheroes in a reality reminiscent of contemporary society. It is a vulgar and violent participant within the genre, filled with moments of metalevel commentary that cannot be ignored in their contribution to super-intertextuality. This film evaluates the narrative moments and mythic tropes implemented within the *Spider-Man* franchise. *Kick-Ass* reveals the search for identity and understanding personal limitations occurring through sections of Dave's (Aaron Johnson) narrative, paralleling moments from that of Peter's coming-of-age in *Spider-Man*, but also including insightful comments upon the prototypical narrative line.

Dave's identity creation occurs under the guise of realism and his costume offers similar piecemeal construction like the first version of Peter's Spider-Man outfit. However, his process pushes Dave away from the realm of the sexual and reaffirms ideas about his socially-grounded desires (even if naively). He begins with the purchase of the costume — a bastardized scuba suit and hiking boots — and ends with the search for and birth of his alternate identity. In contrast to the prolonged artistic sequence from *Spider-Man* and professional appearance of the costume, the text places Dave in full costume in order to give a different feeling to the identity process; he knows what the visual attire will be but is unaware of any implications branding will have on this alternate persona. The sketching scene, as borrowed from *Spider-Man*, parallels an earlier scene where Dave gazes upon his teacher's breasts instead of his textbook. The scene continues to build Dave's motivations through the shifting images from the teacher bending over to a low angle shot from the hero's right shoulder onto the poorly drawn self-portrait of him in costume; block-lettering of the words

"Kick Ass" accompany the sketch. Dave goes from costume to identity in his drafting process, which reverses the process enacted by Peter. This reversal plays into the branding of the superhero; their branding will be their primary signifier to the citizenry that they seek to protect. By Dave going from costume to empowerment, he places more value on protecting the citizenry from any of society ills. Peter begins this structural process that *Kick-Ass* discusses and mocks through media-specific terms, but both texts work toward understanding the importance of their superheroes being able to toggle between branded identities and personal identities as they operate as social advocates. In *Spider-Man* and *Kick-Ass*, this trope of identity creation acts as a tool to ingratiate the audience into the process of developing an alternate persona as a need for the superhero. As they begin to uncover their individualized social advocacy and continue the maturation process from teenager to man, the alternate identity becomes a catalyst for learning lessons about the role of the individual in society. Coupled with the developments of the alternate identities, the superheroes and villains in *Spider-Man* and *Kick-Ass* go through a process of testing and exploring the capabilities of their powers.

Peter's initial engagement with his abilities depicts the majesty and delight newfound powers bring; he sprints across the rooftops bellowing with delight. His fleeting moments of fear and uncertainty occur when he first attempts to swing across a gap using his web. The text reveals Peter through a low angle enhancing the feelings of uncertainty as he searches for his limitations. At the actual moment of departure from the rooftop, the narrative disregards moments of uncertainty and presents Peter through the empowering high angle shots. There is no inherent sense of advocacy built by the testing of these powers. Peter fails to recognize any sense of commitment to the rest of society as he begins to see his skills extend beyond his previous understandings of self and his relationship, or a lack of one, to Mary Jane. The first *Spider-Man* film enacts a conversation about how the superhero's alternate identity binds with his abilities. *Kick-Ass* explicates a metalevel commentary on whether individualized social advocacy actually requires powers. This investigation then becomes an avenue to engage the spectators and their own search for individualized social advocacy as they may be in a similar situation as the characters of *Kick-Ass*.

For Dave, the testing sequences require more planning and foresight, as he possesses no superpowered gifts at this point in the narrative. He does not begin by jumping from rooftop to rooftop, but rather he opts to practice by jumping from the wall to a tire laid out to approximate the distance between rooftops. Within the mise-en-scène, the text zooms out to show the reality of the distance in comparison to the diminutive stature of Dave, reinforcing his inability. This sequence replicates the narrative spirit of *Spider-Man*, but does so in a way that continues to ground Dave's lack of abilities. However, when Dave endures his neurological shift, an additional testing sequence occurs, with his friends opting to punch and strike him with a lunch tray. They are not aware of his alternate identity, but this moment serves to show how the deadened nerve endings do offer benefits for Dave and Kick-Ass, and they appear in a lunchroom setting like where Peter's first web was slung.[7] *Kick-Ass* interacts with the tropes of *Spider-Man* to explore the unrealistic portrayal of Peter as an individual. The connection between *Spider-Man* and *Kick-Ass* underscores Dave's lack of actual superpowers. He does not need the Force for his individualized social advocacy, and it becomes a burden on a viewer to question whether they have any motivation to construct their own version of social advocacy in a post–9/11 society in a manner similar to Dave.

Within the *Spider-Man* franchise, Doctor Octopus (Alfred Molina) and Venom (Topher Grace) explore the failures associated with using powers for selfish purposes without going through a ritualized process requiring the character to come to terms with potential social requirements of their powers; the follies of rushing towards empowerment manifest within Doctor Octopus and Venom in *Spider-Man 2* and *Spider-Man 3*, respectively. Doctor Octopus appears as a man who has his family taken from him, paralleling what happens to Big Daddy (Nicolas Cage) in *Kick-Ass*, and turns to a life of crime to further his research and to obtain his revenge. His character becomes a textual response to the individualized social advocacy being developed through Peter because he attempts to take his villainous advocacy. The text depicts Doctor Octopus in this manner to show the errors associated with trying to force empowerment. Through Venom, the text creates a parallel narrative line, building upon some of the desires voiced by Peter; he similarly wants to work at the *Daily Bugle* and marry the girl of his dreams. *Spider-Man 3* positions Peter and Venom as in a binary opposition, more comparable than any of the other villains in the franchise, and uses these similarities to explore values associated with developing individualized social advocacy and trying to forcefully empower the individual. Venom's alternate persona, Edward Brock, attempts to cheat his way into his aspiration by digitally forging the photo of Spider-Man robbing the bank instead of trying to earn his position by working hard like Peter. Through the villains, the *Spider-Man* universe explores the issues with trying to forcibly obtain any form of dominance. While these villains do not explicitly engage in social advocacy, they create a model of imposing power on character that *Kick-Ass* investigates. Through Big Daddy and Hit-Girl (Chloë Grace Moretz), the difference between developing individualized social advocacy and forcing its appearance in a character becomes an essential investigation to the development of powers and the form of advocacy that can arise from this process. Big Daddy's identity becomes constructed in conjunction with the quest for vengeance that surges through most of the villains within the *Spider-Man* films and appears as an orphaned construction of Batman's visuals. His effort to transform his daughter into a social advocate to fit his selfish needs functions as a commentary on the usual villain narrative and a perversion of the familial system that so many superheroes seek to protect as part of their individualized social advocacy.

Big Daddy offers a structure around Hit-Girl that enacts a sense of empowerment, but he perverts his paternal role by molding his daughter into a pristine killing machine, which eliminates a conventional childhood. The introduction to this character primes the tonal mockery Big Daddy and Hit-Girl impart on the narrative by mixing gunshots and familial affection. The text implements an establishing shot with the characters in the upper right hand corner of a vacant lot. Mindy, or Hit-Girl, expresses her fear to her father, Big Daddy, who responds by urging her to "be a big girl." His fatherly conversation about shooting her suggests the gunshot will only hurt for a second, and he replaces her name with the affectionate moniker, "Sugar," showing the familial bond at work. This training sequence endeavors to condition her to not fear a gun by showing the effectiveness of her bullet proof vest. When he finally pulls the trigger, he cocks the gun and says, "You're gonna be fine, Baby Doll." The two characters engage in a typical father-daughter bartering scenario to finish out the training session. He wants to shoot her two more times without her flinching, and she wants ice cream and bowling. These interchanges reflect the familial element heroes want to protect, but Big Daddy has other motives and goals in mind. He empowers his daughter, and it costs her a socially normative identity. The value of that identity is moot, but she should have enough agency to develop her own individualized social advocacy through a series of events depicting the value of her protecting the citizenry. He perverts the familial network through the conditioning process; Hit-Girl's lack of fear serves as an empowering characteristic for her.

The construction of Big Daddy's need for vengeance and its motivating abilities become narrated through remediated sequences merging comic artwork with the cinematic text, and while he appears visually constructed as a mockery of Batman, his narrative fall from the regulatory role of the police force to vigilante murderer is more indicative of a villain-like Doctor Octopus, who loses his familial network and turns to a life of crime. The text uses a sequence of graphic art similar to a graphic novel to convey the origins of his revenge. Frank D'Amico (Mark Strong) is the crime boss who attempted to get Big Daddy on his payroll when he was still a cop. Big Daddy declined the offer and lost his wife and his sanity in the process. His vengeance against Frank stems from the failures of the regulatory structures that are supposed to protect the citizenry and the loss of his family. By having nothing left to believe in or protect, Big Daddy loses the drive to protect and serve the citizenry and seeks only personal satisfaction. With this selfish drive — a perversion of the hero's advocacy that parallels Big Daddy's perversion of familial values and roles, he constructs his daughter in his own image, and her childhood is transformed into a series of exercises that craft Big Daddy's perfect protégé. Advocacy and the social networks, which superheroes, superheroines and villains construct, appear as motivating factors for their actions, but with super-intertextuality, these texts converse about the nature and values of this advocacy. The familial network becomes a source of stability for the individual who sacrifices himself or herself for the betterment of society, and these texts interact with the empowering and destructive implications of their presence that are brought to light when examined under the optic of super-intertextuality.

The costuming trope works in tandem among these texts to show the need for alternate identities as the superheroes attempt to establish their individualized social advocacy. Dave's creation of identity shows how unimportant a quality costume really is if the superhero has the drive to protect the citizenry. The conversation among the *Spider-Man* films and *Kick-Ass* discusses the value in having a private and public persona as they interact with the citizenry, with Dave stating that powers should not matter if there is a desire within the individual to improve society. In addition, the films' comments on the coming-of-age narrative and the development of social advocacy become further realized and entwined as the super-intertextual discourse explores the voiced and masculine narrations within the text and their contributions to the development of the social advocate.

Voices and narration evolve from branding and training as additional signifiers for identity and offer additional tactics for texts to shape a character's narratives and developments as they participate in the coming-of-age maturation process. Male voiceovers initiate the trend of masculine narration in the *Spider-Man* franchise and *Kick-Ass*, and additional aural and visual components suggest added moments of masculine narration, which these texts use to develop the individualized social advocacy of superheroes.

## Masculine Voices and Narration in the Spider-Man *Films and* Kick-Ass

There appears to be a repeated use of male voiced narration in the manner by which the coming-of-age narrative is constructed throughout the *Spider-Man* films and *Kick-Ass*. Its use becomes a tool for the *Spider-Man* texts to introduce and prime the emotional tones of the texts and an area for *Kick-Ass* to expand its metalevel commentary evaluating the same narrative tool. The use of the male voiceover in the *Spider-Man* texts occurs only at the beginning and end of the films and helps to inflect the text with thematic and emotional appeals. Unfortunately, these voice moments work against parts of Peters development of individualized social advocacy. Peter exists and operates on dual narrative levels, diegetic and extradiegetic, as he relates information and emotions to the audience using his male and virile narration. What follows is an analysis of these cinematic voiced introductions as depictions of Peter's maturation process and development of a social advocacy. His voiceovers at the beginning of the films prime the viewership to the narrative's emotional commentary of the diegesis, while there also exists a masculine and romantic tone within the narration.[8]

With his introduction in the first film, Peter asks the audience "Who am I? Do you really want to know? My story is not for the faint of heart." His extradiegetic conversation begins the thematic questioning of identity, which becomes a point of exploration for the diegesis. However, the assumptions loaded into his statement impart a sense of arrogance and self-reflexivity into the discourse on this narrative level. As Peter ponders his own tale of woe, he wants the audience to think about their own ability to understand his personal struggles— as well as to begin to acknowledge their own struggles. However, this prelude to the narrative shifts away from the title sequence to the diegesis, with Peter opining about how this story "is about a girl," with the visual of him running after the bus and the narrative discussing how he wanted to be one of the guys closest to Mary Jane. The extradiegetic level of the narrative has begun to undercut the self-sacrifice of the superhero's advocacy and reinforce notions that the motivation for Peter is romantic desire. This opening attempts to imbue an emotional tint to the text, but it fails to recognize the potential failings in the superhero being guided purely by sexual desire, contrasting with Dave's initial moments of desire. Peter begins this discourse on his character by putting himself in reference to a girl and ignoring the larger social role he is supposedly inheriting with his powers.

In *Kick-Ass*, the voiceover operates as less of a gimmick to imbue theme and tone to the text, which is how it operates in *Spider-Man*. The text values the narrational and self-reflexive potential of the voiceover in a greater way. Dave uses this initial conversation from the extradiegetic and narrative future to give a glimpse into what he sees as reasons why there are no superheroes in his reality and to question some of the overused motifs within the genre. Dave's initial voiceover, far more common than in *Spider-Man*, initiates a conversation with the superhero genre by saying, "I mean all those comic books, movies, TV shows. You'd think one eccentric loner would have made himself a costume." The pervasive nature of the superhero in popular culture should have, in Dave's mind, inspired someone to attempt to do something for society while wearing a costume. Dave already situates himself within the context of the genre's media by acknowledging the pervasive nature of superheroes. However, even though he discusses himself in a manner reminiscent of Peter and Superman, he avoids the notion of self-burdening that Peter attempts to impart, as he does not feel obligated to engage in the activity because of some gift/curse, but because he "just existed." There is also a sexual motivator within Dave, but it is not as inherent to his narration as Peter's. Dave talks more about the graphic sexual releases of an outsider teenager — masturbation — than the romanticism evoked by Peter. Thus, *Kick-Ass* begins to pit the two heroes against each other by offering divergent discourse about the role of romance in superhero cinema. Dave operates with a sexually-grounded approach to females, which is closer to the reality of teenage boys, while the Spider-Man universe depicts women as unattainable love interests because of Peter's gift/curse, and presents them as characters who enhance his burden by showing how he can never have what he desires.

Dave makes a fairly innocuous statement directed at the character of Spider-Man and Superman when he explores his apparent lack of abilities, stating: "I was just a regular guy. No radioactive spider. No refugee status from a doomed alien world. My mother was killed by an aneurism in the kitchen as opposed to the gunman in the alley." He continues to position himself against the stalwarts of the genre. In comparison to Spider-Man and Superman, Dave is nothing, but his conversation about and against these tropes begins to question why the superhero should take up a mask and protect the citizenry. Dave just wants to put on a "mask and help people," offering a more noble motivation for heroism than Peter. This noble motivator acts as a challenge to the apathetic spectator. The super-intertextual discourse builds notions of conflict between the two heroes on the extradiegetic level of their narratives. Their paralleled search for identity marks the way super-intertextuality offers a means for uncovering the repeated visual tactics of the genre. The other voiceovers from the *Spider-Man* films continue to construct the maturation process of the superhero, who struggles to become an adult and to persist in showing how individualized social advocacy becomes paired with the evolution of the teenage superhero into an adult.

*Spider-Man 2* also continues to build the familial and personal elements that Peter laments as something unattainable for Spider-Man. For this extradiegetic Peter, Spider-Man was "given a job to do," which suggests that this is not something Peter wants for his life. He does not feel a sense of attachment to the citizenry he protects and sees it more as an obligation to his powers that he grudgingly performs. This section invites the viewer to question his/her potential commitment to the superhero by showing the awareness enacted by Peter and his reluctance. By introducing this material through an extradiegetic source, the text overpowers the relationship between Peter, Spider-Man and the citizenry. His advocacy becomes lost in this constructed narration because the text endeavors to let Peter's selfishness dominate the voiced introduction. When constructed in this manner, Peter represents a reluctant superhero without a strong connection to the larger social system. The text pieces together the power of the familial and private being overvalued by Peter, who loses his social advocacy through the text's narrative. These voiceovers also construct Mary Jane as something unattainable because of the curse of his powers. Her absence from Peter's life is a personal burden he must endure as he defends the citizenry. The voiceovers fail to convey to the audience any sense of personality and value she may bring to Peter's advocacy. She merely functions as the love he is not meant to possess, which further codes the failings of superhero cinema to meaningfully engage in the depiction of a supporting female character since she is not defined on her merit but through her lack of relationship to Peter. This male voiceover focuses on the personal and romantic roles of Peter and Spider-Man. It curtails the development of the individualized social advocate that becomes essential to the maturation of the hero that parallels the maturation of boy to man.

In *Spider-Man 3*, the voiced narration initially employs a positive tone prompting the discourse on the superhero coming to terms with the roles of advocate and man and succeeding in that process. He has finally begun to obtain balance between his private life and his crimefighting. He remains at "the top of [his] class" in school and functions in a relationship with "the girl of his dreams." This voiced introduction helps depict the final phase of both the superhero's and man's development and prepares the audience for the conclusion of this process. However, it fails to hint at the potential challenges awaiting Peter. Everything about his existence that he has worked so hard to obtain will be under assault by the text's efforts to see if he has actually earned his individualized social advocacy. The voiceover explains his happiness, but fails to explain the final process of his evolution that exists beyond this introduction.

Throughout the *Spider-Man* franchise, the introductory voiceovers lend a masculine flavor to the text's narration. The voiceovers in question relate to Peter's development from boy to man. Each voiceover explores his process of identity creation and his relationships to women. In addition, these voiceovers are tools, which develop and explore the masculine coming-of-age narrative of Peter and Spider-Man. On the other hand, *Kick-Ass* uses other methodologies of masculine narration to construct elements of Hit-Girl's narrative and comes to terms with the coming-of-age narrative of a female superheroine. Melissa Silverstein (2010) explores the complexity of Hit-Girl and the word choice of the character. However, Silverstein avoids exploring the media-specific elements that help to build Hit-Girl's character in a manner employing elements of masculine narration. *Kick-Ass* extends the male voiceover into additional elements that explore other avenues of masculine film narration in a few of Hit-Girl's action sequences.

The text uses a number of narration strategies for constructing Hit-Girl, and implementing extradiegetic aural components provides thematic and character implications in the sequence where Hit-Girl saves Dave from the drug ring. During the devastation, the text focuses on her and keeps her victims' corpses in the background; everything within this sequence works towards showcasing Hit Girl's extraordinary abilities. The chaotic sequence after murdering the gang leader presents a number of countershots of the victims, which are conventionalized at first, but which become self-reflexive, as they typically feature a portion of her body or weapons inflicting harm on them. The montage works as a primer for the type of decimation and domination that she is capable of demonstrating. The aural companion to Hit Girl's murderous rampage is a cover of the theme song to *The Banana Splits Adventure*, a 1969 child's television program featuring actors in animal suits interacting with children, "The Tra La La Song (One Banana, Two Banana)" by The Dickies, an American punk band. The song is remediated to fit the needs of a punk discourse to show how children can be active members of rebellion. The music has no diegetic source in reference to the characters, but it serves to influence the gender "punking" that occurs through Hit Girl's unraveled intertextual code (Barthes 38). By pairing Hit Girl's appearance with a punk version of a child's theme song, the text builds the tone around the character and the sequence. The song thrives as an intertextual line contributing to the text's effort to narrate Hit-Girl; by unraveling this thread, the text bring the viewers to the metalevel discourse from which super-intertextuality interacts with additional primary sources commenting on the gender politics built into the individualized superhero advocacy of Hit-Girl and hinting at the inherent masculinity of this aural component. By using the punk version of a children's song, the text extends the construction of Hit-Girl beyond the narrative's depictions. It adds another dimension through the inclusion of other sources that indicate an inability in the narrative level to fully construct Hit-Girl's persona. These voiced and aural narration effects work to show how the cinematic text constructs the two characters, but with Hit-Girl, a narrative technique constructs her social role without regards to media specificity.

By using the aural companion to her first rampage, the text initiates the process by which Hit-Girl's rebellious creation responds to the prototypical female characters within *Spider-Man*, a distressed damsel like Mary Jane. The text implements a narrative sequence reliant on masculine narration and extends the disregard of media specificity around Hit-Girl; it suggests elements of adroit dominance in her character that respond to the damsel motif. Hit-Girl's physical skills allow her to function as the savior to a captured Dave and Big Daddy, instead of being saved like Mary Jane. Her physical skill provides the text with an opportunity to construct a unique visual sequence through remediation. The sequence creates a first-person point of view for the spectator through the eyes of Hit-Girl as she attempts to rescue Dave and Big Daddy from D'Amico's thugs; the image starts with a heads-up display of night vision goggles, creating a frame for the action to take place, and as that action unfolds, her arms and weapons come into view. The sequence quickly evolves into a shootout reminiscent of first-person shooters, like *Halo* and *Doom*.[9] In this sequence, the camera oscillates between the first-person perspective of Hit-Girl and the third-person, suggesting a shift from video game storytelling to stereotypical film storytelling, and shows how the two mediums can coexist and defies the notion that they are reforming one another (Bolter 59). The text weaves the technologies together in a way that suggests a masculine narration of Hit-Girl's action montage by associating her dominance with the stereotypically male activity of the shooter genre of video games; the text implements the medium to narrate Hit-Girl as a compounding of gender, and simultaneously explore the compounding of media within superhero cinema. Both the film and Hit-Girl exist in constructed middle grounds to argue against conventions of genre, gender and media. Her predilection to the masculine and her age mark a stark departure from the females in *Spider-Man* and many other superhero films. Mary Jane requires rescuing at some point in the narrative; her presence helps Peter Parker come to terms with his own construct of advocacy, but Hit-Girl functions as the savior of captured men. Her advocacy becomes a construct of her father's efforts, but her vengeance in relation to her advocacy after Big Daddy's death comments on the nature of superhero cinema to rely on familial networks to motivate the hero and prompt the coming-of-age scenario. It suggests another moment of failure to fully realize the ideal individualized social advocacy that these texts desperately seek to impart on the viewers.

## Conclusion

In the post–9/11 era, superhero cinema depicts the absolute need for individualized social advocacy and the strong familial or personal networks that these heroes strive to create and protect. The super-intertextual conversation enacted by *Spider-Man, Spider-Man 2, Spider-Man 3,* and *Kick-Ass* evaluates the beginnings of this advocacy for the superheroes/superheroines as protectors of private networks, and the ways in which that effort evolves into the necessary and greater advocacy of the citizenry. The textual network explored the narrative level and ended at a metalevel discourse. This network explores the construction of the superhero's agency as the beginning and the end of the superhero's search for identity. Advocacy becomes this network's primary question of superhero cinema, and this chapter offers a model for exploration within networks to examine the growth of the super-intertextual relationship within superhero cinema. *Pan's Labyrinth* (2006) could be used to decode the social advocacy of Ophelia and expand the reach of superhero cinema. In *Scott Pilgrim VS The World* (2010), the journey to define individualized social advocacy occurs as Scott attempts to save the girl of his dreams. *Hellboy* (2004) and *Hellboy II: The Golden Army* (2008) explore the advocacy of the Other as Hellboy and his team help a world that does not understand them and they explore identity issues within superhero cinema. *The Incredibles* (2004) presents an opportunity to explore individualized social advocacy of a familial unit. These texts construct new channels for super-intertextuality to interact and unravel thematic codes within superhero cinema. Super-intertextuality becomes a new tool for decoding and unlocking the relationships within superhero cinema. And the struggle for legitimacy of these "popular" texts will be aided by exploring how they erode notions of media specificity and how the cultural network begins to envelop the myriad number of texts not explicitly labeled a superhero film, which do, in fact, engage in the same tactics and questions as superhero participants.

## Notes

1. Super-intertextuality exists as a concept born from ideas of intertextuality explored by Meinhof and Smith that there exist "complex ... interactions between texts, producers ... and reader's lifeworlds" (3). Self-reflexivity in these interactions makes intertextuality into super-intertextuality. Stam states self-reflexivity is a text's ability "to scrutinize its own instruments" (151), and when the interactions between texts offer this scrutiny of instruments, super-intertextuality occurs.

2. Barthes engages in some film criticism, but his effort in defining the text leading him to explore the intertext is a literary effort. This is one of the problems with intertextuality in film. The research must either be adapted from literary criticism or look at the study of the intertext and how it relates to the work of specific directors, like *Akira Kurosawa and Intertextual Cinema* by James Goodwin, and not specifically a search for intertextuality in genre.

3. Remediation, as a construction of intertextuality, positions the text as a binary opposition to other ways to construct texts using media. This works against the notion of intertextuality as a concept of inclusion of other texts and expanding the network of connection to include other media.

4. The opposition between "old" and "new" inherently values the "new" over the "old" and assumes that "old" media will eventually succumb to "new" media.

5. In *Windows and Mirrors*, Bolter teams with Gromala to explore the digital arts and avant-garde that is ignored in *Remediation*. It attempts to reconcile some of the issues with *Remediation*, but it does not show how the process of remediation can effectively create symbiotic relationships.

6. Anton Karl Kozlovic (2006) compares and contrasts the repeated themes between Richard Donner's *Superman* (1978) and *Superman 2* (1980) and the *Spider-Man* franchise, which consisted of only two films at the time of publication. However, the author does not explore the possibility that these relationships are larger indicators of superhero cinema and its faculty for new millennium culture, although he begins to acknowledge their importance and highlights the need for thorough application of intertextuality to superhero cinema.

7. Dave's "mutation" occurs after being beaten by some thugs in a failed attempt to stop a carjacking. This is the closest thing he possesses that could be deemed a superpower.

8. Peaslee (2005) explores the subconscious of Peter in *Spider-Man* and *Spider-Man 2* in a way that builds the theoretical notions of a franchise of films as a single text, and this chapter uses a similar approach to the franchise as the text.

9. The merger of media occurring here does not favor one over the other, and demonstrates hypermediacy as its method for engaging in remediation; for Bolter and Grusin, hypermediacy is one of two forms of remediation in which the spectator or user is "aware of the medium or media" (34).

# The *Watchmen,* Neo-Noir and Pastiche

PHILLIP DAVIS

When Zach Snyder's film *Watchmen* was released in March of 2009, it received mixed and tepid reviews. Some critics expressed the confusion of a general audience unfamiliar with the source material. Bruce Bennett, writing for *Spectrum*, stated: "This may be everything Moore's fans have hoped for, but there is little for the average film fan to understand let alone enjoy" (Bennett). Others, however, revealed a more informed perspective that nevertheless identified their let-down.[1] Both types of responses reveal the same underlying thought; *Watchmen* can only be understood in the context of the novel. To some degree this idea is to be expected given the novel's popularity and its notorious history in Hollywood. When the novel was published in 1986, it established an immediate cult following. Hollywood attempted several times to capitalize on this popularity, but these attempts met with little success initially. Up until the time of its filming and release, *Watchmen* was a narrative perennially on the verge of being filmed, yet one that consistently failed to meet production deadlines and studio budgets.[2] By the time of its release, it was highly anticipated. It was almost unavoidable, then, that it would be compared to its source material in early reviews and criticism.

The unfortunate thing about this reading, however, is that it overlooks the intriguing ways that the film operates as a stand-alone narrative. It adapts the material from the novel, it is faithful to its characterizations, and it is generally faithful to the storyline. However, despite its intimate connection with the original, *Watchmen* can be read as a unique narrative: one that performs similar functions as its source, but one that ultimately has to be read in the context of its own historical moment.[3] The novel's dark representation of superheroes acts as an ironic counterpoint to the Regan-era "morning" of corporate expansion and American military adventurism.[4] The film's dark plot and brooding characters serve to underscore the uncertainty of the 21st century.

What makes the film particularly distinct from the novel, we will see, is its ability to function as both a neo-noir film, and as a pastiche of the neo-noir genre.

The *Watchmen* film and novel both rely upon pastiche as an underlying aesthetic. The novel utilizes the four-panel design of the superhero comic to identify the familiar tropes of the genre all in an attempt to exaggerate them, to overload their representations, and to underscore the darker aspects inherent in them. The film utilizes its own raw materials to perform the same tasks. Its medium, however, allows it to function as a critique of the superhero film: a genre of immense popularity and cultural importance in early 21st century America. The film's medium also allows it to function as a critique of the other genres associated with the development of the superhero narrative. As Iain Thompson notes, Rorschach's voiceover represents an homage "to the detective's voiceover in *film noir,*" a genre that was critical to the development of superhero fiction (112). It is one thing to read the character's cryptic comments. It is quite another, however, to *hear* them in the context of the film. The film, in short, is better able to utilize its medium to identify and critique the sources important to the development of the superhero genre.

While the film begins as a critique of the superhero narrative, it ultimately functions as a critique of neo-noir. As the film depicts the events of the narrative, its medium becomes less dependent upon its original source and more responsive to the generic demands of the neo-noir framework. On one level, the film represents these tropes. Its basic plot, the conflict between Rorschach's obsessive search for truth and the larger world's attempt to obscure that truth, consists of a pattern that can be found throughout neo-noir. Rorschach's representation parallels the depiction of neo-noir protagonists: he is a marginalized figure living on the edges of society, he survives his world by relying upon violence, and his violence stems directly from his personal trauma. The world that the film creates conforms to the image of a seedy and corrupt society familiar to the neo-noir film of the 1970s. On another level, however, the film exaggerates its tropes, creating a pastiche through both its characterization of Rorschach and its depiction of place. The isolation of the traditional neo-noir protagonist was always implicit. Rorschach's isolation in the *Watchmen,* in contrast, is both codified by law and perpetuated by his strange behavior. His violence, we will see, takes on absurd dimensions, and his trauma is similarly exaggerated and overwrought. The film's representation of place likewise begins by echoing the bleak urban imagery of neo-noir film, and ends by expanding its depictions to include both an alternate America and world. This paper will focus on the *Watchmen* film's pastiche of the neo-noir genre as it is located in both its treatment of Rorschach and in its depiction of place. As we will see, the film explicitly identifies the neo-noir genre's implicit association with social and historical crisis to represent the sociopolitical concerns of our own era, and events such as the 9/11 attacks. The film's pastiche of the genre ultimately suggests that the complexities of our own era render traditional narrative forms incapable of serving their familiar symbolic purpose any longer. The world, the film implies, is too complex for superheroes, and even too murky for the dark generic patterns of neo-noir film.

## Pastiche and the Neo-Noir Genre

Before proceeding to the film itself, however, some definition is in order. My understanding of pastiche stems from that established by Fredric Jameson in *Postmodernism, Or the Logic of Late Capitalism*. Jameson defines it as "[an] imitation of a peculiar or unique, idiosyncratic style, the wearing of a linguistic mask, speech in a dead language" (17). While pastiche is akin to parody and/or irony, it is distinct in the way that it makes its point without the attendant use of humor, or the assumption of a "normality" to balance one's parody (17). For Jameson, it is symptomatic of the emptiness found in late capitalism. He writes: "the producers of culture have nowhere to turn but to the past: the imitations of dead styles, speech through all the masks and voices stored up in the imaginary museum of a now global culture" (18). Pastiche is, then, an acknowledgment that genres are worn-out, and a willful echoing of these same exhausted tropes.

In identifying pastiche in contemporary American film, Jameson indirectly references neo-noir when he mentions Roman Polanksi's *Chinatown* (1974), a film frequently cited as a definitive example (18).[5] What distinguishes neo-noir from classic noir is the issue of genre. Film noir, as John Irwin points out, is not a genre but more or less a happy accident (206).[6] It emerged from a variety of factors: overabundance of detective narratives that were finally released in the early postwar years, tightening studio budgets which led to increased emphasis on atmospheric lighting and other money-saving techniques, and the appreciation of postwar French critics who had not seen an American film since the 1930s critics who coined the term "film noir" in the first place.[7] Neo-noir, on the other hand, emerged in the late 1960s and early 1970s. These films were produced by a generation of filmmakers well acquainted with both American classic noir, and with European cinematic approaches influenced by noir stylistics. Films such as *Chinatown*, *Death Wish* (1974), and *Taxi Driver* (1976) began by relying on the motifs and techniques of film noir, and ended up creating a stand-alone genre.[8] Neo-noir's self-consciousness its deliberate use of noir stylistics and techniques in order to formulate its own narrative paradigms is what sets it apart from classic noir. As we will see, *Watchmen* identifies this aspect of neo-noir and exploits it in order to create its own pastiche of the neo-noir genre.

Whereas neo-noir shares many of the same traits as the classic variety, it is distinguished by its self-awareness, its freedom from the types of studio controls that constrained classic noir, and its willingness to expound upon the techniques and motifs of its predecessor. The genre is both self-conscious in its reliance upon older tropes, and a deliberate attempt to break from conventions.[9] Pastiche is thus inherent to neo-noir's underlying aesthetic. Richard Martin's *Mean Streets and Raging Bulls* argues that pastiche is either a product of big studios, an attempt to create homogenized products, or a self-referent motif: a deliberate attempt to utilize noir tropes for the purpose of commentary and/or critique (15).[10] In such cases, however, pastiche operates as a means by which filmmakers can situate their narratives in the greater context of pre-existing narrative patterns. As Jarold Abrams claims, neo-noir is largely a meditation on time (7).[11] It is an attempt to recreate a specific moment in American culture and film, while also commenting on the historical crises of post–Vietnam War, post–Watergate America.

The *Watchmen* narratives are directly connected to this same set of historical undercurrents. The novel, published in 1986, makes a pastiche out of the superhero genre. It exaggerates superhero characterizations, exposes the violence, misogyny and racism associated with superhero stories, and ultimately suggests that the driving force behind these legends is a thinly-veiled fascistic will to power.[12] In total, the novel reflects the same cultural conditions that informed neo-noir film. The film expounds upon these elements, but takes its narrative even further. It utilizes pastiche to comment upon the neo-noir genre itself. It suggests that we are in a unique cultural moment beset by an influx of national and global challenges that go well beyond those cited by earlier neo-noir films. We turn now to a discussion of the *Watchmen* film, and to an examination of how the film utilizes pastiche to comment upon its era.

## Rorschach as Neo-Noir Detective

The character Rorschach (Jackie Earle Haley) bookmarks the film. His investigation of the Comedian's (Jeffrey Dean Morgan) death initiates the story. His death concludes it, solves the mystery, and brings his character full circle. He begins the film, we will see, by signifying his disgust for the world around him, and ends it by refusing to go along with the lie the other Watchmen accept. While his obsessive search for truth is one of many narrative threads in the film, it is also among the most important. It is through Rorschach's investigation that the disparate events come together in a coherent fashion. As the film's central detective-figure, Rorschach is the one who is able to see beyond the surface meaning of events, and to recognize the larger plot behind them. Rorschach is also the figure through whom the film is able to transition from a pastiche of the superhero genre into a pastiche of neo-noir.

The film introduces Rorschach in a shot that registers with the familiar motifs of noir and neo-noir. He stands alone, an isolated avenger who looks out upon a desolate urban hell. Steam pours out of a manhole, a motif which parallels *Taxi Driver*'s initial scene. The only light that is visible in the sequence comes from the neon sign of a porn theater, a light that is reflected in the rain-drenched, wet pavement. We do not see Rorschach directly at first, but only see the outline of his shoulder as he stands with his back to the camera. In a voiceover, he states: "October 12th, 1985. A Comedian died in New York." Then as the scene shifts, Rorschach climbs his way to the crime scene. As he enters the Comedian's apartment, we see his physical appearance clearly for the first time; he wears a fedora, mask, and raincoat.

As in classic noir and neo-noir, the juxtaposition of detective and setting is crucial. The city is metonymic for an absurd world in which authority is corrupt, justice is non-existent, and where violence is a given. Rorschach is symptomatic of the city, even while he imagines himself above it. The horrific nature of his voiceover in this sequence, the reference to "retarded children in an abattoir," indicates both the extent of the detective's psychosis, and the potentiality of horror present in the city. Much like Yeats' dancer and the dance, it is impossible to distinguish one from the other: both are part of the same horrifying panorama.

Even while this opening sequence reveals the film's debt to classic and neo-noir, however, it also illustrates its simultaneous pastiche. The opening shot conveys the familiar image of an urban street. Unlike the cinematic realism of *Taxi Driver*, this shot conveys the artificiality of *Watchmen*'s constructs. The dated cars, the ironic "1980s" clothing and fashion, and the entire aesthetic appear highly constructed. Other factors, likewise, break the film's strict adherence to the neo-noir formula. Rorschach's appearance, his mask and "1940s" raincoat and fedora, shatter the continuum of the image. The extreme and convoluted nature of his voiceover makes an absurdity out of the convention. Finally, the film shatters any pretense of realism as Rorschach rappels his way up the entire skyscraper via grappling hook.

This opening sequence reveals two things about the film's aesthetic. First, it reveals an awareness of cinematic convention in its use of noir and neo-noir motifs. At the same time, it conveys a detached representation of these same motifs, a willingness to take them to their utmost extreme. These two aspects appear throughout the film, as we will see. In order to appreciate the film's narrative, however, it will be important to briefly examine the conventions of neo-noir film and to contextualize the social meaning behind them.

Neo-noir stemmed from classic noir; noir stemmed from the pulp fiction of the 1920s and 1930s. Pulp fiction, originating in the "pulp" magazines of those decades, was ultimately codified through definitive generic elements: a detached private investigator, a corrupt social world, and violent and convoluted narratives. Whereas the Victorian and Edwardian detective tale attempted to symbolically resolve social crises through a clearly devised plot, the hardboiled narrative posited a world in which disorder was the dominant feature.

Sean McCann writes that, by the time of hard-boiled fiction's development, "The traditional mystery tale was a myth, illegitimate because it no longer corresponded to the complex realities of an urban industrial society" (18). The hard-boiled genre, then, signified not only changes in an aesthetic, but in American culture as well.

In hard-boiled fiction, the private detective often served as both narrator and as the central narrative consciousness of these works. Figures such as Phillip Marlowe, Sam Spade and Mike Hammer navigated the "mean streets" around them, a dangerous world that required the detective "to embark on a journey in which he compulsively courts a violence that threatens his imminent death" (Forter 13). Though often jaded, and armed with both fists and cynicism, these figures were nevertheless idealistic, embodiments of "neglected popular virtues" (McCann 147). Like Chandler's Marlowe, they maintained their personal moral codes in spite of the deteriorating world around them, remaining true to their personal ethical visions. Because they were outside the official sanctions of law, they were not hamstrung by the limitations of official authority. And because they were true social outsiders, distant from and equally skeptical of upper and lower social classes, they allowed their authors to present a scathing image of the modern world. The detective operated as an aesthetic device, as well as a motif that enabled hard-boiled authors to make a sweeping critique of their culture.

The hard-boiled detective, then, operated in contradistinction to his larger social context. Emerging out of the populist sentiment of the 1930s, hard-boiled fiction operated as a mechanism of critique. It offered a social vision that posited the upper classes as both victims and perpetrators of crime. While representatives of the lower classes and criminal elements were often directly responsible for the crimes committed in these tales, it was the upper classes that were typically responsible in a far more complex capacity.[13] These narratives operate as a means of demonstrating that the pretensions of the wealthy, the idea that they are above the corruption around them, is merely a ruse. More abstractly, they reveal a modern social world made uneasy by the tumultuous conditions of the early twentieth-century.

Due to the fact that the hard-boiled genre developed out of the pulp magazines of the period, it was marketed towards a largely working-class readership. This had a direct impact upon the features of the genre as they were tailored to their target audience. These stories were punctuated by violent action and by tales that privileged action over plot development.[14] When in the hands of a master author like Chandler, however, these base generic components could be turned into a symbolic image of modernity. Violence could be made to represent a deteriorating social world, a world in which the collapse of traditional order generated a Darwinian struggle for survival. Similarly, the convoluted nature of the typical pulp narrative could be utilized as a way of signifying the fragmented nature of modern life. Mysteries were no longer solved; resolutions were no longer achieved; the detective was lucky enough just to survive the events of the narrative.

Classic noir often built upon the narrative structures of hard-boiled fiction in its depiction of isolated, marginalized detectives; corrupt and violent social worlds; and convoluted narratives punctuated by pervasive violence. But classic noir used these same features as a way of signifying its own historical moment. These components no longer identified the class-conflict ridden world of the Depression era, but rather the disorienting conditions of post–World War II American culture.[15] Their narratives represented a darker, more confusing world, and were marketed towards a sophisticated audience aware of Freudianism, existentialism, and other markers of postwar society. Neo-noir built upon this same foundation, elaborating on noir's intellectualizing of hard-boiled fiction's essential narrative components, even while remaining faithful to the same basic narrative patterns. The elements that began as a populist critique of Depression-era society ultimately served as the post-modern devices of neo-noir film.[16]

As Iain Thompson points out, *Watchmen*'s Rorschach is a "hypertrophic development of the Batman archetype" (106–7). Thomson explains it this way. Alan Moore modeled Rorschach after Batman, who was modeled off of the Shadow. The Shadow was in turn "drawn from the notoriously gritty, 'detective' genre of pulp fiction" (107). Even while he was representative of the Batman-type, Rorschach is also an embodiment of hard-boiled fiction's legacy in the superhero genre. As he is represented in the film, he is also an embodiment of the intimate connection between hard-boiled fiction and neo-noir film. His character traits correspond not only to the literary Phillip Marlowe, but to various filmic portrayals of the character, as well as such neo-noir protagonists as Robert DeNiro's character in *Taxi Driver*, Travis Bickle. The film is faithful to the novel's treatment of its figure, but its medium translates the literary Rorschach into the cinematic, neo-noir Rorschach. His place in the context of the film translates him into a latent critique of the isolated avenger, a type familiar to neo-noir since 1971's *Dirty Harry*.[17] Context and setting determine the character's meaning, even as his traits represent a direct carry-over from one medium to another.

*Watchmen* defines Rorschach as a neo-noir protagonist through the following key character traits: he is an isolated figure, separate from both his lager world and fellow Watchmen; he is characterized by his extreme violence, which is directly linked to his sexual anxiety and personality disorders; and, finally, he is obsessed with a personal code of conduct. The film's pastiche operates by overextending these basic elements. Rorschach's isolation is not only abstract; it is codified by the Keene act, and perpetuated by his strange behavior. His violence is over-the-top and extreme; his sexual anxiety is equally magnified and overwrought. Finally, his obsessive ethical drive leads him not only to the brink of destruction, as in classic and neo-noir, but to his ultra-violent death at the hands of Dr. Manhattan (Billy Crudup).

Rorschach can first be identified as a neo-noir protagonist in his social isolation. In the opening scene, the film visually juxtaposes the forces of socially sanctioned law enforcement against Rorschach's status as a marginalized vigilante. The police investigating the Comedian's murder go through the front door. Rorschach, as we have seen, forces his way into the apartment by repelling his way into the loft, and by physically breaking the yellow police tape. Even before we are informed about the Keene act, this visual clue gives us some idea of the vigilante's status in his society.

His isolation, however, is not merely a matter of legality. As Dan (Patrick Wilson) and Lorie (Malin Akerman) — Nite Owl and Silk Specter respectively — dine, Dan relates a "humorous" story about a would-be supervillain known as Captain Carnage, and Rorschach's treatment of him. The Captain is not a supervillain in any sense, but is merely a masochist who is forever pestering Dan and the other Watchmen to "punish" him. This is until Rorschach, in Dan's words, "shoved [him] down an elevator shaft," thus killing him. Lorie and Dan laugh at the morbid tale, a reaction that subtly underscores their assessment of Rorschach as "crazy," a figure who takes his costume and his status as a Watchman far too seriously. Dan's sheer frustration with the detective comes to the forefront much later in the film during a brief moment of dialog when he exclaims: "You [Rorschach] live off of people while insulting them, and nobody complains because they think you're a goddamn lunatic." The statement reveals Dan's inability to comprehend Rorschach, even while it identifies Rorschach's inability to behave according to basic social standards.

While Lorie, Dan and others act as superheroes out of a sense of duty, Rorschach does so because he has an obsessive need to serve the cause of "justice." This isolates him existentially from his allies, removing him further from any true human companionship. The film thus presents his isolation as both something codified by law and perpetuated by the character's hidebound obsessions with his personal moral code.[18] It makes explicit that which was always implicit in classic and neo-noir film: the protagonist's isolation from, and contempt for, his larger social universe. Rorschach himself makes this explicit in the opening scene of the film when he states that: "This city hates me; I've seen its true face."

Ultimately, his code entails his use of violence. The scene depicting his interview with the psychiatrist flashes back to his origin story, the moment when he became Rorschach and abandoned his previous identity, Walter Kovacs. In this sequence, he plays vigilante, hunting for the kidnapper of a six-year-old girl. His investigations lead him to a seedy house belonging to the suspected kidnapper. Inside the house, he discovers a stove which contains ashes and the little girl's underwear. It is this case, he tells his doctor, that forced him to stop being "soft on criminals": that is to say, it is this moment when he stopped letting them live. As the scene progresses, as the kidnapper returns, Rorschach assaults him, ties him to a chair, and splits his skull with the man's own cleaver.

This sequence takes the tropes associated with classic and neo-noir protagonists—the willingness to use violence—but exaggerates it to the point of absurdity. The extreme nature of his moral code, in short, leads him to acts of extreme violence.

Rorschach's violence stems, ultimately, from his personal trauma, sexual confusion, and his loss of traditional masculine authority. This aspect was always implicit in hard-boiled fiction, classic and neo-noir—cultural forms that underscored the tensions associated with changes in gender politics and arrangements.[19] But the film makes this explicit by positing Rorschach as a product of a traumatic childhood, one in which he literally watched his mother working as a prostitute. The film conflates his violence with his sexual trauma in a couple of key scenes. Rorschach kills the kidnapper, in part, because he is horrified by the man's pedophilia. Cryptically, he states prior to the act: "Men get arrested, dogs get put down." His statement reveals the depth of his hatred, and indirectly, the fact that his own psychosexual tendencies underline his acts of brutality. In another flashback sequence, Rorschach, as a child, assaults two bullies. He beats them, and then bites into the flesh of one attacker. This beatdown occurs because one of his bullies called his mother a whore. Finally, in the prison sequence, Rorschach responds to taunts by his fellow prisoners by assaulting one of his enemies with a pan of boiling fat. Once again, the film conflates Rorschach's violence with his internal torment; this scene occurs right after his visit with the psychiatrist.

The film magnifies the link between Rorschach's troubled sexual identity and his violence by making both extreme. The film thus takes traits familiar to its formula and transforms them into a pastiche, overloading and overextending its familiar generic markers until they become absurd. The same process occurs in the scenes depicting Rorschach's death. His obsessive drive leads him, Lorie and Dan to Antarctica, and to the discovery of Ozymandias's (Matthew Goode) role in the murky events. After they uncover his plot, the other Watchmen are given a choice: say nothing as to Ozy's role in the bombing of New York and live with a lie, or refuse and be killed. Everyone agrees to the former condition, everyone except Rorschach. His code, his visceral hatred of crime, and his refusal to go along with the lie force him to accept his fate. He is shot by Dr. Manhattan. His body explodes, leaving the shape of a bloody ink blot, a literal Rorschach, on the Antarctic snow. His choice for personal destruction finds an immediate parallel in the masochism of the neo-noir and hard-boiled protagonist.[20] Once again, however, while this feature is only implicit in hard-boiled fiction, noir and neo-noir, it is rendered explicitly and magnified in *Watchmen*.

Yet Rorschach only makes sense in context of his broader society. And the film's pastiche of neo-noir film can only be appreciated when the character is read against the larger context of his world.

# Watchmen's *Pastiche of Place*

Return for a moment to the opening scene. This sequence, as we have seen, juxtaposes Rorschach and his society: the marginalized detective and the corrupt social world that leads to his deformation. The setting is at once a realistic image and a highly stylized representation. Its gritty urban motifs—its images of porn theaters, urban blight, and slums—realistically portrays the image of a city while also self-consciously evoking the motifs of neo-noir's urban imagery.[21] If Rorschach is a pastiche, an extreme representation of a familiar character type, his world is also a self-conscious construction, an ongoing cinematic citation.

The film's treatment of place is threefold. First, it recreates the familiar urban milieu of neo-noir film. Secondly, it creates an image of an alternate America in an alternate 1985. Finally—and crucially—the film expands its horizons to include not only the U.S. in its representations, but the world as well. The motif of place recreates the patterns of neo-noir film, expands them, and ultimately subverts them entirely.

In the scenes depicting Rorschach's investigations, the film explicitly connects its own narrative to the cinematic tradition of neo-noir. As in movies like *Death Wish* and *Taxi Driver*, the film establishes the theme of social decay through the conflation of literal and metaphorical grime. Rorschach's first visit to Moloch's (Matt Frewer) apartment, for example, juxtaposes the image of porn theaters and prostitutes with the image of the former archvillain's seedy flat. The conflation of physical grime and social decay functions as a symbol of pervasive moral corruption, and as an expressionistic rendering of Rorschach's psychology. Similarly, in its treatment of the kidnapper's house, the image of a shadowy, filthy home is conflated with both the horrific crimes of the criminal, and the tortured mentality of the detective.

The space of Moloch's apartment also serves as the catalyst that takes the plot beyond the limits of the city. In a later scene, Rorschach returns to question Moloch further about his involvement in the Comedian's death. The scene begins as in typical neo-noir fashion; the space of the apartment functions symbolically. But as it progresses, the scene shatters the film's neo-noir stylistics. Rorschach discovers Moloch's corpse, intrusive searchlights fill the apartment, police break down the door, and an unrealistic fight sequence takes place for the next several moments. Action overrides the film's aesthetics in this moment and the expressionistic use of setting gives way to a much more formulaic use of setting as a frame for the battle between the police and Rorschach. Similarly, as the fight spills out onto the streets below, the symbolism of the setting gives way to a much more prosaic function. This abrupt transition in the film's stylistics coincides with the fact that Rorschach, the neo-noir protagonist, is arrested and removed from the film's focus for several scenes. Shortly after this sequence, the plot takes us beyond the seedy streets of Rorschach's investigations and introduces us to its imagined America. By expanding its framework of place, the film stretches its generic patterns.

Neo-noir film signifies the historical crises of post–Vietnam and post–Watergate America.[22] *Watchmen* reveals this aspect of the genre by recreating the generic tropes associated with it, but also by reimagining the historical backdrop of the genre's development. The film achieves this aim by creating an alternate image of America and by presenting it as a nation in the throes of deep social crisis. This aspect of the film's treatment of place allows it to stretch the boundaries of generic representation. It not only links neo-noir paranoia to its urban environment, it links it to the entire nation. We see this process first in the infamous opening montage sequence. This sequence juxtaposes the strains of Bob Dylan's "The Times They Are a-Changin'" against several vignettes of alternate history. These images begin with the familiarity of context: the majority of them are taken from scenes familiar to American culture and history. In one such example, the film presents the image of Times Square in postwar America, the day after Japan surrendered. In another, we see Studio 54 complete with disco-going patrons and 1970s motifs. The sequence operates by subtly altering the familiarity of these scenes. In the Times Square image, the female superhero Silhouette is the one kissing the nurse as opposed to the sailor in the original photograph. In the Studio 54 image, we see superhero Ozymandias standing by the familiar club. A later scene depicts Andy Warhol introducing a new image: a collection of repetitive superhero images. The purpose of these scenes is to introduce a scene familiar to American history, to de-familiarize them, and to introduce the audience to the film's alternate America: a place that looks a great deal like the nation, but that is simultaneously alien.

This sequence is shot through with a prevailing sense of foreboding. This is not only an alternate America, it is also a distinctly dark version of it. The image of Silhouette and her lesbian lover murdered in their bedroom and the sight of former Watchman Mothman being led away to a mental institution reinforce this dark tone. In the middle of the opening montage, there is an image that depicts Rorschach's childhood. He is sitting in his apartment hallway, watching a prospective john waiting to enter his mother's bedroom. The man is reading a newspaper, the headline of which reads: "RUSSIANS HAVE A-BOMB." This image is crucial. It reinforces the dark mood of the entire montage, but it also explicitly identifies the connection between the neo-noir genre and historical crisis, a feature that was only implicit in neo-noir film. The scene sets up the film's pastiche of the neo-noir genre, but it also identifies the ambitious scope of its aims. The film is not merely interested in recreating the patterns of neo-noir; it also intends to reconstruct its historical backdrop through its depiction of an alternate America.

We see the nature of this imagined nation in a couple of key scenes, both of which occur as flashbacks during the Comedian's funeral. The first sequence is taken from Dr. Manhattan's memory of the Comedian, specifically their involvement in the Vietnam War. In this version of events, the United States wins the war thanks to the involvement of both the Comedian and Dr. Manhattan. As the two Watchmen stand in a bar during a post-war celebration, the Comedian tells Dr. Manhattan: "If we had lost this war, I think it would have driven us crazy as a country." As the scene progresses, it reveals the depth of irony inherent in the statement. The statement is ironic, first of all, because it contradicts the outcome of real events as it posits the United States as the victor in the war. More importantly, however, the scene also reveals that sanity is a highly relative term. During their celebration, a Vietnamese woman enters the bar, the woman the Comedian impregnated. She walks up to the Comedian and demands that he take responsibility for the baby. The Comedian responds by insulting and shooting her. The senselessness of his actions reveals his mental instability, as well as the random violence of the war. More importantly, it reflects the insanity of the nation that he represents; the Comedian, at that moment, embodies in microcosm the social breakdown of his nation.

The next scene is taken from Dan/Nite Owl's memory, the moment when he and the Comedian quelled a riot. In some ways, this scene functions like the montage sequence at the beginning. It operates by generating images that are both familiar to real American history and alien to it. Specifically, it reveals a group of protestors carrying signs and protesting the involvement of superheroes. While the riot resembles Vietnam era protests, it is also distinct. The image of a superhero costume burning in effigy, one that resembles Superman's uniform, distances this scene from the real history that it mirrors. The riot continues the themes established in the Vietnam sequence. And as in the earlier scene, the Comedian acts as a microcosm to his broader social macrocosm. His violent actions— his shooting of protestors with grenades and a shotgun — signify the breakdown of America's social fabric. After the riot, Nite Owl exclaims: "What happened to us; what happened to the American dream?" The Comedian replies with a cynical grin: "What happened? It came true." His words explicitly identify the film's imagined America as a place evocative of violence, mayhem and disorder: a place similar to the real nation that spawned neo-noir film, but one that is even more chaotic.

The film's recreation of bleak urban imagery identifies the generic patterns of neo-noir film; its representation of America overextends them. But its representation of the world subverts them entirely. Just as the city streets have to be understood in context to the film's representation of America, its representation of the nation has to be understood within the context of the larger world. The first scene of the film makes this explicit. The Comedian sits in his apartment watching a talk show. The show is a fictionalized version of the *McLoughlin Group* (WRC-TV 1982– ), a panel discussion that features an ironic version of liberal and conservative pundits discussing the Soviet Union's aggressive actions in Afghanistan. The topic of their conversation is far less important than its implications. If the Soviet Union invades Afghanistan, the fear is that this action will ultimately lead to global nuclear conflict. Once again, the film links impending disaster to personal trauma. The Comedian is seconds away from having his home invaded and from being murdered. The film establishes tension through the use of low lighting and tense music, elements that intimate the destruction that is to follow shortly, and elements that are consistent with neo-noir stylistics. As the invaders enter, assault the Comedian, and murder him, the sequence appears to conform to familiar neo-noir patterns.

It is only at the conclusion, however, that we see how this scene actually uses the film's global reach to subvert its generic representations. The Comedian's murder does not merely parallel the threats of nuclear war debated by the panel; it is directly connected to them. Ozymandias plans the murder as part of his elaborate scheme to remove the remaining Watchmen from the national and world picture, to spark tensions between the U.S. and Soviet Union, to frame Dr. Manhattan, and to turn the world's anger towards Manhattan. Indirectly, this will allow him to end the threats of nuclear war between the U.S. and the Soviet Union. When Rorschach discovers the scope of this plot, he is overwhelmed. His sense of resolve and obsessive will collapse into his weeping and willingness to die. Rather than go along with the lie started by Ozymandias— that Dr. Manhattan is the one who levels New York City with an energy blast — he allows himself to be murdered. While the first scene resembles the genre stylistically, then, it sets into motion the very plot devices that will overwhelm both the film's neo-noir protagonist (Rorschach) and overextend the film's representation of the neo-noir genre to the breaking point.[23] As the film's storyline stretches beyond the grimy streets of Rorschach's urban milieu, in short, its representation of the neo-noir genre begins to unravel.

The scene leading to the Antarctica sequence has a similar effect. In that scene, Nite Owl and Rorschach break into Ozymandias's apartment, discovering his culpability in the events they are investigating. Much like the Comedian's death scene, this sequence is steeped in neo-noir stylistics. The empty apartment, the low key lighting and the image of the two marginalized Watchmen all reverberate with motifs of the genre. However, the film breaks its representations by juxtaposing this scene, immediately, with the sequence that follows: the scene that depicts the image of Archie, Nite Owl's ship, flying over Antarctica. Visually, this is a stunning move. In the space of seconds, the film contrasts the darkness and atmospheric moodiness of the earlier scene with the blindingly bright image of the snow, the feel of an action film, and the sound of Jimmy Hendrix's "All Along the Watchtower." In the scene that follows, the film contrasts the visual image of Rorschach in his fedora and trench coat, the costume elements that define him as the film's neo-noir detective, against the snow. His choice to wear his costume regardless of the setting further underscores the hidebound nature of his personality. But the visual contrast of neo-noir protagonist against an unfamiliar setting indicates the degree to which the film has overextended its narrative motifs.

All of these visual motifs prefigure the plot elements that will ultimately dismantle the film's representation of the neo-noir genre: namely Rorschach's discovery of Ozymandias's plot, his subsequent breakdown, and his death. This sequence thus conflates Rorschach's grief and destruction with the symbolic dismantling of the neo-noir framework. In this same sequence, the film makes its most explicit reference to its own historical period. In the novel, Ozy releases a force of genetically engineered worms onto New York. In the film, he releases a blue energy ball that resembles one of Dr. Manhattan's blasts.[24] This levels the city and turns Dr. Manhattan into a global enemy. At the same time, the visual image of a leveled New York City speaks explicitly to the 9/11 attacks. The image of a giant open crater, in particular, links the film's narrative to the event and its aftermath. The film's reference to 9/11 does not just identify the event itself, but all of the issues surrounding it: terrorism, the American government's questionable practices in the years following 9/11, economic decline, America's loss of legitimacy on the world stage. Collectively, all of these elements make up the geopolitics of the contemporary world and challenge the traditional symbolic function of our genres. In its montage sequence, the film identified the connection between the neo-noir genre and social crisis. In its oblique reference to contemporary history, it challenges the genre's ability to function in this capacity any longer.

The film's treatment of place begins by presenting the familiar tropes of neo-noir film in its representation of its urban milieu, and proceeds by de-familiarizing them by stretching them in order to fit the scope of its imagined America. Finally, it subverts them through its representation of its global environment. By the time that Rorschach cracks under the strain of his discovery, the film concludes its representation of the genre. The final scenes in the film depict the same streets that appeared at the beginning. Instead of appearing through the motifs of neo-noir film, however, they appear in daylight. On one level, this leaves the film on an upbeat note. Ozymandias's plan has the result of quelling tensions between the U.S. and the Soviet Union, while Lorie and Dan plan to make a life together. There is simply no longer a perceived need for Rorschach's obsessive brand of watchfulness. But on another level, this conclusion reveals the limitations of genre. The film ends its use of the neo-noir framework abruptly, implying that its tropes are useful only up until a point. *Watchmen*'s oblique reference to 9/11 identifies the genre's traditional function of symbolically representing social crisis. Nevertheless, the film's sudden departure from that framework identifies that it is merely a pastiche, and therefore devoid of the very symbolic potency that it intimates.

## Conclusion

As a film, *Watchmen* shares a connection not only to the cinematic tradition of neo-noir film, but to the superhero movie genre of the post–9/11 American world. It follows in the footsteps of a plethora of films, including *Spider-Man* (2002) and *Spider-Man 2* (2004), *Batman Begins* (2005) and *The Dark Knight* (2008), *Superman Returns* (2006), *Fantastic Four* (2005), *The Spirit* (2008), and a multitude of others. This glut of superhero movies stems in part from prosaic material conditions; it was not until the late 1990s that studios such as Warner Brothers were allowed unprecedented access to superhero franchises.[25] But on another level, this obsession with the superhero genre owes something to the nature of our own moment. Beginning in the summer of 2002, when *Spiderman* added the "patriotic" sequence to its conclusion, studios both directly and indirectly connected American nationalism with the superhero.[26] The immediate trauma of 9/11 was so profound that it necessitated the appearance of symbolic rescuers in the form of familiar costumed heroes.

Watchmen can be viewed as an extension of this process, as a commentary on both the superhero narratives that emerged out of the post–9/11 American world, and of the political and social events of that same period. It may be an accident that a film that soberly ponders the real effects of superheroism follows in the immediate wake of the Bush presidency. In any event, the film was nevertheless able to speak to the specific zeitgeist of its cultural moment. It spoke to an American culture uncertain of its own role and deeply fearful for the future. Despite the costumes and the superficiality of its "1980s" trappings, *Watchmen* is an artifact deeply resonant of our period.

More importantly, the film's questioning of the superhero narrative parallels its pastiche of the neo-noir genre. The world, the film suggests, is too complex for superheroes and too murky even for the dark generic patterns of noir film. Its profound self-consciousness and the way in which it subsumes the motifs of classic and neo-noir indicate that, historically, we are in new territory. The classic noir may have been suitable for the post-war generation, and neo-noir may have been an applicable art form in the latter half of the twentieth century, but our own moment requires something new. The film never answers its own question. It never states what art in our own period should look like, but it nevertheless forces us to ponder the relationship between our narratives and their social context: more specifically, our superheroes and their social context.

## Notes

1. Katrina Montgomery is the best example. In her review, she cites the film as a failure and writes: "I am so disappointed in this film for its own sake, never mind for the sake of the original" (Montgomery).

2. Rjurk Davidson in his article "Fighting the Good Fight?," points out that Hollywood had been planning on making a *Watchmen* film for some time, but that the project kept falling through, and had been passed to various directors until Zach Snyder was selected to direct (19).

3. In *Remediation: Understanding the New Media*, Jay Bolter and Tom Grusin describe the relationship between the cycle of films produced in the late 1990s that were based on Jane Austen's fiction. These films are faithful to their source material, but nevertheless "they do not contain any overt reference to the novels on which they are based, they certainly do not acknowledge that they are adaptations.... The content has been borrowed, but the medium has not been appropriated or quoted"(44). In a similar sense, the *Watchmen* narratives are related to one another, even while remaining unique iterations.

4. Tony Spanakos points out in "Super-Vigilantism and the Keene Act," that the *Watchmen* narrative explicitly questions "the legitimacy of authority" (34). By questioning the authority of superheroes and their attendant violence, the narrative also questions the role of violence perpetrated by socially sanctioned forms of authority. This includes both police forces and the military. By implication, then, the *Watchmen* challenges the moral and ethical basis for military and colonialist actions.

5. Ray Pratt refers to *Chinatown* as "an homage and a pastiche" (115). It is an homage in the sense that it represents the elements of classic noir. It is a pastiche in the sense that it builds upon these same constructs to create its own narrative, establishing itself as the prototypical neo-noir film.

6. Irwin writes: "Virtually none of the studio executives, directors, writers or actors who made these movies [film noir] in the 1940s and 50s would have even heard of the term *film noir*" (207). Irwin maintains, citing Barton Palmer, that noir was created by later French film critics and American film scholars.

7. Richard Martin claims that "classic film noir, as a product of the American film industry, represents an institutionally sanctioned alternative cinema to that traditionally associated with the American studios of the thirties and forties, one that often stretched the limits of established production policies" (15). His assessment views classic noir as a by-product of money-saving technical procedures utilized by smaller studios that, indirectly, created a cycle of films defined by their moody aesthetic elements.

8. Steve Neale argues that film noir "never existed" as a distinct genre (170). However, he also contends that neo-noir can be viewed as a much more coherent generic category (174).

9. The Coen Brothers' 2001 noir comedy *The Man Who Wasn't There*, for example, utilizes a plot that builds upon the motifs created by James Cain. At the same times, it delves into what R Barton Palmer describes sees as a self-conscious "[existentializing]" of "Cain's Materials." (160).

10. On the one hand, he views pastiche as an example of conformity, a by-product of "the age of multi-media conglomeration," where "film franchising" leads indirectly to the homogenization of cultural expression (Martin 28). At the other end of the spectrum, films like *Blood Simple* (1984) and *One False Move* (1992) represent a form of pastiche that attempts to self-consciously use the motifs of classic noir as a commentary on "the concerns of living in the United States today" (22).

11. Abrams argues that the neo-noir protagonist is divided against him/herself temporally: "The character [in neo-noir] is 'divided' against himself, although not so much emotionally as in Shakespeare, as epistemologically: divided in time as two selves, and one is looking for the other" (7). Seeking oneself in these films is largely a matter of seeking oneself as that self existed in a previous moment

12. See J. Robert Loftis's "Means, Ends, and the Critique of Pure Superheroes" for an in-depth discussion of how the *Watchmen* novel exposes the fascism inherent in the superhero fable, particularly in Rorschach's characterization.

13. In Raymond Chandler's *The Big Sleep*, for example, it is the rich and powerful Sternwood family's involvement with Geiger's pornography ring that set the violent events of that novel into motion.

14. See Erin Smith's *Hard-Boiled* for a detailed analysis of the ways in which the formal features of the hard-boiled narrative appealed to its readership.

15. As Sheri Chinen Bisen points out, the motifs of film noir were taken directly from the "austerity, populism and social critique of Depression-era" society (3). They were, then, utilized to speak to the "immediate challenges, concerns and anxieties of wartime"(3). The conventions remained the same, while their symbolic meaning evolved.

16. See Barton Palmer's essay "The New Sincerity of Neo Noir" (2007) for a discussion of the ways in which post-modern neo-noir film could utilize and expound upon the basic conventions of hard-boiled fiction.

17. The motif of the solitary avenger was made popular in 1970s action films, as Eric Lichtenfeld points out, beginning with 1971's *Dirty Harry*, and it would influence an entire genre of 1970s action/neo-noir films (24).

18. In the article "What's So Goddamn Funny," Taneli Kukkonen observes that Rorschach stringently sticks to his perceived set of rules, having, for example, "a propensity for acting in a bizarrely polite fashion at unexpected moments" (207). In essence, Rorschach rigidly sticks to his moral code, even when it causes him to act strangely in the eyes of the people around him.

19. See Megan Abbot's *The Street Was Mine* for a detailed discussion of the relationship between hard-boiled fiction and neo-noir in their respective treatment of gender.

20. This aspect began in hard-boiled fiction, as Greg Forter points out (13). But it is equally present in film noir. Ultimately, it can be located in the manic characterizations of neo-noir protagonists. Specifically, Travis Bickle's actions trigger *Taxi Driver's* imagined apocalypse, as Christopher Sharrett argues, even as it brings him to the brink of personal self-destruction (56).

21. The motif of making the familiar uncanny is key to the *Watchmen* narrative, as Thompson observes (104).

22. See Pratt for a discussion of the historical meaning of the neo-noir film.

23. As Kukkonen argues, Rorschach and the Comedian are both "reduced to tears" at key moments in the narrative (211).

24. The subtle changes between the novel and the film confirm Dennis O'Neill's observations that changes in medium can sometimes radically alter the meaning and significance of superhero narratives (27).

25. Litchenfeld notes that "it is the decade's later years that saw a breaking of the nearly twenty-year stranglehold that DC Comics had held on the comic book film with just the *Batman* and *Superman* franchises" (286).

26. Terry Kading argues: "The superhero comic, in response to 9/11, provides a distinct medium from which to reflect on and explore the fears, insecurities, and varied individual reactions generated by the attacks" (219).

# Smallville

## Super Puberty and the Monstrous Superhero

### SHAHRIAR FOULADI

Premiering in 2001, the television program *Smallville* (The WB/The CW, 2001–2011) frequently depicts a "monstrous" version of the oldest and most venerable superhero, as the pre–Superman Clark Kent struggles with the pubescent emergence of destructive, uncontrollable superpowers. "Monstrosity" is my term for the superhero's corruption by internal or external forces that overturn his traditional role as a protector. According to Peter Coogan, the superhero genre is identified primarily by its protagonist, whose key characteristics are "mission, powers, and identity"(30). The second and third aspects are visually apparent: The superhero has abilities that go beyond those of normal humans and has a heroic identity comprised of a codename, costume, and (often) an alter ego. What is most important in identifying the character as a superhero is his mission. Coogan defines it as "prosocial and selfless, which means that his fight against evil must fit in with the existing, professed mores of society and must not be intended to benefit or further his own agenda" (30). As such, the superhero does not disrupt or extend the status quo; he uses his superpowers in order to maintain order and stop others (the so-called "villains") from changing things. The monstrous superhero is a corrupted figure primarily because his core mission is violated, as he becomes (or is perceived as) a destroyer who disrupts order rather than a protector. In the process, the powers that allow his heroism and define him as a character cause terrifying destruction. Moreover, in some cases, the powers themselves are corrupted, flowing out of the hero's control and instigating the violation of his protective mission. As Scott Bukatman explains in his analysis of mutant superheroes (who fit into the monstrous mold), "their first and most dangerous enemies are their own bodies" (60). This chapter shall explore the portrayal of Clark Kent's monstrous puberty on *Smallville*, as the character suffers through violent physical changes that make him a threat to humans and reveal potential immoral uses of his

161

abilities. In examining Clark's monstrosity, I do close analysis of several episodes of *Smallville* in which his bodily transformations are the focal point. I break down narrative, dialogue, and formal aspects of the television text (mise-en-scène, cinematography, editing, and sound) to establish how his body's monstrosity is represented and its significance.

My argument is premised on the idea that a genre's tendencies reveal actual anxieties and fantasies of viewers/readers; accordingly, elements like monstrosity are repeated when they resonate with the audience. As elucidated by Coogan, genre is "a system of interaction between the producers and audiences of a medium embodied in privileged story forms in which basic social conflicts are narratively animated and resolved" (194–195). To put it simply, generic stories typically follow a set of conventions, which act as a blueprint for producers and determine audience expectations. In animating "basic social conflicts," genre texts reflect real concerns of viewers/readers. Importantly, producers can shift the genre by introducing variations (whether for artistic or commercial reasons) and the audience can change it through its consumption or lack thereof, creating the "system of interaction" between them. Most of the transformations of and deviations from a genre are defined in relation to the accepted and expected conventions. In the case of the superhero genre, monstrosity upends (classical) conventions, creating moments when the protagonist is a threat rather than a protector. The repeated appearances of monstrosity in the superhero genre broadly (after 2000) and the ten seasons of *Smallville*, in particular, show that the constantly corrupted superhero represents an evolution of the genre (a new convention) and meaningfully animates spectator fears and desires.

Instances of superhero monstrosity invariably work to unveil the deep-seated anxieties at the heart of the superhero genre (it commences, after all, during the Great Depression): feelings of powerlessness, distrust and fear of the powerful. The superhero combats these uneasy feelings, offering the fantasy of having great power and creating an idealized world in which pure-hearted overseers protect the weak and punish the criminal. However, the initial anxieties are never completely suppressed, as there is a steady stream of stories about the superhero being corrupted in some way, thereby becoming an unstoppable force of destruction and exposing the impotence of humans. Monstrosity transforms the superhero into something nightmarish, revealing the continued discomfort with individuals possessing such disproportionate power.

The superhero's monstrosity can be traced back to the first evil Superman story from 1933, a character created by Jerry Siegel and Joe Shuster five years before the heroic version. In "Reign of the Superman," the title character uses his telepathic and telekinetic abilities to bend the entire world to his mercy. Thomas Andrae describes this evil Superman as a "social menace who threaten[s] fundamental American values and institutions" and is "obsessed with his power and ... contemptuous of mankind"; thus, the character shows how great power can corrupt, leading to the exploitation of others and even threatening entire nations (124–125). The monstrosity is largely absent in the more heroic Superman that starts the superhero genre in 1938, but there are vestiges of it in some of the superhero's occasionally destructive behavior.[1] In addition, there are consistently superhero comics (regardless of character) in which the monstrous suddenly erupts, as the protagonist somehow turns evil, loses control of his powers, and/or becomes a threat in some manner. However, the large-scale shift in superhero comics does not occur until the 1960s, when Marvel Comics characters like the X-Men, the Hulk, the Fantastic Four, and Spider-Man transform the genre by making the monstrous not just some shadowy specter but a key component. These often darker, younger superheroes (many are teens) actively struggle to control their bodies and use their abilities ethically and are often viewed in the comics as frightening destroyers as much as saviors. The more monstrous superheroes do not become the norm in mainstream film and TV incarnations of superheroes until 2000, with the premiere of *X-Men*. With its mutant protagonists, the film initiates film and TV representations of young superheroes who deal with monstrous morality and dangerous bodies and have a strained relationship with regular humans.

Like much of the film and television superhero media post–2000, *Smallville* is an origin story, depicting a pubescent superhero who struggles with his own monstrosity. Unlike superhero films in which this origin comprises two hours of screen time (or even just a half, a quarter, or less of the running time), the narrative of Clark Kent's development into a superhero takes up the entire ten-year run of the series, a perpetual tease that is the most intricate, extended superhero origin story yet created in film or on television. The program focuses on Clark Kent's high school years for the first four seasons and then follows him as he enters adulthood, not taking on the "Superman" mantle until the end of the show's run. The pre–Superman version of Clark Kent, like most of the superheroes of this era in film and TV, discovers his great abilities and struggles to control and use them properly while simultaneously questioning his moral mission. Reflecting this angst, the show began on the WB network, which was primarily identified with teen audiences, featuring numerous programs about beautiful teens and young adults having difficulty making sense of life, as they balance romance, entry into adulthood, and melodramatic, sometimes fantastical situations. Combining aspects of the teen, horror, and, of course, superhero genres, *Smallville* creates an anxious young Superman who flirts with monstrosity constantly, as—especially in the early seasons—he undergoes the tribulations of puberty amplified by his possession of superpowers.

In undergoing super puberty, *Smallville*'s Clark Kent exhibits the three kinds of (often overlapping) monstrosity that can be found in superheroes: moral, physical, and original sin. The superhero is morally monstrous in cases where he uses his powers to indulge his own desires or to enact excessive violence.

Alternately, the superhero displays physical monstrosity in situations where his powers either flow out of control, causing destruction, or visually mark him as horrifying. Finally, there is original sin monstrosity, in which the superhero's possession of powers or, less commonly, his place of origin leads to humans being harmed or feeling threatened. It is called "original sin" in that the superhero is viewed as a threat or actually becomes dangerous due to his birth as a superpowered being (i.e., his birth is monstrous).[2] On *Smallville*, Clark Kent lacks the certainty about his powers and ethical purpose that is associated with the traditional versions of Superman (i.e., the ones known to the mainstream public), since the show is set before his emergence as a true superhero. As such, he often displays moral monstrosity by making poor or selfish decisions on how to use powers (with occasional deadly consequences), even using them evilly in several instances. Likewise, physically, he exhibits elements of the monstrous: His body escapes his control many times and there is a profound sense of bodily freakishness for the young Clark Kent. The typical shame associated with puberty becomes something more frightening, as the super teen fears his own body and moral development; he has no idea what his strange alien heritage (he is from the planet Krypton) will do to his body and mind and whether he has any control over it. He constantly worries about his original sin monstrosity, as he could endanger humanity or be seen as a menace due to his superhuman abilities (or his place of origin, since Krypton brings various dangerous objects and villains to Earth). Rather than something to be shown off, his abilities are, throughout most of the show's run, something to be hidden, "kept in the closet" in a way similar to secrets about one's sexuality. In this sense and several others, *Smallville* owes much to superhero narratives of characters like the X-Men and Spider-Man, in both comics and film.[3] Like the mutant superheroes, Clark struggles to control his super-powered body, deals with puberty, and fears the revelations of his true, non-human nature.[4] Like Spider-Man, he constantly questions how to use his superpowers, undergoes a process of learning how to use his abilities and how to create a heroic identity, and flirts with darker morality.

In looking at Clark's monstrous puberty on the TV series *Smallville*, I start with the premiere episode of the show and explore how it establishes a pubescent superhero who battles the emerging freakishness of his super body (is he becoming a monster?) and fears the consequences of the super/monstrous body being revealed to the public. It is original sin monstrosity — the superhero's powers (or his place of origin) harming humans or making them feel threatened — that is paramount here as Clark's aberrant puberty marks him as a potential hazard to humanity. In the next section of the chapter, I analyze several of the episodes in which Clark achieves new superpowers, which the show overtly makes analogous to pubescent development. Most of these powers initially have destructive consequences, emphasizing Clark's physical monstrosity. They also highlight the dangerousness of such a powerful individual existing (original sin monstrosity), if he could not gain control of these powers or if he decided to use them for evil purposes (moral monstrosity). In the chapter, it is imperative to tie the portrayals of the kinds of monstrosity on *Smallville* to other live-action superhero media from the post–2000 era (*X-Men* being the primary point of comparison), proving how the genre as a whole has shifted and exhibits similar tendencies broadly.

The primary focus on *Smallville*, rather than any of these other renditions of superheroes, is the result of several key factors. First, it is a question of manageability, as in-depth research and analysis of *Smallville* is less unwieldy than looking closely at numerous superhero films and TV shows. More importantly, as the longest-running live-action superhero representation (with over 200 episodes), the program provides multiple examples of all the variations of the monstrous superhero, offering a myriad of narratives, images, and sounds to analyze. Choosing to concentrate on a program like *Heroes* (NBC, 2006–2010) or the *X-Men* films would not provide nearly the same variety due to the limited number of episodes/films and would result in a lack of attention to certain manifestations of superhero monstrosity. Furthermore, *Smallville* premiered the year after the genre's shift to more monstrous superheroes in 2000 (caused largely by the film and TV industry's targeting of a youthful demographic who primarily identifies with young, conflicted heroes) and will finish in 2011, meaning it has been on television throughout the time that film and TV superheroes have been at the height of their popularity. As a result, *Smallville* both heavily borrows from the era's film superheroes (e.g., the *X-Men*, *Spider-Man*, and *Iron Man* films) and influences them, making it a key text to look at for trends.

The choice of *Smallville* is also due to the fact that it features a version of the first superhero, the one who set up most of the anxieties and fantasies of the genre, providing a connection to the genre's origin and history. Superman is typically the most conservative superhero in that, as the oldest and most recognizable, he resists many of the genre's trends in order to match reader/viewer expectations of the character (which simultaneously results in claims that the character has become outdated and irrelevant).[5] Thus, the overwhelming monstrosity of the teenage and young adult form of the superhero on *Smallville* shows how significantly the genre has shifted. Even Superman suffers through growing pains, as he constantly loses sight of his moral mission, struggles to control his super body, and is often a destroyer as much as a hero.

## Finding the Monster Inside: Clark Kent's Discovery of His Super (Freakish) Body ... and the Quest to Hide It

The first episode of *Smallville* ("Pilot") establishes one of the show's primary thematic elements: Clark Kent (Tom Welling) discovering his potential for moral and physical monstrosity due to his superpowers, fretting about becoming a threat to humanity (original sin monstrosity), and working to control (and hide) his abilities so that they can be used for decidedly un-monstrous ends. The opening scene with the teenage Clark Kent in the premiere shows that he is already obsessed with his own physical monstrosity: He eagerly peruses online newspaper stories titled "Record Breaking Teen Becomes Fastest Man Alive" and "Six-year-old Korean Boy Lifts Car Off Injured Father" (his only two powers at this point are super speed and strength) as if looking for confirmation that his own freakish body is not unique and will not result in being marginalized. This interest in freakish bodies is contrasted with the preceding shot of an idyllic farmhouse and fenced-in cows (shown while gentle country-ish guitar music plays in the background) and the following scene that depicts an apparently normal (if stunningly attractive) nuclear family — Clark, his mom (Annette O'Toole), his dad (John Schneider) — having breakfast in the kitchen on their Midwest farm. The implication is that the surface appearance of a nostalgically "normal" American family is largely illusory, as Clark's anxiety over his body dominates the lives of the Kents. Clark's hopes for normalcy — or, as he expresses it, to "go through high school without being a total loser" — are thwarted by his potential physical monstrosity, as his powers may escape his control or "out" him as a superpowered being, and by his potential moral monstrosity, as he may get upset and use his powers for selfish, destructive ends. When the family's breakfast conversation turns to the subject of Clark's desire to join the football team, his father immediately squelches the idea since his superpowers create danger for other students and give Clark an unfair advantage, especially if he uses them without restraint.

Though he already has some knowledge of his super speed and strength, the first episode of *Smallville* exhibits Clark discovering the extent of his power and his increasing fear of being outed as a monster. Instructed by his parents to keep his powers secret — as reflected in their discussion about joining the football team — Clark struggles with the potential to have all three kinds of monstrosity due to his body: moral (he may use his powers selfishly), physical (his freakish body may be a source of horror or destruction), and original sin (the revelation that he has superpowers, regardless of how he uses them, may cause him to be seen as a threat to humanity). Ironically, his attempts to hide his potential monstrosity lead to him being socially unpopular, as he cannot participate in activities or show off who he truly is.

The first moment in the premiere episode in which Clark deals with the discovery of his powers is when Lex Luthor (Michael Rosenbaum) accidentally hits him with his speeding Porsche. The aftermath of the impact is shown in a slow-motion long shot (and two subsequent slow-motion shots from different angles that repeat part of the fateful action and unveil more of it) as Clark is thrown sideways off of the bridge and Lex's car flies straight into the water below. After Clark rips Lex out of his submerged car and rescues him, Lex mouths: "I could have sworn I hit you." In a close-up shot with the now-broken bridge in the background, Clark responds in a stunned manner: "If you did, I'd be ... I'd be dead." He is then shown in a close-up turning to look at the off-screen bridge, followed by a long shot of the bridge (with Clark out of focus in the lower-right foreground) as the camera slowly zooms toward it. The surprise on Clark's face and the emphasis on the accident site underscore that Clark himself did not know the extent of his own strength and did not believe he could survive such a collision.

He not only realizes his extreme physical freakishness, but also confronts the fear that he may be outed by Lex. Like most teenagers, he remains afraid of being socially outcast and feels vulnerable about his body. Furthermore, Clark's fear that revelation will lead to horror is compounded with the apprehension that he will be seen as a threat to humanity, an invader of some sort that puts the world at risk (several characters see him as this sort of threat in future seasons). Appropriately, the pivotal accident scene ends with a close-up of Lex looking toward the camera as Clark walks away off-screen, the camera then racking focus to the heavily damaged Porsche being lifted out of the water in the background, as Lex turns to look at it. At the conclusion of the shot, the camera switches its focus back to Lex in the foreground, as he turns to look off-screen at Clark again, this time more suspiciously. The implication — which is expressed concretely later in the first season — is that Lex does not believe he could have survived an accident in which the front of his car was ripped off unless something unexplainable happened. His skepticism reinforces Clark's dread at being revealed as superhuman.

Rather than depicting Clark's pubescent discovery of greater powers as something entirely positive, *Smallville* falls in line with the post–1960 comic book tradition and post–2000 filmic tradition of seeing superhuman abilities as both a curse and a blessing. Clark voices his alienation later in the episode when he asks his dad, "How about this, is this normal?" and proceeds to stick his hand in a wood chipper, remove it unscathed, and say, "I didn't dive in after Lex's car, it hit me at sixty miles an hour. Does that sound normal to you? I'd give anything to be normal." Thus, superhuman strength is something horrifying to him, as it stops him from having the kind of experiences a typical human teenager would have; he is constantly wary that his body will unintentionally hurt others, give him an unfair advantage, or reveal his threatening alienness. Taking his teenage alienation to literal levels, Clark soon learns that he is from another planet; after revealing the truth about his origin to him, his father tells him he waited so long to tell him in order "to protect him." The implication is that until this point his alien origin might have been too difficult for him to conceal and too horrifying. However, now that he is growing up and becoming even more superhuman, he has to know so that he understands that he may be going through a very strange, inhuman puberty. As his potential monstrosity increases, so do the fears of revelation.

In the first four seasons (covering Clark's high school years), the show is largely about the danger of Clark's super body escaping his control and/or openly marking him as a freak.[6] Though most obvious in episodes where Clark discovers new powers (which will be covered shortly), Clark's out-of-control body can also be seen in his encounters with green kryptonite, meteor rocks from the remnants of his home planet that are poisonous to him. In "Pilot," we are introduced to kryptonite when we meet his love interest, Lana Lang (Kristin Kreuk). Following a medium close-up of Clark looking off-screen intently, we see a slow motion shot of a pretty girl (Lana) as non-diegetic romantic music plays. We are subsequently presented a long shot of Clark approaching Lana, while numerous students stand in the foreground and background. However, Clark (accompanied by some non-diegetic comical music) soon trips and falls down, dropping all his books and inciting the mockery of his schoolmates. One of his best friends even says that he becomes "a total freak show" whenever he approaches Lana. A close-up of Lana's green necklace reveals its role in Clark's clumsiness; for non–Superman fans who do not already recognize this green rock, it is revealed later in the episode (and in subsequent episodes) that it is a remnant of a meteor rock from Clark's home planet of Krypton (a.k.a., "kryptonite") and it can harm and potentially kill Clark. Clark spends the rest of the scene in a medium close-up, in serious pain and struggling to pick up his books, while Lana talks to her boyfriend, who laughs that Clark looks like he is "going to hurl." In a similar incident later in the episode, Lana's boyfriend (now wearing her necklace) challenges Clark to a fight, but Clark's body is rendered totally helpless by the kryptonite. He collapses to the ground in a close-up, high angle shot, grimacing in pain. Unable to resist, he is tied up in a field as "the scarecrow," a yearly rite of passage for an unfortunate freshman student.

Green kryptonite has a role throughout the show to make Clark impotent, thwarting his potential heroism and serving to make him look weak and cowardly. In cases where it halts his heroism, kryptonite exemplifies original sin monstrosity in that something from Clark's origin endangers humans, since it does not allow Clark to save people in peril. In addition to making Clark look weak and jeopardizing his life and mission, kryptonite's visibly harmful effect on Clark is dangerous in that it can reveal some of his abnormality (regular humans do not get sick because of green rocks) and his greatest weakness; villains who learn of its power over Clark often try to use it to torture Clark, convince him to do morally reprehensible things, or kill him (e.g., in the episode "Extinction").

Though clearly examples of his super body being self-destructive (and of original sin monstrosity since he is rendered unable to save people), Clark's misadventures with green kryptonite do not quite qualify as cases of physical monstrosity. Clark's powers do not become unintentionally destructive to others (in fact, they are nullified) and, though his body acts abnormally, he is typically not revealed as a horrifying superpowered being. Instead, his reactions to kryptonite often create the illusion of a young man going through regular puberty, as Clark's unusual body results in behavior that is interpreted by others as social ineptness, usually in the form of excessive anxiety or wimpiness (typical human freakishness, not shocking superhuman freakishness). So, if he falls short of outing his super body and being labeled a monster when he encounters kryptonite, he ironically marks himself as painfully average — i.e., not super at all. Thus, even when the superhero succeeds in hiding and controlling his powers, the possession of a super body can still have negative effects, fitting in with the shifts of the genre post–2000 in film and TV that make powers often as much of a curse as a blessing.

## Emerging/Overflowing Superpowers: Sexual Awakening, Destruction, and Nearly Being Outed as a Monster

> "Great, so I'm maturing into a fire-starter!"
> Clark Kent, in the episode "Heat" on Smallville

The most frightening manifestations of Clark's super puberty in the early seasons of Smallville are when he loses control of his body, becoming unintentionally destructive and risking revelation. These cases of monstrous physicality are usually conterminous with the discovery of new powers, as he undergoes a puberty which is unknowable since no one else on Earth has experienced it. A comparison with the X-Men films throughout this analysis is fruitful, as Clark Kent embodies many facets of Bukatman's depiction of mutant characters, who "are distinguished by (a frequently maudlin) emotionalism" and constant difficulties controlling their own bodies (66). Though he battles with his body in a similar manner, Clark does differ in several significant ways from the mutants Bukatman describes: He is a solitary alien rather than one of many mutated humans (making his bodily changes even more mysterious), has multiple powers to master, has a clearer purpose for his powers (helping people), and is essentially invulnerable, resulting in little physical risk to his own body. Moreover, whereas the bodies of mutants remain their greatest enemies throughout their lives, Clark's struggles with his body are largely transient, as he gains control over each of his abilities quickly and firmly. Each new power commences a short narrative that ends in triumph, with Clark closer to becoming Superman, an all-powerful, totally-in-control superhero (though kryptonite promises to remain a problem he cannot overcome). An analysis of several early season episodes will show how Clark's teenage physical monstrosity results in destruction, danger of revelation, and the need to tame his own body, and how all of this coincides with pubescent sexual and social maturation and trauma.

The first episode devoted to the pubescent changes of Clark's body is the first season's "X-Ray," which features Clark's discovery and attempted control of his unwieldy X-ray vision. He initially experiences the power after a trauma: A character who appears to be his friend Lex Luthor (in reality, a shape-shifting mutant) responds to Clark's greeting by angrily throwing him through a store window with inhuman force, the latter emphasized with slow motion footage of the largely impervious Clark Kent flying through the window like a ragdoll. Seemingly betrayed by his friend, who shockingly appears to have superpowers too, Clark's confused face gives way to a medium point-of-view shot of "Lex." This shot suddenly (via special effects) transforms into a moving X-ray image of "Lex" running away, his skeleton appearing to glow with the green of the town's meteor rocks. Therefore, social/emotional distress (betrayal by his friend) and physical pain (being thrown) have triggered another trauma: the initiation of a new superpower, which has appeared without advance warning.

The second appearance of this new power in the episode is more explicitly tied to emerging sexuality and teenage awkwardness. While in gym class, Clark glances at Lana, shown in a medium close-up in her workout clothes, sweaty from exercising and heading to the locker room. After she looks in Clark's general direction, he is framed in medium close-up and then close-up as he scrunches his face in agony and complains that his "head hurts." The alluring presence of Lana is evidently what has activated this physical reaction, which, as is clarified a few seconds later, is related to the initiation of his X-ray vision. Threatened with ten laps of running for his slowness and forced to climb the rope in gym class, Clark is socially shamed by the coach. Things get worse when Clark suddenly looks horrified while climbing the rope; as we cut to a medium close-up shot of his friend Pete (Sam Jones III) on the adjacent rope, Pete's image frighteningly turns into an X-ray, exposing his circulatory system with its flowing rivers of blood.[7] The sense of humiliation increases when Clark lets go of the rope and falls a long way to the ground, the coach asking, "Kent, are you all right? Kent, what happened up there?" as Clark lies on the ground.

The scene ends with the most sexual use of his new power yet: A close-up of Clark looking off-screen gives way to a point-of-view shot of a wall, the camera zooming toward it and then X-raying through its interiors (aided by special effects) until it reveals the girl's locker room, with various half-naked teenage girls. Clark's eyes are then framed in an extreme close-up, as he shakes his head, trying to stop his ability from working (and perhaps wondering if it is all a dream). Next, we see Lana approach her locker while only wearing a towel; another extreme close-up of Clark's eyes as he furrows his brow in shock; a medium shot of Lana turning her back to the camera and dropping her towel; and finally a medium close-up of Clark with a goofy grin on his face, ecstatic about what he is seeing. Thus, his powers are triggered by sexual arousal and here climax in his access to the naked body of his love interest. This peek into the girl's locker room operates as wish-fulfillment for both Clark and the audience (what pubescent boy hasn't dreamt of X-ray vision?), but also is a moment of moral monstrosity in that he is (unintentionally) using his powers for personal gain and is violating the privacy of others. Furthermore, despite the pleasurable, sexual moment, the overwhelming effects of his new ability have been negative: He has embarrassed himself in gym class and nearly revealed his powers by falling from the rope without injury.

The very next scene depicts him meeting with his parents in an attempt to tame pubescent powers that are potentially monstrous in so many ways: their immoral usage, their ability to out him as an alien and, most prominently, their destructive uncontrollability.[8] Clark rails at the abnormal body that threatens to reveal his freakishness: "You guys, I can see through things! How do you control that?" His mother offers an analogy to human development: "You gotta practice, Clark. Your eyes have muscles, just like your legs." The parallel to the human body reminds that Clark's body is going through the changes of puberty any teenager undergoes; it is only the scale and dangerousness that is different. As Clark follows his parents' advice and practices his new power, it pays off almost immediately: He discovers the identity of the Lex Luthor imposter and, by the end of the episode, stops the villain and saves Lana from certain death using his X-ray vision.

The super puberty of characters like Clark clearly has a special draw for teenage boys, who comprise a significant part of the audience for superhero films and TV shows (and of course comics as well). In "A Boy for All Planets," Miranda Banks discusses how the changes Clark and other superpowered teens endure parallel those of most teenagers:

> The development of power and vulnerability can be seen as a metaphor for the experience of every teenager. Max [from *Roswell*] and Clark's transformations are like alien puberty: they often feel uncomfortable at first with their growing abilities, and sometimes letting people know about how their bodies are changing makes them feel more vulnerable [24].

Clark's discovery of new powers is like the discovery of physical changes for teenage viewers, as they change in perhaps "uncomfortable" ways that can be embarrassing and scary. By adding superpowers to the mix, *Smallville* and other superhero texts ratchet up the drama of puberty to life-or-death proportions, reflecting perhaps how some teenagers actually feel as they change. Moreover, superpowered puberty is, in many ways, a fantasy of puberty that appeals to teens and (to a lesser extent) adults who underwent a more mundane or difficult process of growing up. Clark does not just get taller or stronger, but gets super strength, super speed, heat vision, and X-ray vision, abilities that are the stuff of male teenage fantasies. Even when Clark's body flows out of control, there is something impressive about the level of power he displays. In addition, he always figures out how to make his pubescent changes work to the benefit of himself and the world. Significantly, not all superhero puberty is so positive, as mutants in the X-Men world experience more traumatic changes as their powers ostracize and constantly overwhelm them. However, even mutants present the fantasy of attainting abilities beyond those of regular people. In Clark's case, none of his anxious bodily transformations can be characterized as negative in the end; the viewer knows that each difficult adjustment brings Clark closer to becoming Superman, an adult superhero characterized by his amazing powers and steadfast morality. The triumphant nature of Clark's (often scary) pubescent development ultimately defuses some of the anxieties about puberty for teen male viewers.

The episodes in which Clark discovers his body's changes always follow the same pattern: From something monstrous that could hurt Clark and others, his new powers develop into something that he can use in his heroic actions. In other words, the episodes are about growing up — going through puberty on a super scale. Unlike the constantly overflowing bodies of the mutant superheroes discussed by Bukatman, Clark's mastery of his X-ray ability appears very complete and he never struggles with its control again. Despite the total taming of his abilities (i.e., powers initiate only at Clark's behest), all of Clark's powers continue to contain monstrous potential. His X-ray vision could still out him as a freak, cause him to be seen as a threat to humanity (he endangers privacy and is a superpowered alien living among humans), render him unable to fulfill his role as a superhero (if it somehow escapes his control again), and be used by him for nefarious purposes.[9] The latter use is referenced when, at the end of the episode "X-Ray," Clark asks his mother, "Mom, if you could see anything, what would you do?" and she responds, "Learn to close my eyes." Her advice is a plea to use his powers responsibly, to refrain from morally dubious uses for personal gain or pleasure, and to maintain control.

The next significant new power Clark obtains is heat vision, which is even more explicitly linked to sexuality and more dangerously threatens both Clark and others, but is still tamed by the end of the episode "Heat" during the second season. The power first emerges while Clark struggles to watch a sex education film in class due to being distracted by his attractive new substitute teacher (Krista Allen). As the film mentions things like "intercourse," we see Clark looking behind himself, followed by medium shots of his provocatively dressed teacher, the camera sometimes tilting down to show her bare legs. Following an extreme close-up of her cleavage, a series of shots show Clark's new power erupt (a very appropriate word in this case): first, a close-up of Clark's face as he stares behind himself and begins to blink his eyes rapidly, as if in pain; next, an extreme close-up of Clark's face as he turns to the front of the room, his eyes glowing as the camera moves closer and we hear sound effects meant to resemble fire shooting; and, finally, a long shot of Clark (facing the camera) at his desk shooting short bursts of fire out of his eyes, with streaming motion lines marking their path. As if the sexual nature of his heat vision were not clear enough, there is then a shot of the screen at the front of the classroom displaying the image of an egg with sperm surrounding it; Clark's heat bursts (which, in their transparent form, do resemble sperm) penetrate the filmic egg at the same time as the sperm. The implication of all these images is that his new ability is directly triggered by typical teenage sexual feelings, taking puberty into unprecedented, destructive directions since, in the first instance of Clark's power, the film screen bursts into flames and the school has to be evacuated.

Clark's monstrous eruption shows the dangerousness of the super body; in particular, this ability is frightening to Clark himself because, he explains: "All my other abilities didn't involve things bursting into flames." Clark starts a minor fire, but he could have easily burned down the entire school or killed a fellow student if he were simply looking in a different direction. The scene exemplifies physical monstrosity, but also original sin monstrosity in that his heat vision makes him a danger to people around him. In addition, uncontrolled heat vision holds further possibilities of original sin monstrosity in that it could expose him as a disproportionately powerful alien (a menace just for existing) and could render him unable to act heroically in certain situations, thereby indirectly endangering people.

The more destructive second eruption of his new power occurs while sitting at a coffee shop alone with his love interest, Lana. Sitting in close proximity to Clark, Lana is framed in extreme close-up discussing how Lex has acted on his "passion" and wondering if she and Clark will ever "be able to do the same" (hinting at the sexual tension between them). The romantic underpinnings of the scene quickly get to Clark, as he is shown in extreme close-ups quickly blinking and looking away. After he gets up and twirls around with his eyes closed in complete panic, Clark's eyes suddenly let forth a long sustained burst of fire, which is depicted burning the expensive equipment in the coffee shop and then causing it to explode. Lana, who does not see Clark's eyes, screams and cowers in close-up at the horror of the raging fire. Rather than protecting her, as he normally would, Clark is shown fighting to close his eyes but is unable to counteract his super hormones. Thus, Clark's body has become a danger to everyone in his life, as it can damage property and kill people with dreadful haste. The monstrousness of his pubescent development is emphasized by Clark's subsequent remark: "I was afraid it wasn't gonna stop"; since there is no precedent for his body's changes, there is a sense that each new power controls him (rather than the other way around) and that his body may continue to experience strange, hazardous changes perpetually. It is why Clark somewhat seriously exclaims: "Great, so I'm maturing into a fire-starter!"

In both violent eruptions, the super body becomes not only monstrously unstable and dangerous, but a source of embarrassment and near-public exposure and reminds of the morally monstrous potential of superpowers. Even more so than his X-ray vision, Clark's heat vision is a metaphor for the sexual maturation of every teenager. The context and physical appearance of the new ability make it resemble premature ejaculation: Clark gets so excited that he cannot stop his body from bursting forth. After the first bursts, in particular,

Clark appears ashamed — looking dazed, covering his mouth and lowering his head, and then spinning around in place while everyone else exits — as if he has sexually malfunctioned in the most public, horrible way possible. Furthermore, the look of embarrassment is indicative of how the power threatens to expose him as a physical freak and a menace to humanity. Clark sees his own body as monstrously freakish, dramatically telling his parents: "Hi, I'm Clark. I'm the kid who can lift up tractors and see through walls." The series of unexplained fires eventually leads to Clark being arrested as an arsonist (aided by a frame job by the villain) in the same episode. Even though his powers are not unveiled, his damming role in the fires is, recalling the negative social costs of having a super body that escapes control. Despite Clark's desire to hide his new power, his uncontrolled outbursts of heat (physical monstrosity) endanger humans (original sin monstrosity), engaging the dark potential of immoral usage: With heat vision, an angry or selfish Clark could simply point his eyes at something or someone and destroy it. Thus, the accidental destruction — i.e., unintentional monstrosity — reflects how each new power bears new possibilities for intentional moral monstrosity.

Destructive powers that overwhelm the superhero and are triggered by sexual development represent a generic trend that was initiated in film and TV by 2000's X-Men. Describing the mutant bodies presented in X-Men texts, Bukatman writes: "They are traumatized, eruptive bodies; the energies that are normally unleashed only in battle now continually threaten to overspill their fragile vessels. The mutant superhero is both armored and flowing" (68). Much of this description also applies to Clark on Smallville, because he and the X-Men mutants both possess strong bodies that are not always under their control (especially fitting for pubescent characters). The powers of the mutants often wildly flow out of them like Clark's heat vision does in the episode just described. However, as mentioned earlier, Clark's experiences with superpowers are not precisely like those of the mutants, as his body is not at all "fragile" and is generally much more "armored" (controlled, protected) than "flowing" (unrestrained). Clark is traumatized by his eruptive body, but he largely overcomes the initial ordeal of each new power and regains command over his body; he does not "continually" lose control the way mutants usually do. In fact, the frequency of Clark's out-of-control body is largely due to the fact that he achieves multiple new powers, each requiring a process of taming. In contrast, mutants can struggle for a lifetime with one power.

In one of the opening scenes of X-Men, teenager Marie (a.k.a., "Rogue") exhibits the traumatic overflowing of mutant powers when her pubescent sexuality activates her ability to absorb the energy of anyone she touches. Initially, Rogue (Anna Paquin) is alone in her bedroom with her love interest, both of them reclining on her bed. The sexually charged atmosphere gives way to several extreme close-ups of them kissing. With her first manifestation of powers, her love interest suddenly opens his eyes as veins start protruding all over his face.

As he has seizures, all she can do is scream and run into the corner of the room, saying: "I just touched him" and yelling to her parents: "Don't touch me!" Thus, like several of Clark's abilities, her power appears for the first time when she is sexually aroused. She is immediately cast as monstrous: She has a strange and dangerous body, can kill humans simply by touching them, and can potentially use her powers for nefarious purposes. Her experience is similar to Clark's in that she undergoes a kind of super puberty, though there is less hope for her to tame her power and it marks her as more aberrant (how can she ever live as a regular teen if she cannot touch?). Though she gets some control over it, she chooses in the third film of the series (*X-Men: The Last Stand*, 2006) to have her power removed so she can be with her superpowered boyfriend. The dangerous uncontrollability of her mutant power (even after several years) and the need to remove it are in direct contrast to Clark on *Smallville*, who usually gains a handle on each new power in a remarkably short amount of time, learning to use it to protect the world.

Although he is not going through puberty, another *X-Men* character, Cyclops (James Marsden), bears similarities to Clark in his possession of violent optical powers that threaten to erupt out of his body. Cyclops's eyes shoot destructive beams that he cannot control without a specially made visor, meaning that his eyes are always covered. As Bukatman recounts of the comic book version of the character, "the struggle of Cyclops involves holding back this energy, containing it within himself; to release it would be to destroy his own sense of being (the woman he loves can never see his eyes, he realizes)" (68). Likewise, in the film, his "sense of being"—he sees himself as a hero—will be destroyed if the energy from his body flows out uncontrollably and transforms him into a monster. This potential transformation is glimpsed in a scene at a train station in *X-Men*, as Cyclops and his heroic teammate Storm (Halle Berry) are confronted by villains. After having his visor knocked off, he is shown in several shots wildly shooting red beams from his eyes, including a close-up that depicts his eyes aglow with firing red beams (somewhat of a devilish image). He eventually shoots the roof off of the train station, the rubble injuring and possibly killing some of the nearby people, a clear case of physical monstrosity and original sin monstrosity. Forced to close his eyes or risk hurting more people, Cyclops is left totally helpless and unable to help his friends.[10] The depiction of overflowing, dangerous power from Cyclops's eyes is echoed in Clark's introduction to heat vision on *Smallville* (the episode aired two years after *X-Men*'s release). However, Clark again differs from the mutant superhero in that he tames his power by the end of one episode, regaining his capability to appear "normal." Cyclops, in contrast, is never able to gain physical control over his abilities. He can only manage his optical powers by technological means, usually wearing an oversized visor that marks him as aberrant (e.g., a mother in the same scene recoils on seeing him). Thus, when he is wearing his visor, he is seen as physically monstrous and a threat (i.e., original sin monstrosity), even when his abilities are restrained.[11] Finally, as Bukatman suggests, Cyclops's power is, if not directly tied to sex, a clear barrier to intimacy (68). Like Rogue's power and Clark's heat vision before he controls it, Cyclops's optical beams endanger his romantic partners.[12] If he were ever to let his partner look into his eyes while he looked into hers, he would kill her almost instantly.

All of these monstrous, overflowing and impotent super bodies are subsequently put under control to an extent. In terms of the characters discussed here, Rogue learns some control and then removes her powers, Cyclops wears a visor, and Clark, of course, learns to control his heat vision and other abilities. After a scene in which Clark is unwilling to look his father in the eyes for fear of killing him, his father takes him out to a field away from buildings and has him practice. By the next scene, Clark is gleefully using his heat vision to make popcorn and light candles, boasting: "Next time I have a date, I'll be able to take her out without setting her on fire" (i.e., he can hide his physical monstrosity and avoid original sin monstrosity by not hurting anyone). His power is also instrumental is stopping the villain at the end of the episode. Clark's education on how to utilize his powers properly is shepherded by his adoptive parents, the Kents, in these early seasons, as they teach him how to restrain his eruptive body and use it to help others. His parents serve a function similar to *X-Men*'s Professor Xavier (Patrick Stewart), whose mutant school brings control to unwieldy, potentially monstrous powers so that they will not be a danger to others and/or themselves; as Bukatman explains, "Under the tutelage of Professor X, the mutants are sited both inside and outside society; their powers move from uncontrolled and eruptive to controlled and articulate" (70). We do not see many scenes of mutants learning to control their powers in the *X-Men* films (there is some practicing of already proficient abilities), but it is implied that there is some rigorous training to help mutants gain command of their bodies. Likewise, many superhero films and TV shows of this era provide sequences in which the superhero trains his body with or without help, putting it under control.[13]

Despite these widespread depictions of superhero training, nearly total control of powers is achieved by only the non-mutant superheroes. For the mutants of the *X-Men* films, their bodies constantly threaten to overflow or fail; the dangers of puberty (or simply development) with superpowers never completely subsides as they continue to imperil themselves and everyone around them. In contrast, superheroes like Spider-Man and Superman typically exhibit extreme command of their powers once they train their bodies. This control, however, does not prevent rare cases in which unusual circumstances cause superpowers to ebb and flow wildly. For instance, Clark's heat vision on *Smallville* escapes his control at least two other times, but both instances are due to otherworldly factors. In the first situation, during the second season's episode "Rosetta," Clark is temporarily controlled by Kryptonian technology that abruptly forces him to create a symbol using his heat vision. In the second instance (episode "Perry," third season), he is unable to restrain any of his powers, as solar flares (he gets his powers from the sun) cause the super energies in his body to fluctuate wildly. Other destructive consequences in this episode include losing his super speed in the middle of the street, causing a car accident; suddenly running at super speed, outing his secret to a reporter; and receiving a spike in his strength that causes him to throw a tractor across town, nearly killing the same reporter and destroying expensive equipment. These are, again, clearly extraordinary conditions, as Clark usually exhibits a mastery over his (established) abilities that mutants generally lack.

As is typical of the superhero genre in film and TV after 2000 — especially as it increasingly depicts teenage protagonists learning to use powers and aims for a youthful demographic — *Smallville* shows how the superhero's monstrous side constantly erupts in stories and special effects visuals in which his body flows uncontrollably. Ultimately, Clark grapples so much with his abilities because he acquires them gradually over a period of time, reflecting the experience of puberty. He is a transitional figure, on the path to being all-powerful as Superman but still going through changes (and even after puberty, he continues to face the challenges of growing into a superhero). As a result, even when he controls one superpower, other abilities threaten to appear violently at any time. For example, his acquisition of super hearing initially results in him being crippled by excessive sensitivity to sound (and, related to this ability, he goes blind for a time), making him unable to save others in several cases; likewise, in the episode "Whisper," in which he achieves super breath, he destructively sneezes numerous times. Clark's struggle is similar to that faced by most post–2000 film and TV superheroes, especially as they master their emerging powers. However, on *Smallville*, Clark Kent is the epitome of the monstrous superhero, the show's longevity allowing the careful and detailed depiction of a super puberty that involves the discovery and attempted control of destructive abilities. His powers embody the superhero's potential to be both a superhero and a destroyer and, fittingly, Clark vacillates between the two roles throughout the series.

## Notes

1. See Andrae for further analysis of how Superman's menacing qualities are gradually shed around the time of the U.S.'s involvement in World War II. To view evidence of Superman's moral monstrosity in his very first heroic appearance, see Jerry Siegel and Joe Shuster, Untitled story, *Action Comics* #1 (June 1938), rpt. in *Superman in the Forties* (New York: DC Comics, 2005).

2. The character's "birth" as a superpowered being does not necessarily coincide with his literal birth, since he can acquire superhuman abilities later in life. For instance, Peter Parker (a.k.a. Spider-Man) acquires his abilities as a teenager after a radioactive spider bites him. In contrast, Superman and the various X-Men characters are born with superpowers (even if they do not manifest until later).

3. *Smallville* premiered a year after the first *X-Men* film and one year before the first *Spider-Man* film. Despite being released after *Smallville*, *Spider-Man* and its sequels conceivably still had a direct influence on the show during its ten-year run. Regardless, the similarities between various superhero films and TV shows indicate generic trends in this era.

4. The *X-Men* films draw a strong parallel between mutants and other minorities, especially homosexuals.

5. See Lev Grossman, "The Problem with Superman," *Time*, 10 May 2004, Web, 14 December 2010. <http://www.time.com/time/magazine/article/0,9171,1101040517-634695,00.html>

6. Though the dangers of his body escaping his control and/or outing him as a superpowered alien are more pronounced in the first four seasons, there are still many episodes in subsequent seasons where there is much anxiety that Clark's true identity will be revealed. In addition, there are a few more instances of his abilities destructively escaping restraint.

7. This is less intense than the earlier X-ray that reveals skeletal structures, suggesting the variability of his X-ray ability and the difficulty he will encounter in controlling it properly.

8. Though X-ray vision is not directly that destructive, its initial uncontrollability is depicted as disorienting Clark, which can potentially cause Clark's super body to slam into objects and people with devastating consequences.

9. Similarly to kryptonite, uncontrolled superpowers (a result of his birthplace of Krypton, like the poisonous rock) qualify as original sin monstrosity when they disrupt Clark from performing his direct heroic objectives—e.g., when his power goes out of control *while* he is trying to save humans from harm. His inability to act endangers humans that would normally be saved by him.

10. This is another example of original sin monstrosity, since superpowers indirectly endanger others by paralyzing the superhero, rendering him unable to save people as he normally would.

11. Cyclops also wears sunglasses that serve to hold back his eye beams without marking him as visibly monstrous; in fact, the sunglasses can be said to make him look "cool." However, they do not allow him to direct his beams at targets, making his powers largely useless.

12. Aside from heat vision, Clark struggles to have intimacy because his super body could kill someone during sex. In fact, Clark does not have sex unless he has temporarily lost his powers or has a partner with similar abilities, until the ninth season's episode "Escape," when extensive training teaches him more control over his powers.

13. Though his body does not have superpowers, Bruce Wayne/Batman in *Batman Begins* (2005) spends much of the first half of the film training his body and mind to control and use his overwhelming anger. Thus, despite the fact that his body is not out of control or inhumanly destructive, the need to tame his rage makes him resemble the superpowered hero with the overflowing body.

# Films and Television Programs

*Æon Flux*. Dir. Karyn Kusama. Perf. Charlize Theron, Marton Csokas, Jonny Lee Miller, and Sophie Okonedo. Paramount, 2005. Film.

*Alias* (ABC, 2001–2006).

*American Splendor*. Dir. Shari Springer Berman, Robert Pulcini. Perf. Paul Giamatti, Shari Springer Berman, and Harvey Pekar. HBO Films, 2003. Film.

*Any Given Sunday*. Dir. Oliver Stone. Perf. Al Pacino, Cameron Diaz, and Dennis Quaid. Warner Bros., 1999. Film.

*Armageddon*. Dir. Michael Bay. Perf. Bruce Willis, Billy Bob Thornton, Ben Affleck, and Liv Tyler. Touchstone Pictures, 1998. Film.

*The Asphalt Jungle*. Dir. John Huston. Perf. Sterling Hayden, Louis Calhern, and Jean Hagen. Metro-Goldwyn-Mayer, 1950. Film.

*Avatar*. Dir. James Cameron. Perf. Sam Worthington, Zoe Saldana, Sigourney Weaver, and Stephen Lang. 20th Century–Fox, 2009. Film.

*The Avengers*. Dir. Joss Whedon. Perf. Chris Evans, Robert Downey, Jr., Chris Hemsworth, and Mark Ruffalo. Marvel Studios, 2012. Film.

*Batman* (ABC, 1966–1968).

*Batman*. Dir. Tim Burton. Perf. Michael Keaton, Jack Nicholson, and Kim Basinger. Warner Bros., 1989. Film.

*Batman & Robin*. Dir. Joel Schumacher. Perf. George Clooney, Arnold Schwarzenegger, and Chris O'Donnell. Warner Bros., 1997. Film.

*Batman Begins*. Dir. Christopher Nolan. Perf. Christian Bale, Michael Caine, Katie Holmes, and Liam Neeson. Warner Bros., 2005. Film.

*Batman Forever*. Dir. Joel Schumacher. Perf. Val Kilmer, Tommy Lee Jones, and Jim Carrey. Warner Bros., 1995. Film.

*Batman Returns*. Dir. Tim Burton. Perf. Michael Keaton, Danny DeVito, and Michelle Pfeiffer. Warner Bros., 1992. Film.

*Ben Hur*. Dir. William Wyler. Perf. Charlton Heston, Jack Hawkins, and Stephen Boyd. Metro-Goldwyn-Meyer, 1959. Film.

*Beverly Hills 90210* (Fox, 1990–2000).

*The Banana Splits Adventure Hour* (NBC, 1968–1969).

*The Big Sleep*. Dir. Howard Hawks. Perf. Humphrey Bogart, Lauren Bacall, and John Ridgely. Warner Bros., 1946. Film.

*Blood Simple*. Dir. Joel and Ethan Coen. Perf. John Getz, Frances McDormand, and Dan Hedaya. River Road Productions, 1984. DVD.

*Buffy the Vampire Slayer* (WB, 1997–2003).

*Captain America: The First Avenger.* Dir. Joe Johnston. Perf. Chris Evans, Hugo Weaving, and Sebastian Stan. Paramount Pictures, 2011. Film.

*Catwoman.* Dir. Pitof. Perf. Halle Berry, Sharon Stone, and Benjamin Bratt. Warner Bros., 2004. Film.

*Charlie's Angels.* Dir. McG. Perf. Cameron Diaz, Drew Barrymore, Lucy Liu, and Bill Murray. Columbia, 2000. Film.

*Charlie's Angels Full Throttle.* Dir. McG. Perf. Cameron Diaz, Drew Barrymore, Lucy Liu, and Bernie Mac. Columbia, 2003. Film.

*Charmed* (WB, 1998–2004).

*Children of a Lesser God.* Dir. Randa Haines. Perf. William Hurt, Marlee Matlin, and Piper Laurie. Paramount, 1986. Film.

*Chinatown.* Dir. Roman Polanski. Perf. Jack Nicholson, Faye Dunaway, and John Huston. Paramount, 1974. Film.

*Commando.* Dir. Mark L. Lester. Perf. Arnold Schwarzenegger, Rae Dawn Chong, and Dan Hedaya. 20th Century–Fox, 1985. Film.

*Constantine.* Dir. Francis Lawrence. Perf. Keanu Reeves, Rachel Weisz, and Shia LaBeouf. Warner Bros., 2005. Film.

*The Corn Is Green.* Dir. Irving Rapper. Perf. Bette Davis, Casey Robinson, and Rhys Williams. Warner Bros., 1945. Film.

*Crouching Tiger, Hidden Dragon* (*Wo Hu Cang Long*). Dir. Ang Lee. Perf. Yun Fat Chow, Michelle Yeoh, and Ziyi Zhang. Asia Union Film and Entertainment, 2000. Film.

*CSI: Crime Scene Investigation* (CBS, 2000–).

*Dangerous Minds.* Dir. John N. Smith. Perf. Michelle Pfeiffer, George Dzundza, Courtney B. Vance, and Robin Bartlett. Hollywood Pictures, 1995. Film.

*Daredevil.* Dir. Mark Steven Johnson. Perf. Ben Affleck, Jennifer Garner, and Colin Farrell. 20th Century–Fox, 2003. Film.

*Dark Angel* (Fox, 2000–2002).

*The Dark Knight.* Dir. Christopher Nolan. Perf. Christian Bale, Heath Ledger, Aaron Eckhart, Michael Caine, Maggie Gyllenhaal, Gary Oldman, and Morgan Freeman. Warner Bros., 2008. DVD.

*The Dark Knight Rises.* Dir. Christopher Nolan. Perf. Christian Bale, Gary Oldman, Morgan Freeman, and Michael Caine. Warner Bros., 2012. Film.

*Dead Poets Society.* Dir. Peter Weir. Perf. Robin Williams, Robert Sean Leonard, and Ethan Hawke. Touchstone Pictures, 1989. Film.

*Deep Impact.* Dir. Mimi Leder. Perf. Robert Duvall, Tea Leoni, Elijah Wood, and Morgan Freeman. Paramount, 1998. Film.

*The Departed.* Dir. Martin Scorsese. Perf. Leonardo DiCaprio, Matt Damon, Jack Nicholson, and Mark Wahlberg. Warner Bros., 2006. Film.

*Die Another Day.* Dir. Lee Tamahori. Perf. Pierce Brosnan, Halle Berry, and Toby Stephens. Metro-Goldwyn-Meyer, 2002. Film.

*Die Hard.* Dir. John McTiernan. Perf. Bruce Willis, Alan Rickman, and Bonnie Bedelia. 20th Century–Fox, 1988. Film.

*Dirty Harry.* Director Don Sigel. Perf. Clint Eastwood, Andy Robinson, and Harry Guardino. Malpasso Studios, 1971. Film.

*Drunken Master.* Dir. Woo-ping Yuen. Perf. Jackie Chan, Siu Tien Yuen, and Jang Lee Hwang. Seasonal Film Corporation, 1978. Film.

*Elektra*. Dir. Rob Bowman. Perf. Jennifer Garner, Goran Visnjic, and Will Yun Lee. 20th Century–Fox, 2005. Film.

*Enter the Dragon*. Dir. Robert Clouse. Perf. Bruce Lee, John Saxon, and Kien Shih. Warner Bros., 1973. Film.

*Erin Brockovich*. Dir. Steven Soderbergh. Perf. Julia Roberts, Albert Finney, and David Brisbin. Jersey Films, 2003.DVD.

*Fantastic Four*. Dir. Tim Story. Perf. Ioan Gruffudd, Michael Chiklis, Jessica Alba, and Chris Evans. 20th Century–Fox, 2005. Film.

*The Fresh Prince of Bel-Air* (NBC, 1990–1996).

*From Hell*. Dir. The Hughes Brothers. Perf. Johnny Depp, Heather Graham, and Ian Holm. 20th Century–Fox, 2001. Film.

*Ghost Rider: Spirit of Vengeance*. Dir. Mark Neveldine, Brian Taylor. Perf. Nicolas Cage, Idris Elba, and Ciarán Hinds. Columbia, 2012. Film.

*Ghost World*. Dir. Terry Zwigoff. Perf. Steve Buscemi, Thora Birch, and Scarlett Johansson. United Artists, 2001. Film.

*The Godfather*. Dir. Francis Ford Coppola. Perf. Marlon Brando, Al Pacino, James Caan, and Robert Duvall. Paramount, 1972. Film.

*Goldeneye*. Dir. Martin Campbell. Perf. Pierce Brosnan, Sean Bean, Famke Janssen, and Judi Dench. United Artists, 1995. Film.

*Goldfinger*. Dir. Guy Hamilton. Perf. Sean Connery, Honor Blackman, and Gert Frobe. United Artists, 1964. Film.

*Goodfellas*. Dir. Martin Scorsese. Perf. Ray Liotta, Robert De Niro, Lorraine Bracco, and Paul Sorvino. Warner Bros., 1990. Film.

*Green Hornet*. Dir. Michel Gondry. Perf. Seth Rogen, Jay Chou, Christoph Waltz, and Cameron Diaz. Columbia Pictures, 2011. Film.

*Green Lantern*. Dir. Martin Campbell. Perf. Ryan Reynolds, Mark Strong, Blake Lively, and Peter Sarsgaard. Warner Bros., 2011. Film.

*Hancock*. Dir. Peter Berg. Perf. Will Smith, Charlize Theron, and Jason Bateman. Columbia, 2008. Film.

*Harry Potter and the Chamber of Secrets*. Dir. Chris Columbus. Perf. Daniel Radcliffe, Rupert Grint, and Emma Watson. Warner Bros., 2002. Film.

*Harry Potter and the Deathly Hallows: Part I*. Dir. David Yates. Perf. Daniel Radcliffe, Rupert Grint, and Emma Watson. Warner Bros., 2010. Film.

*Harry Potter and the Goblet of Fire*. Dir. Mike Newell. Perf. Daniel Radcliffe, Rupert Grint, and Emma Watson. Warner Bros., 2005. Film.

*Harry Potter and the Half-Blood Prince*. Dir. David Yates. Perf. Daniel Radcliffe, Rupert Grint, and Emma Watson. Warner Bros., 2009. Film.

*Harry Potter and the Order of the Phoenix*. Dir. David Yates. Perf. Daniel Radcliffe, Rupert Grint, and Emma Watson. Warner Bros., 2007. Film.

*Harry Potter and the Prisoner of Azkaban*. Dir. Alfonso Cuaron. Perf. Daniel Radcliffe, Rupert Grint, and Emma Watson. Warner Bros., 2004. Film.

*Harry Potter and the Sorcerer's Stone*. Dir. Chris Columbus. Perf. Daniel Radcliffe, Rupert Grint, and Emma Watson. Warner Bros., 2001. Film.

*Heat*. Dir. Michael Mann. Perf. Al Pacino, Robert De Niro, Val Kilmer, and Jon Voight. Warner Bros., 1995. Film.

*Hellboy*. Dir. Guillermo del Toro. Perf. Ron Perlman, John Hurt, Selma Blair, and Rupert Evans. Columbia, 2004. Film.

*Hellboy II — The Golden Army.* Dir. Guillermo del Toro. Perf. Ron Perlman, Selma Blair, Doug Jones, and Luke Goss. Universal, 2008. Film.

*Heroes* (NBC, 2006–2010).

*High Noon.* Dir. Fred Zinnemann. Perf. Gary Cooper, Grace Kelly, and Thomas Mitchell. United Artists, 1952. Film.

*Hulk.* Dir. Ang Lee. Perf. Eric Bana, Jennifer Connelly, Sam Elliott, and Nick Nolte. Universal Pictures and Marvel Entertainment, 2003. Film

*Inception.* Dir. Christopher Nolan. Perf. Leonardo DiCaprio, Joseph Gordon-Levitt, and Ellen Page. Warner Bros., 2010. Film.

*The Incredible Hulk.* Dir. Louis Leterrier. Perf. Edward Norton, Liv Tyler, Tim Roth, and William Hurt. Universal/Marvel, 2008. Film.

*The Incredibles.* Dir. Brad Bird. Perf. Craig T. Nelson, Holly Hunter, Samuel L. Jackson, and Jason Lee. Walt Disney, 2004. Film.

*Iron Man.* Dir. Jon Favreau. Perf. Robert Downey, Jr., Gwyneth Paltrow, Terrence Howard, and Jeff Bridges. Paramount/Marvel, 2008. Film.

*Iron Man 2.* Dir. Jon Favreau. Perf. Robert Downey, Jr., Gwyneth Paltrow, Don Cheadle, and Mickey Rourke. Paramount/Marvel, 2010. Film.

*The Karate Kid.* Dir. John G. Avildsen. Perf. Ralph Macchio, Pat Morita, and Elisabeth Shue. Columbia, 1984. Film.

*Kick-Ass.* Dir. Matthew Vaughn. Perf. Chloe Moretz, Lyndsy Fonseca, and Aaron Johnson. Touchstone Pictures, 2010. Film.

*Kick-Ass 2: Balls to the Wall.* Dir. Matthew Vaughn. Perf. Chloe Moretz, Lyndsy Fonseca, and Aaron Johnson. Marv Films, 2012. Film.

*Kill Bill.* Dir. Quentin Tarantiono. Perf. Uma Thurman, David Carradine, Luci Liu, and Michael Madsen. Miramax, 2003/2004. Film.

*The Kingdom.* Dir. Peter Berg. Perf. Jamie Foxx, Jennifer Garner, Jason Bateman, and Chris Cooper. Universal, 2006. Film.

*Lara Croft: Tomb Raider.* Dir. Simon West. Perf. Angelina Jolie, John Voigt, and Noah Taylor. Paramount, 2001. Film.

*Lara Croft Tomb Raider: The Cradle of Life.* Dir. Jan de Bont. Perf. Angelina Jolie, Gerard Butler, Ciarán Hinds, and Chris Barrie. Paramount, 2003. Film.

*The League of Extraordinary Gentlemen.* Dir. Stephen Norrington. Perf. Sean Connery, Stuart Townsend, Peta Wilson, and Tony Curran. Angry Films, 2003. Film.

*Lost* (ABC, 2004–2010).

*The Maltese Falcon.* Dir. John Huston. Perf. Humphrey Bogart, Sidney Greenstreet, and Peter Lorre. Warner Bros., 1941. Film.

*The Man Who Shot Liberty Valance.* Dir. John Ford. Perf. John Wayne, James Stewart, and Vera Miles. Paramount, 1962. Film.

*The Man Who Wasn't There.* Dir. Joel and Ethan Coen. Perf. Billy Bob Thornton, Frances McDormand, and Michael Badalucco. Good Machine, Gramercy Pictures, 2001. DVD.

*Megamind.* Dir. Tom McGrath. Perf. Will Ferrell, Jonah Hill, and Brad Pitt. DreamWorks, 2010. Film.

*Men in Black II.* Dir. Barry Sonnenfeld. Perf. Tommy Lee Jones, and Will Smith. Amblin Entertainment, Columbia, 2002. Film.

*Mission: Impossible.* Dir. Brian De Palma. Perf. Tom Cruise, Jon Voight, and Ving Rhames. Paramount, 1996. Film.

*Moonraker*. Dir. Lewis Gilbert. Perf. Roger Moore, Lois Chiles, and Michael Lonsdale. United Artists, 1979. Film.

*Munich*. Dir. Steven Spielberg. Perf. Eric Bana, Daniel Craig, Geoffrey Rush, and Ciaran Hinds. Dreamworks/Universal, 2005. Film.

*Murder, She Wrote* (CBS, 1984–1996).

*Mystic River*. Dir. Clint Eastwood. Perf. Sean Penn, Tim Robbins, Kevin Bacon, and Laurence Fishburne. Warner Bros., 2003. Film.

*Nip/Tuck* (FX, 2003–2010).

*Oldboy*. Dir. Chan-wook Park. Perf. Min-sik Choi, Ji-tae Yu, and Hye-jeong Kang. Tartan, 2003. Film.

*On Her Majesty's Service*. Dir. Peter R. Hunt. Perf. George Lazenby, Diana Rigg, and Telly Savalas. Danjaq, Eon Productions, 1969. DVD.

*One False Move*. Dir. Carl Franklin. Perf. Bill Paxton, Billy Bob Thornton, and Cynda Williams. IRS Media, 1992. DVD.

*Pan's Labyrinth*. Dir. Guillermo del Toro. Perf. Ivana Baquero, Doug Jones, and Sergi López. Picturehouse, 2006. DVD.

*The Prodigal Son*. Dir. Sammo Hung Kam-Bo. Perf. Biao Yuen, Ching-Ying Lam, and Sammo Hung Kam-Bo. Image Entertainment, 1981. Film.

*The Pursuit of Happyness*. Dir. Gabrielle Muccino. Perf. Will Smith, Thandie Newton, and Jaden Smith. Columbia, 2006. DVD.

*Raiders of the Lost Ark*. Dir. Steven Spielberg. Perf. Harrison Ford, Karen Allen, and Paul Freeman. Paramount, 1980. Film.

*Rambo: First Blood Part II*. Dir. George P. Cosmatos. Perf. Sylvester Stallone, Richard Crenna, and Charles Napier. TriStar Pictures, 1985. Film.

*Rocky*. Dir. John G. Avildsen. Perf. Sylvester Stallone, Talia Shire, and Carl Weathers. United Artists, 1976. Film.

*Schindler's List*. Dir. Steven Spielberg. Perf. Liam Neeson, Ralph Fiennes, and Ben Kingsly. Universal, 1993. DVD.

*Scott Pilgrim vs. The World*. Dir. Edgar Wright. Perf. Michael Cera, Mary Elizabeth Winstead, and Kieran Culkin. Universal Pictures, 2010. DVD.

*Sex and the City* (HBO 1998–2004).

*She's the Man*. Dir. Andy Fickman. Perf. Amanda Bynes, Laura Ramsey, and Channing Tatum. DreamWorks, 2006. Film.

*Sin City*. Dir. Robert Rodriguez, Frank Miller, Quentin Tarantino. Perf. Mickey Rourke, Clive Owen, Bruce Willis, Jessica Alba, and Benicio Del Toro. Dimension Films, 2005. Film.

*Six Feet Under* (HBO, 2001–2005).

*Smallville* (The WB/The CW, 2001–2011).

*Snake in Eagle's Shadow*. Dir. Woo-ping Yuen. Perf. Jackie Chan, Siu Tien Yuen, and Jang Lee Hwang. Seasonal Film Corporation, 1978. Film.

*The Sopranos* (HBO, 1999–2007).

*Spider-Man*. Dir. Sam Raimi. Perf. Tobey Maguire, Kirsten Dunst, and Willem Dafoe. Columbia, 2002. Film.

*Spider-Man 2*. Dir. Sam Raimi. Perf. Tobey Maguire, Kirsten Dunst, Alfred Molina, and James Franco. Columbia, 2004. Film.

*Spider-Man 3*. Dir. Sam Raimi. Perf. Tobey Maguire, Kirsten Dunst, James Franco, and Topher Grace. Columbia, 2007. Film.

*Spider-Man Reboot*. Dir. Marc Webb. Perf. Andrew Garfield. Sony Pictures Entertainment, 2012. Film.

*The Spirit*. Director Frank Miller. Perf. Samuel L. Jackson, Gabriel Macht, and Scarlet Johannson. Lionsgate, 2008. Film.

*Stagecoach*. Dir. John Ford. Perf. John Wayne, Claire Trevor, and Andy Devine. United Artists, 1939. Film.

*Superman*. Dir. Richard Donner. Perf. Christopher Reeve, Gene Hackman, Margot Kidder, and Marlon Brando. Warner Bros., 1978. Film.

*Superman II*. Dir. Richard Lester. Perf. Christopher Reeve, Gene Hackman, and Margot Kidder. Alexander Salkind, 1980. Film.

*Superman III*. Dir. Richard Lester. Perf. Christopher Reeve, Richard Pryor, and Margot Kidder. Cantharaus Productions, 1983. Film.

*Superman IV: The Quest for Peace*. Dir. Sidney J. Furie. Perf. Christopher Reeve, Gene Hackman, and Margot Kidder. Cannon Films, 1987. Film.

*Superman Returns*. Dir. Bryan Singer. Perf. Brandon Routh, Kevin Spacey, and Kate Bosworth. Warner Bros., 2006. Film.

*Syriana*. Dir. Stephen Gaghan. Perf. George Clooney, Matt Damon, Alexander Siddig, and Jeffrey Wright. Warner Bros., 2005. Film.

*The Tall T*. Dir. Budd Boetticher. Perf. Randolph Scott, Richard Boone, and Maureen O'Sullivan. Columbia, 1957. Film.

*Taxi Driver*. Director Martin Scorsese. Perf. Robert DeNiro, Jodie Foster, and Harvey Keitel. Columbia Pictures, 1976. Film.

*Thor*. Dir. Kenneth Branagh. Perf. Chris Hemsworth, Anthony Hopkins, and Natalie Portman. Marvel Studios, 2011. Film.

*To Sir, with Love*. Dir. James Clavell. Perf. Sidney Poitier, Judy Geeson, and Christian Roberts. Columbia, 1967. Film.

*Transformers*. Dir. Michael Bay. Perf. Shia Lebouef, Megan Fox, Josh Duhamel, Jon Voight, and John Tuturro. Paramount/Dreamworks, 2007. Film.

*24* (FX, 2001–2010).

*Unbreakable*. Dir. M. Night Shyamalan. Perf. Bruce Willis, Samuel L. Jackson, and Robin Wright. Touchstone, 2000. Film.

*Underworld*. Dir. Len Wiseman. Perf. Kate Beckinsale, Scott Speedman, Michael Sheen, and Shane Brolly. Lakeshore, 2003. Film.

*V for Vendetta*. Dir. James McTeigue. Perf. Natalie Portman, Hugo Weaving, John Hurt, and Stephen Rea. Warner Bros., 2006. Film.

*Watchmen*. Dir. Zack Snyder. Perf. Malin Akerman, Billy Crudup, Matthew Goode, Jackie Earle Haley, Jeffrey Dean Morgan, and Patrick Wilson. Warner Bros./Paramount, 2009. Film.

*The West Wing* (NBC, 1999–2006).

*Winchester '73*. Dir. Anthony Mann. Perf. James Stewart, Shelley Winters, and Dan Duryea. Universal, 1950. Film.

*Without a Trace* (CBS, 2002–2009).

*The Wolverine*. Dir. Darren Aronofsky. Perf. Hugh Jackman. 20th Century–Fox, 2012. Film.

*X-Men*. Dir. Bryan Singer. Perf. Hugh Jackman, Patrick Stewart, Ian McKellen, Famke Janssen, James Marsden, Halle Berry, and Anna Paquin. 20th Century–Fox, 2000. Film.

*X2: X-Men United*. Dir. Bryan Singer. Perf. Hugh Jackman, Patrick Stewart, Ian McKellen, Famke Janssen, James Marsden, Halle Berry, and Alan Cumming. 20th Century–Fox, 2003. Film.

*X-Men: First Class*. Dir. Matthew Vaughn. Perf. James McAvoy, Michael Fassbender, Kevin Bacon, and January Jones. 20th Century–Fox, 2011. Film.

*X-Men: The Last Stand*. Dir. Brett Ratner. Perf. Hugh Jackman, Halle Berry, Patrick Stewart, Ian McKellen, Famke Janssen, Ellen Page, and Kelsey Grammer. 20th Century–Fox, 2006. Film.

*The Young Master*. Dir. Jackie Chan. Perf. Jackie Chan, Pai Wei, and Biao Yuen. 20th Century–Fox, 1980. Film.

*X-Men Origins: Wolverine*. Dir. Gavin Hood. Perf. Hugh Jackman, Live Schreiber, Danny Huston, Kevin Durand, and Ryan Reynolds. 20th Century–Fox, 2009. Film.

*You've Got Mail*. Dir. Nora Ephron. Perf. Tom Hanks, Meg Ryan, and Greg Kinnear. Warner Bros., 1998. Film.

# Works Cited

"99 Most Desirable Women." *AskMen.com*. AskMen Mag. 28 June 2006. 10 Nov. 2010.

Abbot, Megan. *The Street Was Mine: White Masculinity in Hardboiled Fiction and Film Noir*. New York: Palgrave Macmillan, 2002. Print.

Abrams, Jerold J. "'A Homespun Murder Story:' Film Noir and the Problem of Modernity in *Fargo*." Mark Conrad, ed. 7–20 in *The Philosophy of The Coen Brothers*. Lexington: University of Kentucky Press, 2009. Print.

Ackerman, Spencer. "Batman's 'Dark Knight' Reflects Cheney Policy." *The Washington Independent*. 21 July 2008. Web. 13 May 2009.

Agamben, Giorgio. *Homo Sacer: Sovereign Power and Bare Life*. Trans. Daniel Heller-Roazen. Stanford: Stanford University Press, 1998. Print.

_____. *State of Exception*. Trans. Kevin Attell. Chicago: University of Chicago Press, 2005. Print.

Altman, Rick. *Film/Genre*. UK: BFI, 2006. Print.

Anders, Lou. "Two of a Kind." *Batman Unauthorized: Vigilantes, Jokers, and Heroes in Gotham City*. Ed. Dennis O'Neil. Dallas: Benbella Books, 2008. 17–33. Print.

Andrae, Thomas. "From Menace to Messiah: The History and Historicity of Superman."*American Media and Mass Culture: Left Perspectives*. Ed. Donald Lazere. Berkeley: University of California Press, 1987. Print.

Ansen, David. "The Wounded Superhero: In 'Hancock,' Will Smith Attempts to Deconstruct the Superhero Genre, to Sub-super Effect." *Newsweek*. 1 July 2008. Web. 11 Jan. 2010.

"All Time Box Office: Opening Weekends." *BoxOfficeMojo.com*. IMDb.com. Web. 21 December 2010.

Arendt, Hannah. *The Human Condition*. Chicago: University of Chicago Press, 1958. Print.

_____. *On Violence*. Orlando: Harcourt, 1970. Print.

Aristotle. *Poetics*. Trans. by Stephen Halliwell. Cambridge: Harvard University Press, 1995.

Baker, R. C. "*The Dark Knight*: Selling Tickets—and a Muddled Political Message." *Village Voice*. 29 July 2008. Web. 13 May 2009.

Banks, Miranda J. "A Boy for All Planets: *Roswell*, *Smallville*, and the Teen Male Melodrama." *Teen TV*. Eds. Glyn Davis and Kay Dickinson. London: British Film Institute, 2004. 17–28. Print.

Banks, William C., Renée de Nevers, and Mitchel B. Wallerstein. *Combating Terrorism: Strategies and Approaches*. Washington, D.C.: CQ, 2008. Print.

Baron, Cynthia, and Sharon Marie Carnicke. *Reframing Screen Performance*. Michigan: University of Michigan Press. 2008. Print.

Barthes, Roland. "Introduction to the Structural Analysis of Narratives." *Image Music Text*. Trans. Stephen Heath. New York: Hill and Wang, 1977. 79–124. Print.

_____. "Myth Today." *Cultural Theory and Popular Culture*. Ed. John Storey. USA: Prentice Hall, 1998. 109–118. Print.

_____. *Mythologies & Mathima*. 1957. Trans. K. Xatzidimou and I. Ralli. Athens: Rappa, 1979. Print.

_____. "Theory of the Text." Trans. Ian McLeod. *Untying the Text: a Post-structuralist Reader*. Ed. Robert Young. Boston: Routledge & Kegan Paul, 1981. 31–47. Print.

Baudrillard, Jean. *The Spirit of Terrorism*. New York: Verso, 2002. Print.

_____. *The Transparency of Evil: Essays on Extreme Phenomena*. New York: Verso, 1993. Print.

Bennett, Bruce. "Watchmen" *Spectrum*: http://www.madaboutmovies.org/. Web. 10 May 2010.

Benshoff, Harry M., and Sean Griffin. *America on Film*. Oxford: Blackwell, 2004. Print.

Binh, Pham. "The Politics of The Dark Knight." *Dissident Voice*. 31 July 2008. Web. 13 May 2009.

Bisen, Chinen Sheri. *Blackout: World War II and the Origins of Film Noir*. Baltimore: Johns Hopkins University Press, 2005. Print

Bolter, J. David, and Richard A. Grusin. *Remediation: Understanding New Media*. Cambridge: MIT Press, 2000. Print.

Booker, Keith M. "May Contain Graphic Material." *Comic Books, Graphic Novels, and Film*. Westport: Praeger, 2007. Print.

Boucher, Geoff. "Christopher Nolan on 'Dark Knight' and Its Box-Office Billion: It's Mystifying to Me." *Los Angeles Times*. 27 Oct. 2008. Web. 13 May 2009. <http://latimesblogs.latimes.com/herocomplex/2008/10/christopher-nol.html>.

_____. "Christopher Nolan Revisits and Analyzes His Favorite Scene in 'Dark Knight.'" *Los Angeles Times*. 28 Oct. 2008. Web. 13 May 2009.

Bradley, William. "Dark Knight America." *The Huffington Post*. 20 August 2008. Web. 13 May 2009.

Breen, Margaret Sönser. "Heroes and Monsters. The Politics of Survival in *Spider-man* and 'A Long Line of *Vendidas*.'" *Truth, Reconciliation, and Evil*. Ed. Margaret Sönser Breen. Amsterdam: Rodopi, 2004. 181–96. Print.

Bronner, Stephen E. *Blood in the Sand: Imperial Fantasies, Right-wing Ambitions, and the Erosion of American Democracy*. Lexington: University of Kentucky Press, 2005. Print.

Brooker, Will. *Batman Unmasked*. New York, London: Continuum, 2000. Print.

Brown, Jeffrey. "Gender, Sexuality, and Toughness: The Bad Girls of Action Film and Comic Books." *Action Chicks: New Images of Tough Women in Popular Culture*. Ed. Sherrie A. Inness. New York: Palgrave Macmillan, 2004. Print.

Bukatman, Scott. *Matters of Gravity: Special Effects and Supermen in the 20th Century*. Durham: Duke University Press, 2003. Print.

_____. "X-Bodies: The Torment of the Mutant Superhero." *Matters of Gravity: Special Effects and Supermen in the 20th Century*. Durham: Duke University Press, 2003. 48–78. Print.

Burns, Elizabeth. *Theatricality. A Study of Convention in Theatre and in Social Life*. London: Longman, 1972. Print.

Burrows, Jim. "The Good, the Bad, and the Beautiful: Strong Women in Comics." *Jimb on Comics*. Web. 15 April 2010.

Butler, Judith. *Bodies That Matter*. New York: Routledge, 1993. Print.

_____. *Gender Trouble: Feminism and the Subversion of Identity*. New York: Routledge, 1990. Print.

_____. "Performative Acts and Gender Constitution." *Writing on the Body*. Eds. K.

Medina, N. Conboy, and S. Stanbury. New York: Columbia University Press, 1997. 401–17. Print.

Cabrera-Balleza, Mavic. "Grrl Power and Third Wave Feminism," *Women in Action* Aug. 2003: 1. Print.

Caldeira, Teresa. *City of Walls: Crime, Segregation, and Citizenship in São Paulo.* Berkeley: University of California Press, 2000. Print.

Chang, Justin. "Aeon Flux." *Variety* 401.4 (2005): 48. Print.

"Color: Meaning, Symbolism and Psychology." *Squidoo.* n.p. Web. 10 Nov. 2010.

Coogan, Peter. *Superhero: The Secret Origin of a Genre.* Austin: Monkey Brain Books, 2006. Print.

Cox, David. "Why the Dark Knight Is So Dim." *The Guardian.* 28 July 2008. Web. 15 February 2009.

Crouse, Richard. "'Dark Knight' Has Reviewer Seeking New Words for Awesome." *CTV.* 18 July 2008. Web. 13 May 2009.

Cusick, James. "Part VII: The Fear That Could Paralyse the World." In "Five Years On: How 9/11 Changed the World." Iain Macwhirter, Trevor Royle, Neil Mackay, Graeme Virtue, James Cusick, Ian Bell, and Barry Didcock. *The Sunday Herald.* 10 Sept. 2006. Seven Days: 4+. Print.

Dargis, Manohla. "A New Eden, Both Cosmic and Cinematic." *New York Times.* 18 Dec 2009. C1. Print.

_____. "Showdown in Gotham Town." *New York Times.* 18 July 2008. Web. 13 May 2009.

Darius, Julian. *Batman Begins and the Comics.* Honolulu: Sequart.com Books, 2005.

"*The Dark Knight* Production Notes." Web. 4 March 2010. PDF.

Dasgupta, Sudeep. "Multiple Symptoms and the Visible Real: Culture, Media, and the Displacements of Vision." *Invisible Culture* 10 (2006): 1–16. Print.

Davidson, Rjurick. "Fighting the Good Fight?: Watching *The Watchmen.*" *Screen Education* 54 (Winter, 2009): 18–23. Print.

Dawson, Jeff. "Has the New Batman Plundered Its Plot from 9/11?" *Times Online.* 20 July 2008. Web. 13 May 2009.

de Beauvoir, Simone. *Le Deuxième Sexe.* Paris: Gallimard, 1949. Print.

de la Durantaye, Leland. *Giorgio Agamben: A Critical Introduction.* Stanford: Stanford University Press, 2009. Print.

Dennis, Rick. "No Rust on This Iron Man." *The News.* 18 Oct 2008. C5. Print.

Derrida, Jacques. *Dissemination.* Chicago: Univesity of Chicago Press, 1981. Print.

_____. "The Law of Genre." Trans. Avital Ronell. *Critical Inquiry* 7.1 (1980): 55–81. Print.

Dimenberg, Edward. *Film Noir and the Spaces of Modernity.* Cambridge: Harvard University Press, 2004. Print.

"Director Bryan Singer Talks ... "X Men.'" *joblow.com.* JoBlow's Movie Emporium. n.d. Web. 10 August 2010.

Dixon, Winston Wheeler. *Film and Television After 9/11.* Carbondale: Southern Illinois University Press, 2004. Print.

Doane, Mary Ann. "Film and the Masquerade: Theorizing the Female Spectator 1982." *Issues in Feminist Film Criticism.* Ed. Patricia Erens. Bloomington: Indiana University Press, 1990. 41–57. Print.

Dray, Stephanie. "The Politics of The Dark Knight: Serious Commentary on the Masks We Hide Behind." *Associated Content.* 31 July 2008. Web. 13 May 2009.

Dudley, Michael. "Batman's Take on 9/11 Era Politics? Drop the Fearmongering." *AlterNet.* 25 July 2008. Web. 15 Feb. 2009.

Easthope, Anthony. *What a Man's Gotta Do: The Masculine Myth in Popular Culture.* Boston: Unwin Hyman, 1990. Print.

Ebert, Roger. "*The Dark Knight.*" *rogerebert.com.* 16 July 2008. Web. 3 Oct. 2010.

Eisenberg, Carol. "Dark Knight May Owe Its Bite to Nolan Team's English Sensibility." *Muckety*. Muckety LLC. 23 July 2008. Web. 13 May 2009.

Epaminondas, George. "25th-Century Style: ARE YOUniversity READY FOR IT?" *In Style* 1 Sept. 2005: 367. Print.

Fischer-Lichte, Erika. "Theatricality: A Key Concept in Theatre and Cultural Studies." *Theatre Research International* 20.2 (1995): 85–89. Print.

Fitzpatrick, Liza. *The Art of Avatar: James Cameron's Epic Adventure*. New York: Abrams, 2009. Print.

Flanagan, Martin. "Teen Trajectories in *Spider-Man* and *Ghost World*." *Films and Comic Books*. Eds. Ian Gordon, Mark Jancovich, Matthew McAllister. Jackson: University Press of Mississippi, 2007. 137–159. Print.

Fleming, Mike. "Chris Nolan to Meet Actresses for Batman 3." *Deadline*. 11 Nov. 2010. Web. 15 Nov. 2010.

Florence, Brandi L. *Busting Out All Over: The Portrayal of Superheroines in American Superhero Comics from the 1940s to the 2000s*. Unpublished Master's Thesis, University of North Carolina at Chapel Hill, Chapel Hill, 2002.

Foerster, Heinz von. "Through the Eyes of the Other." *Research and Reflexivity*. Ed. Frederick Steier. London: Sage, 1991. 63–75. Print.

_____. *Understanding Understanding. Essays on Cybernetics and Cognition*. New York: Springer, 2003. Print.

Forter, Greg. *Murdering Masculinities: Fantasies of Gender and Violence in the American Crime Novel*. New York: New York University Press, 2000. Print.

Franklin, Daniel P. *Politics and Film: The Political Culture of Film in the United States*. Lanham, MD: Rowman and Littlefield, 2006. Print.

Fotopoulou, Sophia. "Phoenix — The Symbol of Rebirth." *Newsfinder*. 22 Sep. 2002. Web. 2 September 2010.

Freud, Sigmund. *Three Essays on the Theory of Sexuality*. Trans. and ed. James Strachey. London: Hogarth Press, 1962. Print.

Frye, Northrop. "Archetypal Criticism: Theory of Myths." *Anatomy of Criticism; Four Essays*. By Northrop Frye. Princeton: Princeton University Press, 1957. 131–239. Print.

Gardies, André. *Le récit filmique*. Paris: Hachette, 1993. Print.

"Gaze," *Art & Popular Culture*. n.d. Web. 20 Nov. 2010.

Geertz, Clifford. *The Interpretation of Cultures*. New York: Basic, 1973. Print.

Gleiberman, Owen. "Aeon Flux: When Good Actresses Do Bad Movies of Good Cartoons." *Entertainment Weekly* 16 Dec. 2005: 63. Web. 16 Oct. 2010.

_____. "Catwoman: Not the Cat's Meow, but Berry Sure Looks Great in Leather." *Entertainment Weekly* 30 July 2004: 47. Print.

Goffman, Erving. *The Presentation of Self in Everyday Life*. New York: Anchor, 1959. Print.

Goodwin, James. *Akira Kurosawa and Intertextual Cinema*. Baltimore: Johns Hopkins University Press, 1994. Print.

Greenblatt, Stephen. *Renaissance Self-Fashioning: From More to Shakespeare*. Chicago: University of Chicago Press, 1980. Print.

Grossman, Lev. "The Problem with Superman." *Time*. 10 May 2004. Web. 14 December 2010.

Haraway, Donna J. *Simians, Cyborgs, and Women. The Reinvention of Nature*. London: Free Association Books, 1991. Print.

Hard, Robin. *The Routledge Handbook of Greek Mythology: Based on H.J. Rose's Handbook of Greek Mythology*. London: Routledge, 2004. Print.

Hawkins, Harriet. *Classics and Trash*. Canada: University of Toronto Press, 1990. Print.

Herman, Judith. *Trauma and Recovery: The Aftermath of Violence — from Domestic Abuse to Political Terror*. New York: Basic Books, 1997. Print.

Hollows, Joanne, and Rachel Moseley. "Popularity Contests: The Meanings of Popular Feminism." *Feminism in Popular Culture.* Eds. Joanne Hollows and Rachel Moseley. Oxford: Berg, 2006. 1–22. Print.

Holt, Jason. "A Darker Shade: Realism in Neo-*Noir.*" *The Philosophy of Film Noir.* Ed. Mark T. Conard. Lexington: University Press of Kentucky, 2006. 23–40. Print.

Housel, Rebecca. "Myth, Morality, and the Women of the X-Men." *Superheroes and Philosophy. Truth, Justice and the Socratic Way.* Eds. Tom Morris and Matt Morris. Chicago: Open Court, 2005. 75–88. Print.

Howard, Tom. "100 Sexiest Women in the World 2007 — The Top Ten." *FHM.com.* FHM Mag. 27 Jan. 2007. Web. 2 Nov. 2010.

"Imdb User Reviews." (2008): n. pag. Web. 15 May 2010.

Inness, Sherri A. (1999). *Action Chicks: New Images of Tough Women in Popular Culture.* New York: Palgrave Macmillan, 2004. Print.

Irwin, John. *Unless the Threat of Death Is Behind Them: Hard-Boiled Fiction and Film Noir.* Baltimore: Johns Hopkins University Press, 2006. Print.

Jameson, Fredric. *Postmodernism, or, The Cultural Logic of Late Capitalism.* Durham: Duke University Press, 1991. Print.

Janoff-Bulman, Ronnie. *Shattered Assumptions: Towards a New Psychology of Trauma.* New York: The Free Press, 1992. Print.

"Jessica Alba." *UGO.com.* UGO Entertainment Mag. n.d. 2 Nov. 2010.

John of the Cross. *Dark Night of the Soul.* Trans. Mirabai Starr. New York: Riverhead Books, 2002. Print.

Johnson, Derek. "Will the Real Wolverine Please Stand Up? Marvel's Mutation from Monthlies to Movies." *Film and Comic Books.* Eds. Ian Gordon, Mark Jancovich and Matthew P. McAllister. Jackson: University Press of Mississippi, 2007. 64–85. Print.

Johnson, Kerri L., Leah E. Lurye, and Jonathan B. Freeman. "Gender Typicality and Extremity in Popular Culture." *The Psychology of Superheroes: An Unauthorized Exploration.* Eds. Robin S. Rosenberg and Jennifer Canzoneri. Dallas: Benbella Books, 2008. 229–244. Print.

Juergensmeyer, Mark. *Terror in the Mind of God: The Global Rise of Religious Violence.* 3rd ed. Berkeley: University of California Press, 2003. Print.

Kading, Terry. "Drawn Into 9/11: But Where Have All the Superheroes Gone?" *Comics As Philosophy.* Ed. Jeff McLaughlin. Jackson: University of Mississippi Press, 2005. 207–35. Print.

Kakalios, James. *The Physics of Superheroes.* New York, Gotham Books, 2005. Print.

Kaveney, Roz. *Superheroes! Capes and Crusaders in Comics and Films.* London: I. B. Tauris, 2008. Print.

Keegan, Rebecca. *The Futurist: The Life and Films of James Cameron.* New York: Crown, 2009. Print.

Kerstein, Benjamin. "Batman's War on Terror." *Azure.* 34 (Autumn 2008): n. pag. Web. 13 May 2009.

King, Barry. "Articulating Stardom." *Screen,* 26.5 (1985): 27–50. Print.

King, Geoff. *Spectacular Narratives: Hollywood in the Age of the Blockbuster.* London: I. B. Tauris, 2000. Print.

Klavan, Andrew. "What Bush and Batman Have in Common." *Wall Street Journal.* 25 July 2008. Web. 13 May 2009.

Kozlovic, Anton Karl. "Spider-Man, Superman — What's the Difference?" *Kritikos: An International and Interdisciplinary Journal of Postmodern Cultural Sound, Text and Image* 3 (2006). 3 July 2006. Web. 5 Dec. 2010.

Kristeva, Julia. *The Kristeva Reader.* Ed. Toril Moi. Oxford: Basil Blackwell, 1986. Print.

_____. *Pouvoirs de l'horreur. Essai sur l'abjection.* Paris: Seuil, 1980. Print.

Kukkonen, Taneli. "What's So Goddamn Funny? The Comedian and Rorschach On Life's Way." *The Watchmen and Philosophy: A Rorschach Test*. Ed. Mark D. White. Hoboken: John Wiley, 2009. 197–214. Print.

Lacan, Jacques. "Le stade du miroir. Théorie d'un moment structurant et génétique de la constitution de la réalité." *Communication au 14e Congrès psychanalytique international, Marienbad, International Journal of Psychoanalysis*, 1937.

Lara, María Pía. "Narrating Evil. A Postmetaphysical Theory of Reflective Judgement." *Rethinking Evil. Contemporary Perspectives*. Ed. María Pía Lara. Berkeley: University of California Press, 2001. 239–50. Print.

Lee, Stan. *Son of Origins of Marvel*. New York: Simon and Schuster, 1975. Print.

Lévi-Strauss, Claude. *Myth and Meaning*. 1978. London: Routledge, 2001. Print.

Lewis, Randolph. "The Dark Knight of American Empire." *Jump Cut. A Review of Contemporary Media* 51 (2009): n. pag. Web. 15 Oct. 2010.

Lichtenfeld, Eric. *Action Speaks Louder: Violence, Spectacle and the American Action Movie*. Westport: Praeger, 2004. Print.

Lindsey, Shelley Stamp. "Horror, Femininity, and Carrie's Monstrous Puberty," *The Dread of Difference: Gender and the Horror Film*. Ed. Barry Grant. Austin: University of Texas Press, 1996. 279–295. Print.

Loftis, Robert J. "Means, Ends, and the Critique of Pure Superheroes." *The Watchmen and Philosophy: A Rorschach Test*. Ed. Mark D. White. Hoboken: John Wiley, 2009. 63–78. Print.

Lorenz, Konrad. *On Aggression*. New York: Bantam, 1966. Print.

Lowry, Brian. "Elektra." *Daily Variety* 286.12 (2005): 4+. Web. 10 Nov. 2010.

_____. "Getting Serious About Comic Book Adaptations: Superhero Pics and Series Have Found a Middle Ground Between Camp and Pretentiousness." *Daily Variety* 284.2 (2004): 4. Print.

Lovell, Alan, and Gianluca Sergi. "Sensual Pleasure, Audiences, and *The Dark Knight*." *Cinema Entertainment: Essays on Audiences, Films and Film Makers*. New York: Open University Press, 2009. Print.

Luhmann, Niklas. "Deconstruction as Second-Order-Observation." *New Literary History* 24.4 (1993): 763–82. Print.

_____, and Katherine Hayles. "Theory of a Different Order: A Conversation with Katherine Hayles and Niklas Luhmann." *Cultural Critique* 31 (1995): 7–36. Print.

Lyotard, Jean-François. *The Postmodern Condition: A Report on Knowledge*. Minneapolis: University of Minnesota Press, 1984. Print.

Lyubansky Mihkail. "Prejudice Lessons from The Xavier Institute." *The Psychology of Superheroes: An Unauthorized Exploration*. Ed. Robin S. Rosenberg. Dallas: Benbella Books, 2008. 75–90. Print.

"Male Gaze." *Columbia Dictionary of Modern Literary Criticism*. Ed. Joseph Childers. New York: Columbia University Press, 1995. Print.

Martin, Richard. *Mean Streets and Raging Bulls: The Legacy of Film Noir in Contemporary American Film*. Lantham: Scarecrow, 1999. Print.

Masters, Tim. "*Inception* Influenced by 007, Says Christopher Nolan." *bbc.co.uk*. 9 July 2010. Web. 3 Oct. 2010.

"Maxim Top 100 for 2007." *Maxim.com*. Maxim Mag. n.d. 2 Nov. 2007. Print.

McCabe Janet, and Kim Akass. "Introduction: Debating Quality." *Quality TV: Contemporary American Television and Beyond*. Eds. Janet McCabe and Kim Akass: I. B. Tauris, 2007. 1–12. Print.

McCann, Sean. *Gumshoe America: Hard-Boiled Fiction and the Rise and Fall of New Deal Liberalism*. Durham: Duke University Press, 2000. Print.

McCoy, Heath. "Beneath the Armour; Iron Man as the First Political Superhero." *Alaska Highway News*, 2 May 2008. B 10. Print.

McDonald, Paul. "Julia Roberts and *Erin Brockovich*: The Cultural and Commercial Paradoxes of Oscar Winning Acting." *Acting on Stage — Acting on Screen*. Ed. Christina Adamou. Athens: Kastaniotis, 2008. 141–153. Print.

McFarlane, Brian. *Novel to Film*. Oxford: Clarendon, 1996. Print.

McGowan, Todd. "The Exceptional Darkness of *The Dark Knight*." *Jump Cut: A Review of Contemporary Media* 51 (2009): n. pag. Web. 15. Oct. 2010.

Meinhof, Ulrike H., and Jonathan Smith. "The Media and Their Audience: Intertextuality as Paradigm." *Intertextuality and the Media: From Genre to Everyday Life*. Eds. Ulrike H. Meinhof and Jonathan Smith. Manchester: Manchester University Press, 2000. 1–17. Print.

Mencimer, Stephanie. "Violent Femmes." *Washington Monthly* Sept. 2001: 15. Web. 3 Nov. 2010.

Miller, Frank, Klaus Janson, and Lynn Varley. *Batman: The Dark Knight Returns*. New York: DC Comics, 1986. Print.

Miller, Prairie. "Angelina Jolie on Filling Lara Croft's Shoes and D-size Cups." *NYROCK*. NYROCK Mag., June 2001. Web. 22 Nov. 2010.

Montgomery, Karina. "*The Watchmen*." *Cinerina*. 6 Mar. 2009. Web.5 March 2010.

Moore, Alan. *The Killing Joke*. New York: DC Comics/Titan Books, 1988. Print.

_____. *The Watchmen*. Illus. Dave Gibbons, John Higgins. New York: D.C. Comics, 2005. Print.

Moore, Omar P. L. "When the Joker Rules Gotham There's No Country for Batmen." *Popcorn Reel*. 18 July 2008. Web. 13 May 2009.

Morris, Tom, and Matt Morris. "Men in Bright Tights and Wild Fights, Often at Great Heights, and, of Course, Some Amazing Women, Too!" *Superheroes and Philosophy: Truth, Justice and the Socratic Way*. Eds. Tom Morris and Matt Morris. Chicago: Open Court, 2005. ix–xiii. Print.

Moyers, Bill, and Joseph Campbell. *The Power of Myth*. Ed. Betty Sue Flowers. New York: Doubleday, 1988. Print.

Muir, John Kenneth. *The Encyclopedia of Superheroes on Film and Television*. Jefferson: McFarland, 2008. Print.

Mulvey, Laura. "Visual Pleasure and Narrative Cinema." *Screen* 16.3 (1975): 6–18. Rpt. in *Issues in Feminist Film Criticism*. Ed. Patricia Erens. Bloomington: Indiana University Press, 1990. Print.

_____. *Visual and Other Pleasures*. London: Macmillan, 1989. Print.

Neale, Steve. *Genre and Hollywood*. London: Routledge, 2002. Print.

_____. "Prologue: Masculinity as Spectacle: Reflections on Men and Mainstream Cinema." *Screening the Male: Exploring Masculinities in Hollywood Cinema*. Eds. Steven Cohan and Ina Rae. New York, London: Routledge, 1993. 9–20. Print.

Norden, Martin F. "The 'Uncanny' Relationship of Disability and Evil in Film and Television." *The Changing Face of Evil in Film and Television*. Ed. Martin F. Norden. Amsterdam: Rodopi, 2007. 125–43. Print.

"The Objectification of Women in Graphic Novels." *Fantasymagazine.com*. n.p. Web. 2 Nov. 2010.

O'Day, Marc. "Beauty in Motion, Gender, Spectacle and Action Babe Cinema." *Action and Adventure Cinema*. Ed. Yvonne Tasker. London: Routledge, 2004. 201–218. Print.

Official Web Site of the Olympic Movement. *Olympic.org*. n.d. Web. 15 Nov. 2010.

O'Neill, Dennis. "The Crimson Viper Versus the Maniacal Morphing Meme." *Superheroes and Philosophy: Truth, Justice and the Socratic Way*. Eds. Tom Morris and Matt Morris. Chicago: Open Court, 2005. 21–28. Print.

Orr, Christopher. "Batman as Bush, Ctd." *The New Republic*. 25 July 2008. Web. 13 May 2009.

Palmer, Barton. "The New Sincerity of Neo-Noir: The Example of *The Man Who Wasn't*

*There.*" *The Philosophy of Neo-Noir.* Ed. Mark T. Conrad. Lexington: University of Kentucky Press, 2007. 151–166. Print.

Palmer, William J. *The Films of the Eighties: A Social History.* Carbondale and Edwardsville: Southern Illinois University Press, 1993. Print.

Peaslee, Robert M. "With Great Power Comes Great Responsibility": Central Psychoanalytic Motifs in *Spider-Man* and *Spider-Man 2.*" *PsyArt: An Online Journal for the Psychological Study of the Arts* (2005). 20 July 2005. Web. 5 Dec. 2010.

Peirce, Charles S. *Collected Papers of Charles Sanders Peirce.* Volume II. Eds. Charles Hartshorne and Paul Weiss. Cambridge: Belknap Press of Harvard University Press, 1965. Print.

Pratt, Ray. *Projecting Paranoia: Conspiratorial Visions in American Film.* Lawrence: University of Kansas Press, 2001. Print.

Prince, Gerald. *A Dictionary of Narratology.* Lincoln: University of Nebraska Press, 2003. Print.

Reynolds, Richard. *Superheroes.* London: BT Batsford, 1992. Print.

Ricoeur, Paul. *The Course of Recognition.* Trans. David Pellauer. Cambridge: Harvard University Press, 2005.

_____. "Universal Civilization and National Cultures." Paul Ricoeur. *History and Truth.* Evanston: Northwestern University Press, 1965. Trans. Charles A. Kelbley. 271–284. Print.

Richardson, Niall. "The Gospel According to Spider-Man." *The Journal of Popular Culture* 36.4 (2004): 694–703. Print.

Rickey, Carrie. "Brooding, Brilliant 'Dark Knight.'" *The Philadelphia Inquirer.* 16 July 2008. Web. 13 May 2009.

Robbins, Trina. *The Great Women Superheroes.* Northampton: Kitchen Sink, 1996. Print.

Robichaud, Christopher. "The Joker's Wild: Can We Hold the Clown Prince Morally Responsible?" *Batman and Philosophy: The Dark Knight of the Soul.* Eds. Mark D. White and Robert Arp. Hoboken. NJ: John Wiley, 2008. 70–81. Print.

Rosenberg, Alyssa. "The Invisible Woman: After a Summer of Blockbuster Comic-Book Flicks and Record Ticket Sales to Women, Why Have We Yet to See a Superheroine Movie?" *The American Prospect.* 19.9 (Sep. 2008): 39–41. Print.

Rosenberg, Robin S., and Jennifer Canzoneri, eds. *The Psychology of Superheroes: An Unauthorized Exploration.* Dallas: Benbella Books, 2008. Print.

Rutenberg, J. "Media Report; World Events Bring Restraint in Levy Case." *The New York Times.* 24 May 2002. Web. 18 August 2009.

Schager, Nick. "The Dark Knight." *Slant.* 17 July 2008. Web. 13 May 2009.

Scheffer, Bernd. "Das Gute am Bösen. Teuflisch gute Kunst." *Das Böse heute. Formen und Funktionen.* Ed. Werner Faulstich. Paderborn: Fink, 2008. 257–70. Print.

Schenk, Ken. "Superman: A Popular Culture Messiah." *The Gospel According to Superheroes. Religion and Pop Culture.* Ed. B. J. Oropeza. New York: Peter Lang, 2005. 33–48. Print.

Schmitt, Carl. *Political Theology: Four Chapters on the Concept of Sovereignty.* Trans. George Schwab. Chicago: The University of Chicago Press, 2005. Print.

_____. *The Concept of the Political.* Trans. George Schwab. New Brunswick: Rutgers University Press, 2007.

Schoenmakers, Henri. "Acting and (Re)presentation: Intrinsic Qualities in Theatre Performances of the Present." *Acting on Stage — Acting on Screen.* Ed. Christina Adamou. Athens: Kastaniotis, 2008. Print.

Schrader, Paul. "Notes on *Film Noir.*" *Film Genre Reader.* Ed. B. K. Grant. Austin: University of Texas Press, 2003. 229–242. Print.

Schulze, Laurie. "On the Muscle." *Fabrications: Costume and the Female Body.* Eds. Jane Gaines and Charlotte Herzog. London: Routledge, 1990: 59–78. Print.

Schwartz, Missy. "Elektracuted: Does Jennifer Garner's Dud Opening Doom Superchick Flicks?" *Entertainment Weekly* 28 Jan. 2005: 20. Web. 1 Nov. 2010.

Sears, Bart. "Brutes and Babes." *Wizard* 1.13 (1992): 38–39. Print.

Sharrett, Christopher. "The American Apocalypse: Scorsese's *Taxi Driver.*" *Persistence of Vision* (Summer, 1984): 56–64. Print.

Siegel, Jerry, and Joe Shuster. "Reign of the Superman." *Science Fiction: The Vanguard of Future Civilization.* Vol. 1 # 3. Jan. 1933. 4–14. *Internet Archive.* Web. 25 January 2010.

_____. Untitled story. *Action Comics* #1. June 1938. Rpt. in *Superman in the Forties.* New York: DC Comics, 2005. 10–22. Print.

Silverstein, Melissa. "The Politics of Hit-Girl." *The Huffington Post.* 15 Apr. 2010. Web. 19 Dec. 2010.

Skoble, Aeon J. "Superhero Revisionism in *Watchmen* and *The Dark Knight Returns.*" *Superheroes and Philosophy: Truth, Justice and the Socratic Way.* Eds. Tom Morris and Matt Morris. Chicago: Open Court, 2005. 29–49. Print.

Smith, Erin. *Hard-Boiled: Working-Class Readers and Pulp Magazines.* Philadelphia: Temple University Press, 2000. Print.

Spanakos, Anthony. "Governing Gotham." *Batman and Philosophy: The Dark Knight of the Soul.* Eds. Mark. D. White and Robert Arp. Hoboken: John Wiley, 2008. 55–69. Print.

_____. "Super-Vigilantes and the Keene Act." *Watchmen and Philosophy: A Rorschach Test.* Ed. Mark D. White. Hoboken: John Wiley, 2009. 33–46. Print.

Stam, Robert. *Film Theory: An Introduction.* Malden: Blackwell, 2000. Print.

Stern, Jessica. *Terror in the Mind of God: Why Religious Militants Kill.* New York: Harper-Collins, 2003. Print.

Stevens, Dana. "No Joke: The Dark Knight Reviewed." *Slate.* 17 July 2008. Web. 6 Dec. 2008.

Sturken, Marita. *Tangled Memories: The Vietnam War, the AIDS Epidemic, and the Politics of Remembering.* Berkeley: University of California Press, 1997. Print.

Talalay, Rachel. "Bigelow's best director award doesn't help women in film — it may hurt them." *Vancouver Sun.* 17 April 2010. Web. 3 July 2010.

Tasker, Yvonne. *Spectacular Bodies: Gender, Genre, and the Action Cinema.* London: Routledge, 1993. Print.

_____, and Diane Negra (eds). *Interrogating Postfeminism: Gender and the Politics of Popular Culture.* Durham: Duke University Press, 2007. Print.

Titus, Jordan. "Gnashing of Teeth: The Vagina Dentata Motif in 'Bad Girl' Comics." *International Journal of Comic Art.* 2. 2 (2000): 77–99. Print.

Thomson, Iain. "Deconstructing the Hero." *Comics as Philosophy.* Ed. Jeff McLaughlin, Jackson: University of Mississippi Press, 2005. 100–129. Print.

Travers, Peter. "*The Dark Knight.*" *Rolling Stone Movies.* 18 July 2008. Web. 3 Oct. 2010.

Treat, Shaun. "How America Learned to Stop Worrying and Cynically ENJOY! The Post-9/11 Superhero Zeitgeist." *Communication and Critical/Cultural Studies* 6.1 (2009): 103–09. Print.

Tudor, Andrew. "Critical Method ... Genre." *The Film Studies Reader.* Eds. Joanne Hollows, Peter Hutchings and Mark Jancovich. London: Arnold, 2000. 95–98. Print.

Turan, Kenneth. "A Bat Never Out of Hell." *Los Angeles Times.* 17 July 2008. Web. 3 Oct. 2010.

Turner, Graeme. *Film as Social Practice.* 4th ed. London: Routledge, 2006. Print.

"Twisted Sisters: A Collection of Bad Girl Art." *Whole Earth* Spring 1998: 29. Web. 22 Sep. 2010.

Tyree, J. M. "American Heroes." *Film Quarterly.* 62.3 (Spring 2009): 28–34. Print.

Van Biema, D. "Mother Teresa's Crisis of Faith." *Time.* 23 Aug. 2007. Web. 17 August 2009.

Wandtke, Terrence R. "Introduction. Once Upon a Time, Once Again." *The Amazing Transforming Superhero! Essays on the Revision of Characters in Comic Books*. Ed. Terrence R. Wandtke. Jefferson: McFarland, 2007. 5–32. Print.

Waxman, Sharon. "Halle Berry Mixes Sexiness with Strength." *New York Times*. 21 July 2004: E1. Web. 6 Nov. 2010.

Weber, Samuel. *Theatricality as Medium*. New York: Fordham University Press, 2004. Print.

Weintraub, Steve. "Exclusivo: Omelete entrevista Louis Leterrier, o diretor de O Incrível Hulk — Parte 1," 10 June 2008. Web. 14 August 2010.

"Who Is the Hottest Comic Book Girl?," *YouTube.com*. 2009. 18 July 2010.

Williams, Linda Ruth. "Ready for Action: *G. I. Jane*, Demi Moore's Body and the Female Combat Movie." *Action and Adventure Cinema*. Ed. Yvonne Tasker. London and New York: Routledge, 2004. 169–185. Print.

Williams, Raymond. *Marxism and Literature*. Oxford: Oxford University Press, 1977. Print.

Wolfe, Alan. *Does American Democracy Still Work?* London: Yale University Press, 2006. Print.

Zajko, Vanda. "Women and Greek Myth." *The Cambridge Companion to Greek Mythology*. Ed. Roger D. Woodard. Cambridge: Cambridge University Press, 2007. 387–406. Print.

Zakaria, Fareed. *The Post-American World*. New York: W.W. Norton, 2008. Print.

Zimmer, Ben. "SKXAWNG!" *New York Times Magazine*. 6 December 2009. P. 20. Print.

# About the Contributors

**Christina Adamou** is a lecturer in film theory in the Film Studies department at the Aristotle University of Thessaloniki, Greece. She has edited a collection on acting and has published articles and book chapters on gender, superhero films, acting, audiovisual translation, Samuel Beckett and the history of Greek television.

**Phillip Davis** received his Ph.D. in American literature from the University of Tulsa, where he is working as an adjunct instructor. His academic interests include Modernism, American Literature, American Culture of the 1930s, film and popular culture. He is currently working on adapting a chapter from his dissertation, "We Were Both Under a Strain: Irony in 1930s American Modernism and Mass Culture," for publication.

**Shahriar Fouladi** is a Ph.D. candidate in the Visual Studies program at the University of California at Irvine. His dissertation explores monstrosity in the superhero genre, with particular focus on Superman and the TV series *Smallville*.

**Vincent M. Gaine** is a doctoral graduate of the University of East Anglia. His research interests include film and philosophy, classic and contemporary Hollywood, quality television, audience and reception, adaptation, genre and auteur-structuralism. He is the author of *Existentialism and Social Engagement in the Films of Michael Mann* (Palgrave Macmillan, 2011).

**Richard J. Gray II** is an assistant professor of French at Carson-Newman College in Jefferson City, Tennessee. His fields of study include interdisciplinary approaches to French literary studies, language, cultural studies, and Women's Studies. He is the coauthor of "Exploring *Niggerdom*: Racial Inversion in Language Taboos in *Chappelle's Show*," *The Comedy of Dave Chappelle*, ed. Kevin Wisniewski (McFarland, 2009).

**Frank Habermann** is a research assistant at the German Department of Ludwig-Maximilians-University, Munich, Germany. His Ph.D. dissertation is about the limits of literary theory and the correlation between theory and ineffability. He has published on cybernetics and *Battlestar Galactica*, semiotics and German realist novelist Gottfried Keller, and the poetics of theoretical approaches to phenomena of presence.

**Betty Kaklamanidou** is a lecturer in film history and theory in the Film Studies department at the Aristotle University of Thessaloniki, Greece. She is the author of two books in Greek, *When Film Met Literature* (2006) and *Introduction to the Hollywood Romantic Comedy* (2007), and has participated in various international conferences. Her fields of study include film and politics, adaptation theory, genre and gender, and contemporary Greek cinema. In March 2011, she was awarded a Fulbright Scholarship to conduct research in the United States.

**Christine Muller** is a Ph.D. candidate in American studies at the University of Maryland, College Park. She explores her primary interest in cultural trauma through life writing, popular culture and literature texts relating to September 11.

**Johannes Schlegel** is a Ph.D. candidate and lecturer at the English department of Georg-August-University, Göttingen, Germany. His research focuses on gothic and horror studies, literary and cultural theory, and contemporary (popular) culture. He co-edited the collection *Challenging Evil. Time, Society, and Changing Concepts of the Meaning of Evil* (2010).

**Justin S. Schumaker** is a student in the Film and Media Studies graduate program at Texas Tech University. His main research interests include genre studies and interactive narratology with emphasis on graphic novels and video games.

**Anthony Peter Spanakos** is an assistant professor of political science and law at Montclair State University. He was twice a Fulbright Visiting Professor (Brazil 2002, Venezuela 2008) and has written a number of scholarly and popular articles on political economy in Latin America, Asian and Latin American foreign policy, democratization and developing countries, and popular culture and political philosophy. These works have appeared in numerous publications, including *Reforming Brazil* (co-edited by Spanakos), *Batman and Philosophy*, *Watchmen and Philosophy*, and *Iron Man and Philosophy*.

# Index